OUR LADY
OF
FÁTIMA

OUR LADY

OF

FÁTIMA

By WILLIAM THOMAS WALSH

INTRODUCTION BY
MONSIGNOR WILLIAM C. McGRATH
DIRECTOR, OUR LADY OF FÁTIMA
PILGRIM VIRGIN TOUR

IMAGE BOOKS
DOUBLEDAY
NEW YORK LONDON TORONTO SYDNEY AUCKLAND

AN IMAGE BOOK
PUBLISHED BY DOUBLEDAY
a division of Bantam Doubleday Dell Publishing Group, Inc.
1540 Broadway, New York, New York 10036

IMAGE, DOUBLEDAY, and the portrayal of a deer drinking
from a stream are trademarks of Doubleday, a division of
Bantam Doubleday Dell Publishing Group, Inc.

First Image edition published in 1954 by special arrangement with
The Macmillan Company. This Image edition published May 1990.

NIHIL OBSTAT: John M. Fearns, S.T.D.
                Censor Librorum

IMPRIMATUR: ✠ Francis Cardinal Spellman
                Archbishop of New York
                April 2, 1947

Library of Congress Cataloging-in-Publication Data

Walsh, William Thomas, 1891–1949.
     Our Lady of Fátima / by William Thomas Walsh ; introduction by
William C. McGrath.
        p.   cm.
     ISBN 0-385-02869-5
     1. Fatima, Our Lady of.   I. Title.
BT660.F3W33   1990   92-40278
232.91'7'0946945—dc20   CIP

ISBN 0-385-02869-5

FOREWORD

At Fátima, Portugal, on October 13th, 1917, seventy thousand people witnessed one of the greatest miracles of all time. The sun suddenly turned pale, emitted brilliant rays of multicolored light, spun three times on its axis and then, to the horror of the assembled multitude, "power-dived" dizzily towards earth. A terrified cry rose from the crowd as thousands fell to their knees thinking the end of the world was at hand.

Among those present was a correspondent for one of the major News Services in this country. Next day, from Lisbon, he cabled a long and impressive story about the Miracle of the Sun. But it was never published. Chicago and New York were in the middle of the World Series and the long dispatch became a one-inch item relegated to page 24, literally snowed under with details of singles, errors, batting averages and home runs. This incident has been advanced as one of the explanations for the great "conspiracy of silence" concerning one of the most momentous happenings of our generation.

Explain it as you will, the fact is that almost a quarter of a century went by before whisperings of the Fátima story began to make themselves heard around the United States. In the early forties it was featured in a few pamphlets and occasional articles in religious magazines, read and duly noted by a comparatively small and devoted *clientele*.

Then—suddenly—the picture changed. Almost overnight Fátima became a subject of universal interest. People were speaking of war as a punishment from God for sin; of a "peace plan from Heaven", brought to earth by the Mother of God, in person; of the grim necessity—in the face of the gravest crisis ever to confront humanity—of making sacrifices, of doing penance and of praying, especially of praying the Rosary, for peace and the conversion of Russia. A new book had just been published, entitled OUR LADY OF FÁTIMA, and it had jolted us out of the complacency of our Fool's Paradise.

As its author, William Thomas Walsh, pointed out the second World War could have been prevented had men listened to the warnings of the Mother of God. The spread of world Communism, the annihilation of nations behind an ever widening iron curtain, the persecution and martyrdom of innocent people—all this had been shown the world at Fátima in a disturbing preview of things to come unless men ceased offending the Son of God, "already too grievously offended."

Belatedly—but, thank God, at last—people were beginning to see in its frightening perspective the real nature of the struggle convulsing the world. We were in mortal combat, to the finish, not merely against flesh and blood but against Principalities and the Powers of Darkness. While there was no doubt as to the final outcome, the world was already paying a ghastly price for its frustration of the saving efforts of the Mother of God through sinful revolt against her Divine Son.

It was only to be expected, people said, that pious writers should tell the story to the comparatively few readers of religious magazines. It was quite another thing—and America sat up and listened—when one of the most illustrious of contemporary historians lent the prestige of his name to an exhaustive study and documented story of apparitions that, in one way or in the other, would change the course of history. Certainly a perusal of OUR LADY OF FÁTIMA jolted *me* out of my own benighted complacency in this regard; "jolted" me, I might add, into accepting an assignment of lectures and sermons on the message of Fátima that has now carried me into 44 states over an uninterrupted period of more than six years.

At the time Dr. Walsh became interested in the story of Fátima, he was recognized as a most distinguished author and scholar. Born in Waterbury, Connecticut, he was educated in his own state and graduated from Yale with an A. B. in 1913. His early career was devoted to teaching in his native state of Connecticut but it was not until he became a professor of English at Manhattanville College of the Sacred Heart that he turned his attention to writing.

While at Manhattanville he began to write the magnificent biographies, *Isabella of Spain, Philip the Second* and *The Life of St. Theresa of Abila*, which established him as one of the outstanding biographers of his era. In rapid succession novels, plays and poetry sprang from his gifted pen. He received the Laetare Medal in 1941. In 1944 the Spanish Government awarded him the Cross of Commander of the Order of Alfonso the Wise; in the same year he received the Catholic Literary Award from the Gallery of Living Catholic Authors. Later, at Madrid, the Spanish Government again honored him with the Cross of Isabella the Catholic. His books had been published in many foreign languages and he is known throughout the entire world.

This was the man who, hearing the story of Fátima, set aside all of his other works to go to Portugal to collect the material for a book which would tell the story of what had occurred in those momentous months in 1917. This book was OUR LADY OF FÁTIMA which more than any other single factor has been instrumental in bringing the miracle of Fátima to the attention of millions of Americans.

This sense of Dr. Walsh's tremendous achievement was uppermost in my mind the day we brought the Pilgrim Virgin statue to the room in St. Agnes Hospital, White Plains, N. Y., where the great Apostle of Fátima lay dying. We spoke of the reception accorded his book and its important bearing upon the very survival of America. Knowing him as we did, we spared him the embarrassment of referring to something that for him was now of even greater import, the exemplary manner in which he himself had *lived* the message of Fátima.

As he spoke to us, quietly and cheerfully, his gaze steadily fixed upon the incomparably beautiful Pilgrim Virgin that had come to him this day from the shrine of Fátima itself, we were impressed as rarely in our lives before with the radiant peacefulness of his expression, a peace that was truly not of this world. After all, we told ourselves, it was not hard to understand. It brought suddenly and arrestingly to our minds the promise of Mary at Fátima to those who would be faithful to her requests that she would assist them at the hour of death "with all the graces necessary for salvation."

Dr. Walsh has left us, but his clarion call still resounds throughout America and the menace to which he awakened us grows more serious with the passing hours. Experts the world over vie with one another in lurid and terrifying details of the possible fate awaiting mankind. Oft repeated appraisal of the effects of a sneak atomic attack by Russia, without the amenity of any declaration of war, leaves no illusion as to what "may happen" unless something decisive and final be done to avert the ever-present danger of atomic madness. Frantically today the world is seeking reassurance and in the political and diplomatic sphere the world is seeking it in vain. For those who will take Mary at her word, that reassurance *is* to be found. *"If my requests are heard"* she tells us, *"Russia will be converted and there will be peace."*

Let us face it. From Russia alone comes the danger of nuclear war that could be the end of this thing we call civilization. However overpowering may be America's ascendancy in atomic weapons, the world well knows that America will never initiate a "preventive" atomic war. Were Russia tomorrow to feel assured of final victory in an all-out atomic struggle we should all too soon be shocked into a realization of the pathetic futility of our contemporary gestures of appeasement and compromise, of our refusal to take a strong and uncompromising stand in the face of an enemy that respects and understands nothing else.

A converted Russia! Therein lies our hope. That it will finally come about we are assured. We have the promise of the Mother of God during the last apparition at Fátima, a promise made on the occasion of the tremendous Miracle of the Sun. *"In the end, my Immaculate Heart will triumph. The Holy Father will consecrate Russia to me, which will be converted and some time of peace will be granted to humanity.*" In the end? Some time of peace? Before—or after —the wholesale slaughter of humanity in atomic war?

That is for you and me to help decide. Actually, we are racing against a deadline, against the time, should it ever come, when Russia's superiority in atomic weapons will usher in a D day of universal death. For the sake of civilization— should God see fit to spare it, which, indeed, we sometimes wonder—we sincerely hope and pray that a faithful response to the message of Fátima on the part of that "sufficient number" will result in the conversion of Russia and the crumbling of world Communism into chaotic ruin.

The Catholic world was electrified by the Holy Father's recent consecration of Russia to the Immaculate Heart of Mary. Lucia, now Sister Maria das Dores, the only living survivor of the three children who saw the apparitions, is reported to have said in an interview last year that the conversion of Russia may be much nearer than is generally realized. In OUR LADY OF FÁTIMA William Thomas Walsh asks you the question that Christians all over the world are asking today: If that consecration were to be implemented by a sustained and concerted spiritual drive by Mary's children the world over, what might the results be? Would they not startle the world out of its somnolence? Might they not usher in that period of peace promised by the Mother of God?

Rt. Rev. William C. McGrath

DIRECTOR, OUR LADY OF FÁTIMA PILGRIM VIRGIN TOUR

April 1954

PREFACE

One of the strangest and most beautiful stories I have ever heard was enacted from 1916 to 1920 in the hill country called the Serra da Aire, in the geographical center of Portugal. Three shepherd children, the oldest ten, the youngest seven, reported six times in 1917 that they had seen a Lady made wholly of light, who stood on a small tree, spoke to them, and vanished. On the last occasion, in the presence of 70,000 people, she performed a startling miracle to prove the truth of what the children said. Two of the little shepherds died in childhood, as she had foretold. Time has verified her other prophecies thus far: the Bolshevik Revolution, which began soon after; the horrors of World War II; the menace that Marxism offers to the entire world at this moment. The Lady said that if her wishes were obeyed, she would convert Russia and there would be peace. If not, every country in the world would be scourged and enslaved.

The third shepherd is still living. She is Sister Maria das Dores (Mary of the Sorrows), a lay sister of the Institute of Saint Dorothy, just forty years of age. I had a long conversation with her last summer. This book is based principally upon her four written but unpublished memoirs, in the light of that conversation.

The message she has lived to reveal is that of no ordinary lady. It comes, I am convinced, from the Queen of heaven and earth, whose beauty, power and goodness have been the theme of prophets and saints for thousands of years. She is that maiden of whom Isaias wrote, "A virgin shall conceive and bear a son . . ." the one of whom King Solomon asked, "Who is she that cometh forth as the morning rising, fair as the moon, bright as the sun, terrible as an army set in array?" It was to her that the angel Gabriel said, "Hail, full of grace! The Lord is with thee. Blessed art thou among women!" and she replied "Be it done to me according to thy word."

This Lady has often changed the course of history. Her Rosary, preached by Saint Dominic, overthrew the Manichean heresy that would have destroyed European society. It kept both faith and the love of freedom alive in Eire for centuries. It won the battle of Lepanto, where Christendom was saved from Moslem domination. It was under her special protection that Columbus set out to discover our western world, changing the name of his flagship from *Mariagalante* to *Santa Maria*; and every night, as dusk came over the uncharted and terrifying waste of the Sargasso Sea, his sailors would assemble on the decks to sing her vesper hymn:

"Hail, holy Queen, mother of mercy,
Our life, our sweetness and our hope,
Hail! . . ."

American Catholics followed this tradition in placing their country under the protection of her Immaculate Conception. And let no one imagine that any sort of Brave New World will be able to efface her memory! For at the end of time, before the consummation of this world, there will appear in heaven—or has it already appeared?—the sign foretold by Saint John in his Apocalypse:

"A woman clothed with the sun, and the moon under her feet, and on her head a crown of twelve stars."

No one who believes in God and the immortality of the soul should find it incredible that the Mother of Christ, the incarnate God, should have revealed herself to privileged persons at various crises in human affairs. Several of these appearances have been established beyond any reasonable doubt—notably, in modern times, the apparitions to Saint Bernadette at Lourdes. But why should she have appeared in Portugal in 1917, and in such a deserted and inaccessible place as the Serra da Aire? It takes all day to get to Fátima, some ninety miles north of Lisboa, first by train and then by bus or taxi; and when one arrives, there is not much to see but a vast moor with sparse vegetation for lean sheep to nibble, and a few wretched villages (by American standards) where humble peasants scrape a bare existence out of a dry reddish soil.

Well, first of all she appears where it pleases God, and her. But the Portuguese have an idea that they were favored partly, at least, because their country has always been called *a terra de Santa Maria*; and in the Serra about Fátima, regardless of revolutions and apostacies in other places, the poor have clung for centuries with unwavering devotion to the recitation of her Rosary. Cova da Iria, the wild place where the apparitions occurred, some two miles west of Fátima, was named from the girl martyr Saint Iria or Irene, who probably had a hermitage there. And eight miles west of Cova da Iria is a tiny antique chapel, square and ugly, where King João I promised Our Lady that if she gave him victory over the Spanish invaders in 1385, he would raise a more fitting temple in her honor. He kept his promise by building, across the road, one of the most beautiful Gothic churches in the world, the incredibly graceful and majestic abbey of Batalha.

The Constable of Portugal, who commanded the army under King João, was Nuno Alvares Pereira, a hero of twenty-five who wielded a sword engraved with the name "Maria." He built six churches in honor of Our Lady, one of the loveliest of them the Carmelite monastery and chapel at Lisboa. It was there, after forty years in the king's service, that he retired to lay his sword at the feet of her image, and to take the habit of her order, with the name Nuno de Santa Maria. Nearly five hundred years later he was beatified by Pope Benedict XV. His sword "Maria" may still be seen at the Carmo at Lisboa, in the hand of a statue of the Prophet Elias.

It was among the mountains hallowed by so many memories and traditions of her that the Lady appeared. And when such a Lady appears anywhere, to give mankind a request and a warning, it is no small matter. My interest in the subject was aroused by what I heard of it from the Reverend Father John C. Rubba, O. P., and the Reverend Father William A. Hinnebusch, O. P. of Providence College. Some of the published accounts, however, were so conflicting that I decided to go to Portugal and try to verify the details before attempting a book. Thanks mainly to their good offices, and to the prayers of several communities of Dominican and Discalced Carmelite contemplatives, I was able to do so under the most favorable conditions. His Excellency, the Most Reverend José Alvernaz, Bishop of Cochin, India, and His Eminence, the Most Reverend Francis Cardinal Spellman of New York were good enough to commend my trip to authorities in Portugal, and I was given every facility for investigation by His Eminence, the Most Reverend Manuel Cardinal Cerejeira, Patriarch of Lisboa, and His Excellency, the Most Reverend Dom José Alves Correia da Silva, Bishop of Leiria, in whose diocese Fátima and Cova da Iria lie. I flew to Lisboa, attended the pilgrimage and processions of July 12–13, 1946, and lived for some time at Cova da Iria and nearby places, interviewing the parents and relatives of the two dead children, besides other witnesses of the miracle of October 1917.

I am indebted to the works and spoken advice of the Reverend Father José Galamba de Oliveira, author of *Jacinta: episódios inéditos das aparições de Nossa Senhora*; the Reverend Father Luís Gonzaga Aires da Fonseca, S. J., professor at the Pontifical Biblical Institute at Rome and author of *Le Meraviglie di Fátima*, and the Reverend Father João de Marchi, I. M. C., author of *Era uma senhora mais brilhante que o sol*. This last is particularly valuable because Father De Marchi has spent three years at Fátima interrogating the chief surviving witnesses, and setting down their exact words with scholarly patience and accuracy. I have taken some of the particulars about Sister Dores' early convent life from Senhor Antero de Figueiredo's *Fátima: Graças, Segredos, Misterios*.

I can never sufficiently thank the Reverend Father Manuel Rocha, who was asked to help me by His Eminence, the Cardinal Patriarch, and whose patience and courtesy were inexhaustible; and my good fellow-pilgrims from America, the Reverend Father Leal Furtado and Mr. Daniel F. Sullivan. Finally, the assistance of my daughter Helen has been indispensable.

The book is not "fictionized." I owe the conversations chiefly to the precise memory of Sister Dores.

The interest of the story in itself—and it would be a great one even if it had been invented, instead of happening—is negligible compared to the truth that it was intended by its divine Author to convey. I came home from Portugal convinced that nothing is so important as making known what the Mother of God asked in those apparitions of 1917, which for some reason have been so neglected, so distorted, so misunderstood. The future of our civilization, our liberties, our very existence may depend upon the acceptance of her commands.

CHAPTER I

Half a mile south of Fátima, on both sides of a winding road paved with flattish cobblestones and scarcely wide enough for two ox-teams to pass, lies the village of Aljustrel. The houses, sheds and patios all join a high stone wall that runs along each side of that narrow "street," and seem to be strung on it like beads of odd shapes and sizes. Windows are few and small, for the northwest blast of winter, cutting across the mountains from the Atlantic, is as pitiless as the parching sunlight of summer; hence these squat one-story dwellings with their red tile roofs and whitewashed stone walls have a veiled and wary look, as if each one could tell an enormous secret if it chose.

If it is a week-day, the men are in the fields; but in and out of the dark interiors pass short, rather handsome women and children with fine eyes, gleaming teeth, and—this from carrying heavy burdens on their heads—straight postures and graceful movements, even under the weight of three or four gallons of water in an earthen jug. Their bare feet, dusty but shapely, seem not to feel the sharp stones, nor are their laughing faces annoyed by the flies, fleas and other insects that buzz, in hot weather, over the patios and the sheds where animals are kept. A burro brays, a dog barks, a rooster crows, a yoke of oxen lumber heavily along the road. The air is seasoned with many odors, among which can be distinguished those of pines and evergreen shrubs, wild mint and onions, sheep, goats and chickens; above all, the distinctive musty and acrid though not exactly disagreeable smell that the soil of Portugal seems to have everywhere. There is nothing here of the overpowering fishiness of Lisboa or Porto, but the red fields are just as insistent in their own way, and the clothes of all these people are laden with the aroma. Such is Aljustrel, where Lucia Abóbora, now the famous Sister Maria of the Sorrows, was born on March 22, 1907.

The cottage in which she grew up was very much like the one where visitors now find that patient and courteous woman with dark honest eyes who is her oldest sister, Maria of the Angels. The living room is severely furnished with a table, a chair, a couple of old wooden chests where food and clothing are stored, a few pious pictures on the bare wall. A breach in the tiled roof, just over a hole in the wooden ceiling, lets in a splash of sunlight, by which one sees better, in a small adjoining room, the old hand loom that used to belong to Lucia's mother. A half-finished rug of white, red and blue woolen stuff still lies entangled in the cords, and sends up a cloud of dust at the slightest touch. The dark kitchen has a spacious fireplace in which a few twigs are feebly burning, even in summer; at other seasons it is lighted by several candles on a piece of board hanging from a wooden ceiling black from the smoke of many winters. There is but one bedroom. An iron bed, with coverings bright and neat, fills half of it, touching three of the undecorated walls. A potted plant stands on the sill of the tiny window; another, with pink flowers, is on the floor. Maria of the Angels explains that the bed was formerly in the house of her parents, and that her sister Lucia was born in it.

Lucia was the youngest, as Maria was the oldest, of the seven children of Antonio Abóbora (or dos Santos), a small farmer and sheep grower who owned pieces of land in various parts of the Serra da Aire. He was a rather good-looking man with dark passionate eyes, who liked conviviality better than going to Mass, and wine more than work. His wife, Maria Rosa, was a devout, almost severe Catholic, short, stout and muscular, with a heavy mannish face which had a grave benignity, but on rare occasions could relax in a motherly smile. There was no nonsense about Maria Rosa, however. She never had time for it.

It was this strong parent who came into Lucia's mind when, in writing her memoirs, she began to examine her earliest recollections. She could remember squirming in those stalwart arms, and being conscious even then of her own personality and her own actions. One of the first things she recalled was learning the "Ave Maria" from her mother's lips. "Hail, full of Grace! The Lord is with thee! Blessed art thou among women!" The ancient prayer, commencing with those words of an angel, is beautiful in any language. But in Portuguese the syllables seem to have acquired a rhythm peculiarly intense and memorable:

"Avé, Maria, cheia de graça, O Senhor é convosco! Bemdita sois vós entre as mulheres, e bemdito é o fruto do vosso ventre, Jesus!

"Santa Maria, Mãi de Deus, rogai por nós pecadores, agora e na hora da nossa morte. Amen."

Lucia has other memories of a more worldly sort. There were, for instance, not a few furious battles in which one or another of her four older sisters always bore off the victory, and left her howling on the floor until her mother snatched her up and caressed her. Lucia could hardly remember the time when she was not under the spell of that passion for dancing to which peasants are given even more than other human beings. This was especially true of her two grown-up sisters, Maria of the Angels and Teresa. And there were plenty of opportunities at Aljustrel. There was sure to be a party somewhere on every holy day—the feast of the Sacred Heart and Saint Anthony's in June, that of Our Lady of the Rosary in October, and of course, Christmas and Easter. Besides this, Maria Rosa was in great demand, either as a patron or as a cook of renowned skill, whenever there was a wedding in any of the dozen hamlets scattered about the Serra; and her older daughters seldom failed to accompany her.

The problem of how to dispose of the baby on such occasions was easily solved. Although she was hardly able to walk, much less dance, Lucia was arrayed in an embroidered skirt with a shiny belt, a splendid kerchief whose corners hung down in back and, what pleased her most, a jaunty little hat glittering with gold beads and bright feathers. She was then carried in the stout maternal arms through the labyrinth of narrow roads that zigzag across the irregular rocky fields between high stone walls; and when the dancing began after supper, she was firmly deposited, for safety from trampling feet, on one of those high wooden chests that form a chief part of the furniture of every kitchen and living room. From that eminence the tiny girl could watch the flushed faces and the twinkling feet, and listen to the fascinating sounds that came from a guitar or a harmonica. Sooner or later, no doubt, she would fall asleep and remain rolled up against the wall until it was time to go home—more often than not when the first streaks of dawn were mounting the eastern sky. For Lucia's sisters could never have enough of waltzes, which were all the rage at that time.

At the Abóbora residence, too, there were plenty of parties. In summer the young people gathered under a large fig tree in the patio, in winter in a shed adjoining the house. On such occasions Maria Rosa would sit at the door of the little room opening on the patio, where she could see all that might be going on inside or outside. Sometimes she had a book open on her lap, sometimes she would chat with some relative or friend while the young people danced or jested. "She was always very serious," according to Lucia, "and everybody knew that whatever she said was like Scripture, and that she must be obeyed in the house." Some of the visitors used to tell her that she was worth all of her daughters put together. Perhaps that was an exaggeration, but she was not displeased.

Maria Rosa was one of the few people in Aljustrel who could read. "I don't know why people like to gad about from house to house," she used to say. "All I want is to stay home quietly and read. These books are very interesting. And the lives of the saints—*que beleza!*" Most of her books, in fact, were pious ones. During the hours of the siesta in the summer and on winter evenings she enjoyed teaching catechism not only to Lucia but to other children of the neighborhood. In Lent she would read accounts of the Passion of our Lord and books about the need of prayer and penance. After supper, when Antonio and his son Manuel had come from the fields, and the candles brightened the glow from the hearth, the older girls and their father liked to repeat old stories of giants, bewitched castles, enchanted princesses. Lucia, of course, found these delightful. But her mother would always seize the opportunity, in between the profane chronicles, to tell something more edifying.

On Sundays Maria Rosa and her daughters—and sometimes Antonio—would hear Mass at the village church of Fátima. This has been greatly altered and in part rebuilt since 1917. The floor of wide boards is halved by a tiled walk that runs from the main door halfway to the altar; then, under a Roman arch, there is a lift in the floor where the old church begins. The walls are tiled in bright blue, white and yellow, from the floor to a height of some six feet. On each side there is a confessional, and toward the front of the church there is a third movable one for emergencies. Instead of pews, there are long rough unstable wooden benches. The bluish green ceiling is high enough to give an impression of dignity and solemnity, if not of grandeur; the dome over the small main altar is deep azure and studded with stars.

Some of the statues are extraordinarily lifelike. There is one of Saint Anthony, for whom the church is named, in a glass case for greater protection. Saint Francis stands near by, his brown habit somewhat incongruously embroidered with gold, to suggest, no doubt, his glorification in Heaven; and the Child Jesus in his arms has a lovely expression in his eyes, which follow the beholder about in a way that must have made quite an impression upon Lucia and other children. This is at the right of the main altar. At the left, in front of the church, stands another which undoubtedly, from her own account, had a strong influence upon the mind of Lucia. It is one of Our Lady of the Rosary, clad in a crimson gown and a blue mantle ornamented with gold, holding in her arms a rather unhappy looking Child. Her own face is uncommonly serious, in fact almost severe and reproving, while the glance of her light brown eyes is arresting and piercing. In one hand she holds a rosary of fifteen decades. Below her there is a statue of the girl martyr Saint Quiteria, in a pink robe spangled with stars and a blue cincture. Here Lucia as a child often knelt to pray.

5

Near the altar of the Sacred Heart now stands a statue of Our Lady of Fátima. Her dark brown eyes look over the right shoulder of the beholder with a soft and appealing affection; her robes are pale blue. But this was not there in 1917.

On the right hand side of the church is a striking Crucifixion. The Christus is very short and stocky, like a Portuguese of the mountains, and is spattered with vivid blood from head to feet. Above is an unusual picture of Our Lady of Mount Carmel. The Child in her arms has a scapular in each hand, and both are gazing out over a vision of hell, into whose flames are falling naked souls of the damned; while others stand in peril, gazing sadly away from the Mother and Infant, though on one side a youth is being plucked from the pit by an angel, and on another a young girl is saved.

On Sundays and feasts the church would be filled with people from the villages of the Serra da Aire, and the open fields round about would be full of family groups, with their earthenware water jugs and lunchbaskets, their burros, mules and carts of various sorts. From his house behind the church, with many a genial word, the parish priest would pass. The bell in the steeple would fling its clear tones for miles through the clean sunny air. The women would crowd to the benches near the sanctuary, while most of the men and boys, save those few who might be going to Communion, would stand in the rear; and then the Mass would begin.

It was customary for children at that time to prepare to receive their first Holy Communion at the age of about nine or ten. It was in 1910, when Lucia was three years old, that Pope Pius X reminded the world of Christ's command, "Suffer the little ones to come to me, and forbid them not." Possibly Maria Rosa had heard of this decree. It seems clear that she resolved, when her youngest daughter was only six, that the time had come for her to receive the hidden Jesus of the Blessed Sacrament; and aided by Caroline, who was then eleven and had received, she drilled her in the questions and answers of the penny catechism. When at last she felt that her pupil was ready for an examination she took her to the church.

The Prior received them with kindness, and then, sitting in a chair on a platform in the sacristy, began to ask the child questions. "Who made the world?" "How many gods are there?" "What is man?" "Why did God make us?" "What must we do to be saved?" And so on through the list that all Catholic children study.

It seemed to Lucia and her mother that she had not done badly. Yet after a little reflection the good priest decided that she was too young, and had better wait for another year.

It was the very day before the First Communion. They had never expected such a crushing blow. Almost stunned by disappointment, they went from the sacristy to one of the benches in the church, and sat with heads bowed, thinking. Lucia began to sob.

It happened that a Jesuit missionary from Lisboa, Father Cruz, had been preaching a triduum at Saint Anthony's to prepare for this First Communion, and was helping Father Pena to hear the many confessions. As he passed through the church, he saw the little girl in distress and stopped to ask what was the trouble. On hearing the story he tested her with questions from the catechism, and then took her back to the Prior in the sacristy.

"This child knows her doctrine better than many of the others who are going to receive," he said.

"But she is only six years old!" objected Father Pena.

The Jesuit persisted. He was a gentle and humble man, but determined; and to the intense joy of Lucia, the Prior finally yielded. Now she must go to the sacrament of penance, so that she could offer a spotless heart and conscience to the divine Guest who was coming next day.

It was at the movable confessional, which had been placed near the sacristy door, that Father Cruz heard her first confession. What a blessing! The famous Jesuit preacher was believed by many in Portugal to be a saint; and he could hardly have talked even with a small child without communicating some of his fervent love of God. He was a tall man of fifty, much bent from study and austerities. When Lucia had finished telling her peccadillões, she heard him say in a low voice:

"My daughter, your soul is the temple of the Holy Spirit. Keep it always pure, so that He can carry on His divine action in it."

She promised, and said her act of contrition. She asked Our Lady to help her receive the Body and Blood of her Son worthily on the next day. Then she arose, and returned to her mother.

Maria Rosa looked embarrassed and out of sorts, and the women about her, for some reason or other, were laughing and whispering. But Lucia paid little attention to this; she was thinking only of what the priest had said. She knelt at the rail before the statue of Our Lady of the Rosary, looked up at the sad face with the searching eyes, and said to her:

"Please keep my poor heart for God."

And "it seemed to me," she wrote years later, "that she smiled, and with a kindly look and gesture told me she would."

Maria Rosa was waiting for her. "Don't you know," she demanded as they started down the road to Aljustrel, "that your confession is a secret, and must be made in a low voice?"

Lucia hung her head.

"Everybody heard you."

Silence.

"They heard everything except the last thing you said to the priest."

Lucia scuffed resolutely along.

"What was the last thing you said to him?" asked her mother.

No reply! Maria Rosa persisted all the way home, but she never learned the secret. Lucia was always a reticent child. As soon as she saw that anyone was trying to make her talk, she would take refuge in a sullen silence that could be very exasperating.

That night her sisters worked late to get her ready for the great event of her life. There was a new white dress to be fitted, a garland of flowers to be woven to crown her dark hair. And when at last they let her go to bed, she was unable to sleep, thinking of all that had happened and all that was going to happen. What if nobody woke her for Mass next morning? Every hour she got up to see what time it was. It seemed as if the dawn would never come.

At last it did, however, and Maria came to call her. No doubt she gave the usual caution not to take a drink, or eat anything, for one must fast before Holy Communion. She made the final adjustments of the white dress and the garland. Then she presented Lucia to her parents, telling her that she must beg their pardon for her sins, kiss their hands, and ask their blessing. The little girl obeyed, and they blessed her.

"And mind you don't forget to ask Our Lady to make you a saint!" added Maria Rosa.

The family set out for the church. When Lucia could not keep up with the others her mother scooped her up in her strong arms, for it was late, and carried her the rest of the way.

There was no need of such haste. Some of the visiting priests from distant places had not yet arrived, and the Missa Cantata did not start for quite a while. This gave Lucia an opportunity to kneel once more before the statue of Our Lady of the Rosary and carry out her mother's instructions.

"Make me a saint!" she whispered. "Please ask Our Lord to make me a saint!"

Again she thought she saw the sad face relax into a smile of encouragement. She was not the first to report such an experience before a statue or a picture; there was little Saint Thérèse of Lisieux, for example, among others. Nor does Lucia attach too much significance to what theologians consider the least reliable sort of locution. "I don't know whether the facts I have written about my First Communion were a reality, or a little girl's illusion," she wrote modestly when her bishop commanded her to commit all her spiritual adventures to paper. "All I know is that they had a great influence in uniting me to God all my life." She remained so long gazing at the smiling Madonna that her sisters had to come and take her away. The procession was already forming.

Lucia was the youngest and smallest of the four long files of children, two of girls and two of boys; and she was the first to receive. When the priest placed the white Host on her tongue, she felt, in her own words, "an unalterable serenity and peace." During all the remainder of the Mass she kept saying in her heart, over and over, "Lord, make me a saint! Keep my heart always pure, for You alone!" And she distinctly heard Him say within her, "The grace that I grant thee today will remain living in thy soul, producing fruits of eternal life."

It was afternoon when the Missa Cantata ended, for the sermon was long, and it took some time for the children to renew their baptismal vows. When they were finally released, they trooped out of the church and separated into little groups, shouting, talking, running, some munching on pieces of bread their mothers had brought.

Lucia remained kneeling in the blue and rosy light that came through the stained-glass windows. Her mother was alarmed, thinking she must be weak from hunger, and dragged her away. But when they got home the child could hardly eat. She was surfeited with the Bread of Angels, and she felt as if no other food would ever attract or satisfy her. For a long time after that people noticed that she seemed absorbed, abstracted, almost dazed.

CHAPTER II

When Lucia's second teeth began to come in, it was evident that nature was not preparing her to be "Miss Portugal." For they were large, projecting and irregular, causing the upper lip to protrude and the heavy lower one to hang, while the tip of her snub nose turned up more than ever. Sometimes in repose her swarthy face suggested a nature that could be sullen, stubborn and defiant, if not perverse. But the appearance was deceptive, for under the stimulus of any emotion, the light brown eyes could flash or twinkle, and the little dimples that creased her cheeks when she smiled contributed to an expression quite charming. Her voice was, and still is, rather high and thin. Older persons often found her too silent and reserved, though quick enough to obey and to help with her strong, stubby hands. Younger children, however, were strongly attracted to her, perhaps because she felt at ease with them and loved to tell them stories by the hour. She had a gift for narration, with a sense of humor and pathos, and under the awkward exterior the instinct of the little ones discovered a sound intelligence and a warm and motherly heart.

Among those most devoted to her were two of her numerous cousins, Francisco and Jacinta (or Hyacinthe) Marto. At first Lucia used to avoid them; in fact she found them rather tiresome and troublesome. As they grew older they began to interest her, and in time there was a perpetual running back and forth between her house and theirs. They were the two youngest children of her father's sister, Olimpia of Jesus, and her second husband, Manuel Pedro Marto.

Lucia was fond of her uncle and aunt. Ti Olimpia had had two children by her first husband, José Ferndandes Rosa; and by Ti Marto, whom she had married in 1897 (when she was twenty-eight and he twenty-four) she had nine more, of whom Francisco was the eighth and Jacinta the last.[1] Compared to sturdy Maria Rosa she looked thin, tall and pale. But appearances are not always trustworthy, for Olimpia has survived her sister-in-law by many years. Her large hands are as capable as ever as she moves lightly about her cottage at Aljustrel, and there is something strangely youthful in the smile that comes easily to the toothless mouth and small shrewd eyes of this woman of seventy-eight, who bore eleven children. She gives the impression of having been a good companionable wife and an affectionate mother, even though she never learned to read or write. In spiritual matters she was content with a decent minimum, and might have been satisfied with less but for the intervention of circumstances hardly to be expected. When I made some remark last summer about all the work she accomplishes, she said simply, as if stating a fact rather than boasting, "I am a strong woman."

Ti Marto is a man of exceptional character, who would command instant respect anywhere. He must have seemed rather a romantic figure to Lucia in the days when she and his children were growing up together. He had the straight carriage, the cropped moustache, the "butch" haircut, the quiet decisive manner, the sophistication of outlook of one who had been a soldier in Africa, and had seen something more of the world than the Serra da Aire. At seventy-four he still stands quite erect, and keeps his gray hair and moustache trimmed closely. He has generous ear lobes, keen honest brown eyes, hands expressive and capable. He too never learned to read or write. But unlike his brother-in-law, Antonio, he never cared much for gaming or carousing. He worked hard, paid his bills, saved a little for rainy days, of which there were plenty, and had enough left over to take Olimpia and the girls occasionally to the Sunday market at Batalha, to buy new shoes for holiday wear, or some finery or other. His conversation has always been salted with the dry wit of those who work outdoors. "There aren't any poor

[1] Francisco was born June 11, 1908; Jacinta, March 11, 1910.

people around here," he remarked last summer as we watched women go by barefoot with great jugs of water on their heads. "Everybody in these mountains has shoes. Of course, if anybody wants to give them anything, they'll take it. But they have enough."

It was inevitable that a man of his natural dignity should be something of a personage throughout the Serra da Aire. I saw him rise to greet the distinguished Archbishop of Évora with great respect but no servility; and they spoke together like those who know that as men they are equals. Nor was there ever any doubt as to who was master in the Marto home. "People always said there was peace in this house," he remarked, "and so there was, because I saw to it. All I had to do was speak, and my boys would keep quiet. They knew that if they didn't they'd get a lambasting.[2] But that wasn't necessary. Just because a burro gives a kick, you don't have to cut his leg off right away."

Francisco was very much like his father. He was a handsome child with fine steady eyes and regular features, and was generally amiable, considerate and obedient. Yet his father is proud of the fact that he had the animal spirits of a normal boy, and now and then had to be taken in hand, as on a certain evening when he decided not to say his prayers. He was never afraid of anything, either. He would go out boldly on the darkest or foggiest night, when others of his age would shrink from the vast unknown of the Serra. Or he would catch wild rabbits or foxes, and make pets of them. He liked to pick up snakes and lizards on the end of his stick, and thrust them in a pool of water to make them drink, or watch them wiggle away. "What a man he would have been!" Ti Marto says from time to time, with a sigh. And Olimpia, with shining eyes, agrees.

Jacinta, two years younger than her brother, had the same fine and even features; but the straight line of her brows,

[2] "*Lampadadas,*" is the Portuguese equivalent. This is one of Marto's reminiscences recorded in the excellent book by Father De Marchi, p. 34.

close above her clear and well spaced eyes, suggested a better intelligence. She was as quick and blithe as a bird, always running or jumping or dancing. Perhaps it was because she had affectionate parents that she gave the impression of being made up wholly of affection—so long as she got what she wanted. For Jacinta had been spoiled a little, too, as the baby of a large family, and she could pout or sulk on slight provocation. This was one reason why Lucia found her annoying when she first began to play with her in 1914. Still, Jacinta was only four! Her father still remembers that she could be very stubborn and independent at times. For some reason she made up her mind to say, "Hail Mary, full of graces," instead of "full of grace," and no one, he told me with some pride, could ever induce her to use the correct singular.

The Martos now live just across the road from their former habitation, between the Abóbora house and Fátima. It is a humble residence, like some of those in Nazareth or Bethany long ago, but Senhora Olimpia was as composed and gracious as any lady in the land as she went about barefoot in her sombre everyday attire of black and gray, to show it to me. There was little furniture in the living room except an old-fashioned clock, no longer functioning, and a massive unpainted wooden chest; nor is there any window there or in one of the two bedrooms. The kitchen is lighted by a small overhead pane of glass, perhaps six by eighteen inches. From the hearth, where a good fire burns in winter, came a feeble glow from a handful of twigs, for the day was very hot. An antique kettle stood by some earthen jugs for water, oil and wine. A rosary hung from a nail in the wall.

Outside was a patio, sheltered by a stone wall and carpeted thick with twigs from a couple of fig trees growing beside a fence. The smell of sheep and goats, mingling with the pleasanter aromas from trees and flowers and the ever-pungent something of the soil, brings fleas and gnats to this inclosure on a summer afternoon. But Olimpia smiles with pride as she displays at one end of it the old outdoor brick oven in which she bakes great loaves of bread once a week. It used to be twice a week when the children were growing up. "Yes, I am a strong woman!" she repeats, closing her mouth resolutely, and looking out across the fence at a striking panorama of fields and pastures between two ranges of mountains. On a high hill opposite were some antique windmills like those that Don Quixote tilted with in Spain; and the quadruple wings slowly revolved and glistened in the fierce July sunshine.

The games that Lucia and her two youngest cousins used to play in or about the two cottages were those that children play everywhere: tag, forfeits, cops and robbers, "Button, button, who's got the button?" and another called, "Pass the ring." When they were tired of such amusements, Lucia would tell them stories, usually the ones she had heard from her parents and elder sisters around the hearth after supper on winter nights: hair-raising tales of witches, fairies and goblins, giants and enchanted princesses, such as Antonio and his older daughters liked to relate, and the holier ones from the more serious lips of Maria Rosa.

What interested Jacinta most was the story of the Passion of Christ, which Lucia, with the native talent that shows sporadically in her four memoirs, must have made graphic enough. Jesus praying alone in the Garden while His friends slept and His enemies plotted; Jesus being scourged while His Mother looked on, weeping; Jesus staggering under His heavy cross and falling on bloody knees under the weight of it; Jesus dying in thirst and agony, and for our sins, not His—all this made a profound impression on the generous hearts of both the Marto children, but especially on that of the little girl. "Poor little Lord!" she would say. "Poor, poor Our Lord! I am never going to commit another sin, if it makes You suffer so much!"

One day, when the children were playing in the Santos house, Lucia's brother Manuel, who was writing a letter at a table, looked up suddenly and said, jokingly:

"Come, Jacinta, give me a hug and a kiss!"

"Ask me for something else," said the little girl.

"No, that's all I want—three kisses," he teased.

"The only one I will kiss is Our Lord. I'll give Him all the kisses He wants." And running to a crucifix that hung on a wall, she covered it with kisses.

This crucifix never ceased to attract her. One day she took it from the wall and was looking at it affectionately when Maria came in and, thinking that Lucia was to blame, began to scold. Didn't she know that holy things were not to play with?

"Maria, don't spank her!" pleaded Jacinta. "It was all my fault. I won't do it again."

Maria gave the rascal a hug, and packed them all out-of-doors, to play in the sunshine. They ran through the patio, and down the sloping field behind the house to the threshing floor. This was a square place paved with concrete on which, for too many years to remember, the Abóboras have shucked the wild bush beans that grow all about the meadows, and have threshed their wheat with flails such as have been used in that country for centuries. There is a good fragrance there, especially when someone has trampled a bit of the wild mint that grows among the beans and the brown grass. The view, too, is excellent. All down the valley, on the dusty green of the olive trees, there is a shimmer of silver, save on the darker verdure of pines, figs or holm oaks, or an occasional field of maize or cabbage.

A few yards from the threshing floor is an old and precious well, one of the few sources of water in that part of the Serra. It is covered by several heavy slabs of stone, very convenient to sit on; and there, hour after hour, in the shade of three olive trees, the children would lie and talk, or simply gaze at the stubble fields where the reddish soil, scattered with jagged rocks and speckled with purple thistles, wild red roses, tufts of brown grass, and withering bush beans with pods standing upright, stretched out into a valley where nothing ever looked quite the same twice. It was especially beautiful there in the early morning or late afternoon. It was heavenly at night when a cool wind came whistling down under the star-pricked vastitude of jet.

When the olive trees were shedding their buds, Maria

Rosa was stern in her insistence that the children keep away from them, if they were going to play about the well. For the buds had a way of getting into the hair, the blouse or the long skirt of Lucia or Jacinta, and then would manage, somehow, to get into the well and spoil the water. Hence if any buds were found on Lucia's clothing at night, she would get a spanking on general principles—literally, in Portuguese, a "scraping." Or next day she would be kept indoors, and would have the additional pain of hearing Jacinta and Francisco chirp under a window, asking why she did not come out.

From the well, too, they enjoyed seeing the new sunlight flood the valley in the morning, and the huge shadows creep from the mountains at dusk, after the sun had disappeared in a splendor of crimson and gold and purple. Jacinta was especially fond of watching sunsets. But she liked even better, after supper, to see the stars come out, and to count them until they became too numerous. What fun to look up at them through the branches of one of the fig trees near the well, and how much larger and more brilliant they seemed there! Lucia called them the lamps of the angels. The moon was the lamp of Our Lady. And the sun? Obviously the lamp of Our Lord.

"I like the lamp of Our Lord best," Francisco would say.

"I don't," returned Jacinta. "It burns and blinds people. I like the lamp of Our Lady."

This dispute seemed destined to go on forever. But in the summer of 1914 it had to yield to one of those catalyses that sometimes occur in families, as if some invisible poison had turned their happiness to discontent and their peace to anxiety and dissension. The agent at work in the Abóbora family was not invisible, to be sure; it was the wine that Antonio drank more and more of with various cronies in those dark little roadside taverns that mysteriously survive, in Portugal, even where habitations are few. The poor man was drinking up not only his fields and his cattle, his self-respect and his old age, but also the health and good-humor of his wife and children. Things had come to such a pass that Maria Rosa had to hire herself out as a domestic nurse, sometimes for all night, sometimes for days at a stretch. She was especially in demand when a baby was born, and sometimes, being very charitable, she would bring home three or four little children to care for while their mother was ill. It fell to the older girls, then, to look after the house and to help Manuel in the fields. Caroline's job had been to pasture the small flock of sheep and goats on family lots in various parts of the Serra. But now she was thirteen, and Maria Rosa decided that she ought to be able to earn some money sewing and weaving. There was no reason why Lucia could not take over the flock. She was seven years old, and a big girl for her age.

All the rest (except Lucia) dissented vigorously. Antonio felt that it would be a disgrace to have so young a child working, and his older daughters agreed. But Maria Rosa, with her stronger will, prevailed as usual.

Lucia was enchanted. It made her feel so grown up to think of being a shepherdess. Francisco and Jacinta, on the other hand, were heartbroken. Now they would have no one to play with, no one to tell them stories. In vain they begged their mother to let them go along, with the sheep of the Martos. At six and four, said Olimpia, they were much too young. So Lucia, after some preliminary instruction from Caroline and the rest, went forth alone one morning, with a long staff to prod the dozen or more sheep and one or two goats that belonged to her father, and slowly made her way down the winding road toward the open fields in the valley.

It was not so very difficult, once she got into the meadows, for there she found plenty of other children who were glad to have her companionship and to initiate her into the pastoral mysteries. There are no lush green meadows in this part of Portugal, and nothing approaching the richness of the Irish fields, where the sheep are twice as large. Still, the Portuguese flocks manage to keep alive and to produce good wool by straying over a considerable area every day, nibbling the sparse grass even when it turns brown in midsummer; and when they find a place they like, they all crowd together and remain for some time munching in peace. This gives the shepherds ample time for games and conversation. Lucia was welcomed on this first day by three girls from a neighboring village, whom she knew slightly: Teresa Matias and her sister Maria Rosa, and one Maria Justino. Their combined flocks were so numerous that they seemed to spread over the Serra, Lucia remembers, "like a cloud."

It was a great deal of fun, if one had good company, to spend the whole day wandering about the wild and beautiful countryside. Usually the young shepherdess would guide her flock between the stone walls of a long winding road to where it crossed the highway from Ourem to Leiria. By the roadside lay the shallow and sluggish waters of what was called the Lagoa, though the children preferred to name it the *barreiro*, or mud-hole. It was not quite as bad as that, for not only did peasants come from miles around to water their sheep, burros and oxen, but the women from several hamlets would bring their laundry there, and almost any day three or four of them could be seen standing up to their knees in the still water, their skirts tied up about their waists, scrubbing on a flat rock or board, while their small children ran naked on the muddy shore or splashed at the shallow edge of the pond. It was here usually that Lucia would meet the other girls. After their flocks had had a good drink, they would herd them all together, and drive them to the pasture where they wished to spend the day.

A favorite place was on some land that Lucia's father owned, about a mile west of the Lagoa, and more than twice as far from Aljustrel, in a great hollow or bowl, whose name, the Cova da Iria, suggests that there perhaps a girl saint's prayers may have won her the courage to protect her virtue even at the cost of life. At all events, there was something about the place that always had a strong appeal for Lucia and her friends. Under the vault of ineffable blue (especially over the northern slope) there was a various undulating scene. The grayish green of innumerable olive trees was broken by the darker tinge and thicker foliage of many evergreens, particularly of the holm oak family. The branches of the *carrasqueira* spread widely and gave a fine shade. The *azinheira* was a dwarfed variety, three to six feet high. In some places the grass grew long enough to be cut as hay. Much of the soil is reddish clay, and seems fit to produce only small wild flowers and thistles; but its barren look is deceptive, for when turned over it packs down and holds moisture even during a long arid summer, and bears diminutive but good potatoes, besides cabbages and corn. Lucia's father owned several cultivated patches in the Cova da Iria.

Sometimes they would spend all day there. Or they would go, after lunch, to a wild place to the south called Valinhos. The ground there was cut up into numerous fields of irregular shape, surrounded by thick stone walls four to six feet high, and so strewn with rocks, far and wide, that the wonder is that it ever occurred to anybody to fence it off for pastureland. Yet there is much good grass among the jagged rocks, and as there are many breaches in the ancient walls, it is easy to herd the sheep from one lot to another; besides, there are some large trees that give a good shade.

From Valinhos the land rises rapidly southward, wall after wall, to the top of a rugged hill called *O Cabeço*, The Head. On the crest of this was an antique windmill (still there, but shorn of its wings) from which one had a magnificent view in all directions for many miles. At the very top, on the southern side, runs a rather irregular ledge from east to west. In one place the crag is hollowed out into a partial cave, which gives some protection when rain or a cold wind comes from the northwest. Scattered about, too, were many boulders and chunks of gray granite. It was fun to play among them or just to sit on them and watch the flocks nibbling on the slope below. Farther down, the checkered landscape spread out in three directions to vast ranges of mountains. Just below, to the south, was a deep green valley from which arose some tall pines that waved and moaned when the wind blew. Beyond them, a few miles away, were several farms much larger than those of Aljustrel. There one could almost always see something interesting: men plowing or sowing or reaping, according to the season, or threshing with the implements of a thousand years ago. Or it was fun to watch, on the far heights, the squarish sails of old mills revolving and veering with the caprices of the west wind. The range at the east was of a sterner sort, like a clump of enormous rocks—from a plane, as a matter of fact, they seem only a small part of one huge piece of calcareous gray that runs for hundreds of miles the length of Portugal. At the other end of the valley are some friendlier mountains, covered with greenery.

It was thrilling to see all this from one place. And such a pleasant place! Everything about Cabeço is clean, fragrant and peaceful. The sunshine seems to laugh there all day long. The wind howls overhead and does no harm. Up there it seems good to breathe, to be alive, to be free.

Lucia began to enjoy her conversations with Teresa Matias and the other girls, all the more as she discovered in herself a certain ascendancy of intellect that could make them do whatever she wished. Teresa, now the mother of nine children, remembers that it was Lucia who led in the dancing and singing, and taught them new songs. One of these was in praise of Our Lady of Mount Carmel, and began thus:

Name of Mary,
   Oh! how lovely!
Save my soul,
   For it is yours!

Lady of Carmel
   Bring me word
To pray three times
   In blessing and praise.

In blessing and praise
   I have to pray.
Lady of Carmel
   Help me, do!

In heaven three bows
   To the weight of the cross,

Pray three times
   Help me, Jesus! Help me, Jesus!
      Help me, Jesus! [3]

One day Lucia and the three other shepherdesses were saying the Rosary together after lunch among the rocks along the ridge at Cabeço, when one of them called attention to a strange white something that was moving majestically from east to west, far over the deep valley. As it approached them it came to a pause over the pine grove, and remained suspended in the air for some little time. Lucia remembers it as "a figure like a statue made of snow which the rays of the sun had turned somewhat transparent." It seemed to have the form of a human being.

"What is that?" asked one of the girls.

"I don't know," said Lucia.

They continued the Rosary, their eyes still fixed upon the mysterious Thing; and as they finished, it disappeared in the sunny air.

Lucia characteristically said nothing about this at home. Others were not so reticent.[4] The news finally got to Maria Rosa, and as usual, she was curious.

"Look here!" she said to her daughter. "They say you've seen I don't know what! What was it you saw?"

"I don't know," replied Lucia. "It looked like somebody wrapped up in a sheet. There were no eyes or hands on it."

"Silly girls' nonsense!" Maria Rosa made a gesture of disgust.

After some time, and at the very same place, the same thing happened again. In fact it happened a third time dur-

---

[3] Op. cit., p. 45.

[4] Senhora Maria da Freitas, a Portuguese writer and daughter of a famous editor of O Seculo, told me in the summer of 1946 that long before she had heard anything about the apparitions at Fátima, a woman of the district repeated to her an apparently absurd tale brought home by her daughter, who said she and some others had seen a "white man without any head floating in the air."

ing the summer of 1915, as nearly as Lucia can establish the date. Maria Rosa, hearing the gossip, was a little more insistent in her questioning.

"Now let us see! What was it you say you saw over there?"

"I don't know, Mother, I don't know what it was." [5]

Neighbors began to twit Lucia about the apparition, and to exchange knowing or pitying glances when she passed. Her older sisters thought it had something to do with the abstraction they had noticed in her since the day of her First Communion, and often, when she seemed to be day-dreaming, one of them would say:

"What's the matter, Lucia? Have you seen somebody wrapped up in a sheet?"

Lucia said nothing. What was the use of talking, when she didn't understand it herself?

[5] Lucia herself tells about these apparitions in her second Memoir, p. 9, written in 1937.

CHAPTER III

Francisco and Jacinta were usually waiting for her at twilight when she drove the sheep into the dusty patio at Aljustrel. The boy was unconcerned, but the little girl would run to meet her, bringing all the news. Every night it was the same. She had asked her mother again to let her tend sheep with Lucia, and her mother had refused. Jacinta took this very much to heart. If the evening happened to be misty or cloudy, she was pensive to the verge of tears. "The angels aren't going to light their lamps tonight," she would say. "And Our Lady's lamp hasn't any oil in it."

While she and Lucia inclosed the sheep for the night, Francisco would sit on a stone in front of the Abóbora cottage, and play a tune on his *pífaro*, a little wooden fife that he treasured. Then he would follow them to the threshing floor near the well, and watch with them until the stars began to come out. But he was never as enthusiastic about this as he was about the rising and the setting of the sun. "No lamp is as beautiful as Our Lord's!" he would insist, and any manifestation of the power of that lamp delighted him beyond measure. The glint of sunlight on drops of dew or on the gilded surface of a pond, the ruddy glare of late afternoon on the windows of houses in a neighboring village—anything of this sort was enough to make him cheerful for the rest of the day. How did it happen that this little peasant, whose parents could not read or write, invariably saw in the sun (like Saint Athanasius and Saint Patrick centuries before) a symbol of the Word of God redeeming the human race?

Considering his age there was a great deal of the detachment and serenity of the saints in Francisco. With all his courage and fortitude, he was peaceful and gentle by nature, and seemed to have a precocious sense of how little the mere *things* of this world amount to. He would not put himself to the trouble of fighting even for what belonged to him. If another boy grabbed his winnings in a game, he would say, "Do you think I care? Keep it."

One day he went to Lucia's house and showed her and some other children a new handkerchief that had been given him. He was very proud of this, and with reason, for it was well made and had a picture of Our Lady embroidered upon it in bright colors. It passed from hand to hand, amid exclamations. Then, mysteriously, it vanished. When at length someone discovered it in the pocket of a certain boy, he insisted that it was his, and struggled to keep it. Francisco was strong enough to take it from him by force. Instead, he shrugged. "Keep it, then. What does a handkerchief matter to me?"

This indifference was his chief defect, in Lucia's opinion, and was probably the reason why other children did not care much to play with him. Lucia sometimes found it so irritating that she would tell him to sit on a stone and keep quiet. Francisco would obey without a word. What did he care? He could always entertain himself. Usually he would take his fife from his pocket and begin to play softly on it.

He had no real desire to be a shepherd. It was Jacinta who wanted to do everything that Lucia did. Yet Francisco loved his little sister more than he did his brother João. And because he preferred her company, he used to second her pleadings with a persistence foreign to his nature, until Olimpia sharply told him to hold his peace.

"It doesn't matter, Mother," he said quietly. "It was Jacinta who wanted to go."

A very different person was the capricious and wilful Jacinta, so much so, adds Lucia, that no one would ever have suspected they were brother and sister, had they not resembled each other so noticeably, with their dark brown eyes, their well-spaced features, their firm comely mouths, the curve of their cheeks. But in temperament, no. The desires of Francisco were few and easy to satisfy. Jacinta wanted everything, and with a passionate insistence. When she made up her mind to be a shepherdess with Lucia, she gave her mother no rest. Yet Olimpia, too, was a strong woman.

Jacinta's dearest ambition was to make her First Communion. If Lucia had received at six, why not she? Whenever there was a new Communion class, the older girl would go with her sister Maria to receive again and to renew her devotion to the hidden Jesus. On one such occasion they took Jacinta along. She was enchanted with everything, most of all with the tiny girls who, attired as angels, fairly showered the Sacred Host with flowers.

The next time they were in the meadows, she made a garland and placed it on Lucia's head.

"Why do you do that, Jacinta?"

"I do as the angels do. I give you flowers."

Jacinta seemed to have reached the pinnacle of happiness when she was given a place at last among the "angels" in a Corpus Christi procession. Yet when Lucia and the other girls cast their offerings at the Host, she was seen to stand still, staring at Father Pena.

"Jacinta," asked Maria afterwards, "why didn't you throw the flowers at Jesus?"

"Because I didn't see Him."

"You should have done as Lucia did."

Jacinta said afterwards to Lucia:

"Then you saw the little Jesus?"

"No. But don't you know that the little Jesus of the Host Whom we never see is hidden, and that we receive Him in Communion?"

"And when you receive Communion do you talk with Him?"

"I talk."

"And why don't you see Him?"

"Because He is hidden."

"I am going to ask my mother to let me go to Communion, too!"

"The Prior won't let you till you are ten."

"But you aren't ten, and you go to Communion."

"Because I knew all the doctrine, and you don't know it."

Thus Lucia became the teacher of a very apt pupil, who was not content to learn by rote, but wanted to know the reason for everything.

"How can so many people at the same time receive the little hidden Jesus?" she would ask. "And how can there be a piece for each one?"

"Don't you see that there are many Hosts, and that the little One is in each one?" And Lucia tried to explain the mystery of the multiplication of the body of Him who had multiplied the loaves and fishes, and had made all things. It was not long, however, before she came to the end of her knowledge, and began to repeat herself.

"Teach us more things," Jacinta would say, encouragingly, "for we know all these things now."

Jacinta managed to persuade her mother that she knew enough catechism to be examined by the Prior, and Senhora Olimpia finally took her to the church.

Father Pena asked her a great many questions. At the end he looked grave and said he feared the child was too young; besides, she did not know enough doctrine.

Poor Jacinta! How she grieved! Yet it was not her nature to brood over past defeats when there were other victories to be gained; and if life brought her some disappointments, they were soon forgotten. One day she ran to Lucia's house with great and evident joy, Francisco following more sedately.

"Guess what? My mother is going to let us tend the sheep!"

It was true, Olimpia had yielded at last. And from then on Francisco and Jacinta, like Lucia, could be seen early in the morning prodding a woolly flock that almost filled the narrow road—Francisco in his long trousers, with a staff and a tasseled stocking cap such as the shepherds of the Serra still wear, Jacinta with a gray checked waist and a black skirt that fell to her ankles, and a kerchief over her dark hair. At the *barreiro* (mud hole) they would wait for Lucia, while the sheep nosed into the brackish water; or if Lucia arrived there first, she would wait for them. Then the three, all barefoot as a rule, would proceed together behind the combined flock of some twenty-five or more sheep, with now and then a goat or two, until they came to some place where there was good grazing.

Jacinta liked to walk in the midst of the flock. Sometimes she would pick up one of the smallest and whitest lambs and carry it wrapped about her neck.

"Why do you do that, Jacinta?"

"To do as Our Lord does," she replied, referring to a holy picture someone had given her, with an image of the Good Shepherd on it. But when they reached their destination in some pasture, she was ready for any sort of game or frolic.

Sometimes they would spend the whole day at Cova da Iria. Sometimes they would play at Valinhos. Their favorite place was the rock-strewn hill called Cabeço, where the cave on the property of Lucia's godfather Anastasio offered so many opportunities for fun, and so extensive and beautiful a view.

Jacinta never tired of chasing the small white butterflies that flitted all day in the warm sweet air on the hillside and along the ridge. If there was anything she liked better than that, it was to pick the wild flowers that grew in great variety and profusion among the scattered rocks. There was a small blossom of brilliant blue that dotted the fields everywhere about Cabeço, and it was not difficult to find wild mint, because it was so fragrant, particularly if it had been crushed by some passing foot. Indeed, there were so many delightful odors combined and flung across the valley by the strong west wind, that it was hard to say just what they were. One could usually distinguish, even above the scent of mint or the aroma from the tall pines in the deep valley below, the more pungent fragrance of a dwarf variety of wild rosemary that the Portuguese call the *alecrim*. They have a popular song about it that recalls the "rosemary—that's for remembrance" of Ophelia:

"*Quem pelo alecrim passou
E um raminho não tirou,*

Rose of the sea—Mary's rose—rose of Mary, star of the sea—
this humble variety of rosemary still grows everywhere about
Cabeço, as if in memory of Jacinta.

Like all children she was fascinated by the discovery of the
echo; and as the echoes at Cabeço happen to be very clear,
loud and deliberate, she and her companions would shout for
an hour at a time across the rustling crests of the pines, and
listen with delight for the slow return of their voices from
the opposite hill. All kinds of names, jingles and jibberish
passed and repassed by that mysterious agency that the Greeks
imagined to be a nymph. But Jacinta was especially fond of
the repercussions of the word "Maria." Sometimes she would
say the whole *Ave Maria,* pronouncing each word only after
the previous one had stopped reverberating:

"*Avé. . .Maria. . .cheia. . .de graça. . . !*"

Sometimes all three would join in this sport, and then it
seemed as if the whole Serra da Aire resounded with the
words spoken by Gabriel two thousand years ago:

"*Blessed. . .art. . .thou. . .among. . .women!*"

What Jacinta liked best of all, however, was to dance.
She was very graceful, and she knew it; nothing seemed
to satisfy the restless energy of her mind and body so much
as flinging her arms and legs about in time to music. Lucia
liked it well enough, but not with the tireless inebriation
that seemed to possess the younger girl. As for Francisco, he
cared nothing for it. Yet, because he loved music, and because he enjoyed seeing the girls dance, he would sit for
hours on a stone playing one tune after another on his pipe,
while they tripped barefoot on the parched clay or the trampled grass. Some of the profaner songs may have been sung
in those mountains since Roman times. Others were holy,
for the Portuguese shepherds, like those of France, have quite
a repertory of Catholic songs inherited from the Middle

---

[1] "He who will pass the alecrim
   And does not stop to pluck a sprig,
   Will not be mindful of his love."

Ages. Francisco's favorite was one called *Amo a Deus no Céu*, which went thus:

"I love God in heaven,
    I love Him on earth,
I love the field, the flowers,
    I love the mountain sheep.

Like my little lambs,
    I learn to jump.
I am the joy of the serra,
    I am the lily of the valley.

I am a poor shepherd girl,
    I pray to Mary always.
In the middle of my flock
    I am the midday sun.

O' i ó ail
Who will let me see Thee?
O' i ó ail
My Jesus, now, this moment?" [2]

One of Jacinta's favorites was an old hymn:

"Hail, noble Patron,
    Thy people's favorite,
Chosen among all,
    As the people of the Lord.

O glory of our land
    Saved by thee a thousand times,
To all true Portuguese
    Thou art their love,
        Their love!

O angels, sing with me!
    O angels, sing forever.
I can't give thanks as you can,

[2] De Marchi, p. 47. Lucia gives a slightly different version in Memoir IV, pp. 4–5.

30

Angels, give them for me,
        Give them for me!

O Jesus, what tender love!
    O Jesus, what love is thine?
Leave the heavenly throne,
        Come make a heaven on earth,
                A heaven on earth!"

There was another one that went,

"In heaven, in heaven, in heaven
    I shall be with my Mother . . .

Virgin pure, your tenderness
    Is the solace of my pain;
Night and day I shall sing
    The beauty of Mary!"

There was nothing of self-conscious piety in the impulse
of these children to sing songs about Christ and Our Lady,
heaven and the angels. Christianity for them was not like a
garment to be put on on Sundays. It was like the air they
breathed, it was a part, and the most important part, of
reality. And because they knew that all things were the crea-
tures of God, they turned just as naturally from time to time
to more secular and even profane songs "of which unhappily,"
wrote Lucia, "we knew plenty." There was this rather cryptic
one, for instance:

"Pretty almond tree,
    What blossoming have you?
It was on your account
    I lost my good name.

I have a bad name now—
    Let it go!
I am going to wash
    In rose water.

I am going to gild
    The green lemon!

Singing is lovely,
   Weeping is no good."

There was a rollicking spring song to which it was great fun to dance:

"Don't sing the *ah la la*, o spring, o spring!
The *ah la la* is all over, how nice, how nice!
Because of the *ah la la*, o spring, o spring!
My mother punished me, how nice, how nice!

   Ah la la . . .
   Ah la la . . .

In this life everything sings, o spring, o spring!
As if to challenge me, how nice, how nice!
The spring sings on the serra, o spring, o spring!
And the laundress at the river, how nice, how nice!

   Ah la la . . .
   Ah la la . . .

At night the screech-owl sings, o spring, o spring!
He tries to frighten me, how nice, how nice!
The girl as she disrobes, o spring, o spring!
Sings songs to the moon, how nice, how nice!

   Ah la la . . .
   Ah la la . . .

The nightingale in the field, o spring, o spring!
Sings all day long, how nice, how nice!
The turtle dove sings in the wood, o spring, o spring!
The squeaking wagon sings, how nice, how nice!

   Ah la la . . .
   Ah la la . . .

Another fine old song was called *A Serrana*:

"Mountain girl, mountain girl,
   With chestnut eyes,
Who gave you, mountain girl,

Such lovely charms?
Such lovely charms,
   I never saw the like!
Have pity on me,
   Have pity on me,
Serrana, serrana,
   Have pity on me!"

When they tired of singing they would play various games.
They were getting rather big now for "Button, button," or
"Pass the ring"; but it was more fun to pitch quoits. As for
cards, they always carried two packs along, one belonging
to Lucia's family, the other to the Martos. Among the best
games with these were "dressing the queens," and "sobering
up the kings." There was another, that Lucia liked, called
bisca.

After their *merenda*, or afternoon snack, they were in the
habit of kneeling wherever they happened to be and saying
the Rosary. Maria Rosa had instructed Lucia to do this; but
without her watchful supervision they were beginning to
gloss over parts of it until they had reduced it to a perfunctory
recital, in which the meditation intended to be part of the
devotion had very little share, and nothing remained of the
words but the first two of each prayer: "Hail, Mary . . .
Hail Mary . . . Hail, Mary;" and "Our Father." Living in
the presence of God in all innocence, and seeing in everything about them the work of His hands and the evidence
of His goodness and power, these three young shepherds
must have seemed neither better nor worse than most other
urchins of the Serra, and ordinary Catholic children everywhere, when their bucolic routine was first interrupted, in
the summer of 1916, by a tremendous and unpredictable experience.

CHAPTER IV

The Serra da Aire had felt very little, thus far, of the misery and despair that had settled over Europe in the spring of 1916. In such remote and inaccessible places life generally pursues its own serene course though armies clash and kingdoms come toppling down. Ti Marto, for example, had felt a natural shock of indignation when King Carlos was assassinated in 1908, and he had never expected much of the liberal Republic of 1910, for he knew the anti-Christian principles and associations of its founders. Yet a true peasant is more interested in the amount of rainfall and the price of wool than in the identity of his rulers in some city many miles away. It was said that the Republic had seized church property, exiled hundreds of nuns, priests, and even the Cardinal Patriarch of Lisboa and other bishops. But the people of Aljustrel still had their good priest at Fátima, and could hear Mass every Sunday. It is doubtful if they realized the harm that had been done to the Church in other parts of the country, particularly in the cities.

It was very much the same when Portugal formally entered the World War in March, 1916. Only a few days previously Pope Benedict XV had made one of his most moving appeals for peace. He had begged all men of good will to have recourse to prayer and mortification rather than hatred, and had warned of the ruin that would come to all Europe if his words were not heeded. Yet with this memorable utterance still reverberating throughout the world, the unchristian rulers of that little Christian country—Christian at least, in history and tradition, and in country places like the Serra da Aire—had taken the decisive step, preferring to follow the voice of England rather than the Pope's; and Portugal was now openly at war. Still, outside of the newspaper propaganda from near-by cities there was little evidence of the change in places like Aljustrel. For it was planting time there, and everything seemed hopeful and cheerful as the sun grew warmer, and the fields turned from reddish brown to green. Lucia, Francisco and Jacinta followed their sheep as usual over the savory hills, watched the rebirth of the world, and sang and danced among the rocks.

Thus passed the spring, and it was summer again. But nothing very notable occured until one fine clear warm day, when they met according to their custom and guided their flocks slowly toward a place known as Couza Velha, a little west of Aljustrel. For some time the sheep nibbled at the new grass on a field there belonging to Lucia's father, while the children played various games near by. They were still amusing themselves, in the middle of the morning, when the sky became suddenly overcast, and a fine mist scudded quickly down on one of those stiff, cold breezes from the invisible ocean to the northwest. They remembered the half-cave at Cabeço, near the rocky crest of the slope on which the sheep were grazing; and as quickly as possible they prodded them up the gradual incline until, seeing them huddled peacefully in the shelter of some trees, they themselves took refuge in the "cave" on the southern brow of the hill.

It is not much of a cave, to tell the truth, for only a little bit of it is roofed. Still, there is enough of a pitch in the great rock that slants upward from the small hollow to give shelter from any light rain or heavy blow from the north or northwest. At any rate, it was the best to be found, and the three continued their games there as gaily as before. After a while they became hungry and ate their lunch. Then they knelt and recited the Rosary. Lucia does not remember whether they said all of it, or merely the skeletonized, "Hail Mary . . . Our Father." She does recall, however, that when they had finished, the rain stopped as suddenly as it had begun, and presently the sun was shining again, fierce and white, in a serene sky. She and the others began to throw stones into the valley below.

They had enjoyed this sport only a few moments when, without warning, a strong wind began to blow across the tops of the pines, which swayed and moaned as never before.

Startled by this, the three left off casting stones, and looked about to see what the cause might be. Then they saw a light far over the tops of the trees. It was moving over the valley from east to west, and coming in their direction. And though the illumination itself was unlike any they had ever seen, Lucia recognized in it the strange whiteness of that "somebody wrapped in a sheet" that she had witnessed the previous year with the three other girls. It seemed indeed to be wholly made up of a radiance more white than snow; and this time it drew so near that when it was just over a squarish rock at the entrance of the "cave," it became distinguishable as the form of "a transparent young man" of about fourteen or fifteen years of age, "more brilliant than a crystal, penetrated by the rays of the sun," as Lucia describes it—or "like snow that the sun shines through until it becomes crystalline." And now they could see that he had features like those of a human being, and was indescribably beautiful.

Stupefied, speechless, they stood regarding him.

"Don't be afraid," he said. "I am the Angel of Peace. Pray with me."

And kneeling on the ground, he prostrated himself until his forehead touched it, saying:

"My God, I believe, I adore, I hope, and I love You! I beg pardon of You for those who do not believe, do not adore, do not hope and do not love You!" [1]

[1] This is a literal translation of the words as Lucia gives them: *"Meu Deus! Eu creio, adoro, espero e amo-vos; peço-vos perdão para os que não creem não adoram não esperam e vos nao amam."* —Memoir II, pp. 10–11. Her two descriptions of the angel are substantially the same: *"Se aproximava iamos divisando as feições, um jovem dos 140 15 anos, mais branco que se fora de neve, que o Sol tornava transparente como se fora de cristal e duma grande beleza."*—Memoir II, p. 10, 1937. And, *"A alguma distancia sobre as árvores que se estendian ao direccão no nascente, uma luz mais branca que a neve, com a forma dum jovem transparente, mais brilhante que um cristal atravesado pelos raios do Sol. A medida que se aproximava, iamos-lhe distinguindo as feições."*—Memoir IV, p. 31, December 8, 1941.

Three times he spoke the same words, while the children, as in a daze, repeated them after him. Then, arising, he said:

"Pray thus. The hearts of Jesus and Mary are attentive to the voice of your supplications."

With that he disappeared, as if he had been dissolved in sunlight.

The children remained kneeling for a long time under the influence perhaps of some supernatural state of ecstacy or suspension of bodily powers, such as many saints have described. "It was so intense," wrote Lucia, "that we were almost unaware of our own existence for a long space of time." They kept saying the Angel's prayer over and over. Not that there was any danger of forgetting it, for the words had been impressed indelibly upon their minds; but it seemed the only thing to do.

"My God, I believe, I adore, I hope, and I love You! I beg pardon of You for those who do not believe, do not adore, do not hope, and do not love You."

Lucia and Jacinta were still kneeling and repeating these words, when they became aware of the voice of Francisco:

"I can't stay this way as long as you can, it hurts my back so much I can't do it."

He had stopped kneeling and was sitting on the ground, exhausted. All of them, in fact, felt weak and dazed. Gradually they pulled themselves together and then began to collect the scattered sheep, for the day was far spent and it was nearly time for supper. None of them felt like talking on the way to Aljustrel.

Just before they parted, Lucia warned the others to say nothing of what they had seen and heard. Why she did this she does not know even to this day. "It seemed the right thing to do," she told me. "There was something intensely intimate about it. It was just something you couldn't talk about."

The Angel of Peace! Who and what could he be? There are angels and angels, there are ranks and hierarchies of angels; and it is nothing new, in the long history of God's People for one of them to appear and to speak. No one with the gift of faith can doubt that the Archangel Raphael guided young Tobias; he is the angel of health, of joy, of happy lovers, of safe travelers. Or that Gabriel told Daniel the time of the Incarnation, and announced to Mary that she was to be the Mother of the Christ; Gabriel, the spirit of consolation, the Power of God. It is to the Archangel Michael, however, that Catholic liturgy applies the name of Angel of Peace—*Angelus pacis Michael.*[2] Yet in keeping with the paradoxical nature of all things Christian, he is also the heavenly warrior, armed with a fiery brand, chief of that embattled flaming multitude

Who rise, wing above wing, flame above flame,
And like a storm, cry the Ineffable Name,
And with the clashing of their sword-blades make
A rapturous music, till the morning break,
And the white hush end all but the loud beat
Of their long wings, the flash of their white feet.[8]

He it was who at the dawn of time cast down the disobedient hosts of Lucifer. It was he who stood by the closed gates of Eden, brandishing his flaming sword. He guards the body of Eve until the Judgment Day. He hid the body of Moses to save God's People from the sin of worshiping it, to which Satan incited them. Some say it was he who led the Hebrews to the Promised Land and shattered the host of Sennacherib. Always the protector of the Synagogue under the Old Law, he naturally became the champion of God's People under the New. Many apparitions have been recorded of him besides the one in Cornwall that Milton refers to in *Lycidas.* In the sixth century, for instance, Saint

[2] Roman Breviary, Hymn for Lauds on his feast of September 29:
"*Angelus pacis Michael in aedes
Coelitus nostras veniat; serenae
Auctor ut pacis lacrymosa in orcum
Bello releget.*"

[8] Yeats: *To Some I Have Talked With by the Fire.*

Gregory the Great saw him sheathing his fiery blade on top of Hadrian's Tomb in Rome, as a sign that God had accepted the penance of the Romans, and would end the pestilence that scourged them for their sins; and many angel voices were heard about the image of Our Lady, which the holy Pope bore at the head of the procession. Finally, it is Michael, according to Saint John in the Apocalypse, who will deal out final and everlasting death to the Dragon at the end of time, after those days in which men shall behold in heaven "A woman clothed with the sun, and the moon under her feet, and on her head a crown of twelve stars."

Whether it was splendid Michael that the children saw at Cabeço, or one of the other six who stand before the throne of God, the effect upon them was profound and lasting. The world could never be the same after such an experience. But this was not all. For the Angel appeared again to them, not merely once, but twice.

The second apparition was a few weeks after the first. It was one of the hottest days of that summer. They had taken their sheep home at noon to inclose them during the blazing hours of the siesta, and were spending the time playing listlessly at the well in the shade of the fig trees behind the Abóbora cottage, apparently with no thought of what was about to happen, when they looked up and saw him there beside them.

"What are you doing?" he demanded. "Pray! Pray a great deal! The hearts of Jesus and of Mary have merciful designs for you. Offer prayers and sacrifices constantly to the Most High."

"How must we sacrifice?" asked Lucia.

"With all your power offer a sacrifice as an act of reparation for the sinners by whom He is offended, and of supplication for the conversion of sinners. Thus draw peace upon your country. I am its Guardian Angel, the Angel of Portugal. Above all accept and endure with submission the suffering which the Lord will send you." [4]

[4] The exact words, as Lucia recorded them were: "*De tudo que*

He was gone. And again the children remained for a long time in a sort of ecstacy or exultation of spirit, adoring the Lord God whose messenger had been revealed to them. When this gradually fell away and they began to feel more like their ordinary selves, Lucia discovered that Francisco had heard nothing of what the Angel had said, although, as before, he had seen him plainly.

"Did you speak with the Angel?" he asked. "What did he say to you?"

"Didn't you hear?"

"No. I saw that you were speaking with somebody. I heard what you said to him, but I don't know what he said."

The next day Francisco said to his sister:

"Jacinta, tell me what the Angel said."

"I'll tell you tomorrow," said the little girl. "Today I can't speak."

On the following day he sought out Lucia again and said:

"Did you sleep last night? I was thinking all the time of the Angel and what it might be he said."

She then repeated the Angel's words on both occasions. The boy's mind was slower than Jacinta's. He had difficulty grasping what some of it meant.

"Who is the Most High?" he asked. "What does it mean, 'The hearts of Jesus and Mary are attentive to the voice of your supplications'?"

Lucia tried to explain. It was not easy, for he would break in constantly with other questions. Besides, the weight of what she calls "the atmosphere of the supernatural" was still to some extent upon them both, even after so long a time. She could not think of what to say. Finally she said, "Some other day! Ask me some other day!"

podeis, oferecei um sacrifício em acto de reparacão pelos pecadores com que Ele é ofendido e de súplica pela conversão dos pecadores. Atrai assim sobre a vossa Patria a paz. Eu sou o Anjo da sua guarda, o Anjo de Portugal. Sobretudo aceitai e suportai com submissão o sofrimento que o Senhor vos enviar."—Memoir IV, p. 32.

He waited patiently, but at the first opportunity he began plying her with new questions.

"Don't talk much about these things!" interrupted Jacinta. Yet with charming inconsistency she went on to say that there was something about the Angel that made her no longer want to talk, sing or play. "I haven't strength enough for anything."

"Neither have I," said Francisco. "But what of it? The Angel is more beautiful than all this. Let us think about him!"

Presently he did begin to grasp what the Angel had meant by sacrifices. From that day forth he vied with the girls in giving up little pleasures and satisfactions for the sinners of the world. All three would spend hours at a time lying prostrate on the ground, repeating over and over the prayer that the Angel had taught.

This must have been in July or August, 1916. As nearly as Lucia can estimate, it was probably late September or October when he appeared for the third and last time. Again they had been playing in the "cave" at Cabeço, while the sheep strayed on the slope below; and after saying their Rosary as usual, they were reciting the prayer in unison:

"My God, I believe, I adore, I hope, and I love You. I beg pardon of You for those who do not believe, do not adore, do not hope, and do not love You."

They had said this but a few times when they saw the same crystalline light come swiftly over the valley, and there he was, beautiful, resplendent, dazzling, hovering in the air before them. This time he held in one hand a Chalice, and in the other, over it, a Host. These he left suspended in the air while he prostrated himself on the ground and said:

"Most Holy Trinity, Father, Son, Holy Spirit, I adore You profoundly and offer You the most precious Body, Blood, Soul and Divinity of Jesus Christ, present in all the tabernacles of the earth, in reparation for the outrages, sacrileges, and indifference with which He Himself is offended. And through the infinite merits of His Most Sacred Heart and of the Immaculate Heart of Mary, I beg of You the conversion of poor sinners."

This he said three times. Then, rising up, he took the Chalice and the Host, and kneeling on the flat rock, held the white disk before him, saying:

"Take and drink the Body and the Blood of Jesus Christ, horribly insulted by ungrateful men. Make reparation for their crimes and console your God."

They could see drops of Blood falling from the Host into the Cup. He placed It on the tongue of Lucia. To Jacinta and Francisco, who had not received First Communion, he presented the Chalice, and they drank of it. At the end he once more prostrated himself on the ground and said the same prayer thrice. The children repeated it with him, Francisco following the others, for he had not heard the words. Then, for the last time, the Angel of Peace faded away into the shimmering sunlight.

The sense of the presence of God on that occasion was so intense, according to Lucia, that it left them weak and abstracted and almost with the sensation of being out of their bodies. It was Francisco, again, who was the first to return to ordinary reality, and to call their attention to the fact that it was growing dark. With such energy as they could muster, they herded the sheep together and drove them home. Yet under their weakness they felt an infinite peace and felicity for which there were no words.

This curious sense of happy debility lasted for days and weeks. It was a long time before Francisco would venture to speak of what he had seen and felt. Finally he said:

"I like very much to see the Angel, but the worst of it is that afterwards we can't do anything. I can't even walk. I don't know what's the matter with me."

A few days later, when he had recovered his normal energy and spirit, he said:

"The Angel gave you Holy Communion. But what was it that he gave me and Jacinta?"

"It was also Holy Communion," put in Jacinta before

Lucia could reply. "Didn't you see that it was the Blood that fell from the Host?"

"I felt that God was in me," he said, "but I didn't know how it was."

Then prostrating himself on the ground, he remained there a long time, repeating the second prayer of the Angel:

"Most Holy Trinity, Father, Son, Holy Spirit, I adore you profoundly and offer You the most precious Body, Blood, Soul and Divinity of Jesus Christ, present in all the tabernacles of the earth, in reparation for the outrages, sacrileges and indifference with which He Himself is offended. And through the infinite merits of His Most Sacred Heart and of the Immaculate Heart of Mary, I beg of You the conversion of poor sinners."

Such is Lucia's account of what happened to her and her cousins when she was nine, and they were eight and six respectively.

CHAPTER V

None of the children ever mentioned the Angel either at home or elsewhere. This became credible to me only after I had gone to Portugal and had spoken with some of the young shepherds who now, at about the same age, go barefoot among the sheep on the Serra da Aire. These short, stocky boys, with their fine eyes and strong flashing teeth, these handsome girls, so straight and shapely, are more precocious than those we know, and are not to be judged by the same standards. Early responsibility has made them resourceful, fearless, and decisive in judgment and expression. Though their formal knowledge is limited, for few can read or write, their brains are not cluttered, at any rate, with misinformation and scraps of half-truths; what they do know they know thoroughly, remember exactly, and can speak without hesitation or fumbling. A barefoot girl of five or six will reply with grace and dignity. Or if she sees fit she can be as silent as a sphinx.

Lucia, even more than most of these *serranas*, was endowed with a reserve so extreme that it was often mistaken for stubbornness or stupidity. It was easier for her to hold her counsel than to talk. Moreover, she had not forgotten the petty persecution she had endured after she and the Matias and Justino girls had seen "someone wrapped in a sheet." If her own mother and sisters had made fun of that, who would believe now that an Angel had come to give her Holy Communion?

Finally, there was something in the experience itself that imposed silence in a subtle but powerful way. Lucia was never able to put this into fitting words, either in childhood or in the years of her memoirs. Yet there it was: an ineffable something which could only be of God, impressing the words of the Angel upon their minds forever, but secretly, in a voice of authority not to be disobeyed.

Their elders seem to have been wholly unaware of what had been going on. What is more lonely and misunderstood than the heart of a child? No doubt these good people of Aljustrel were too busy with their own affairs to notice anything unusual in the conduct of three young shepherds who departed with their flocks early in the morning and were seen no more until they returned for supper. It happened, too, that there were many changes about this time in the life of the small communities on the Serra. One that vividly impressed Lucia's family, for example, was the departure of the Prior, Father Pena, and the arrival of a somewhat more austere priest, Father Boicinha, as his successor. There were the usual gossipings, the usual appraisals of the newcomer, pro and con. The more thoughtful parishioners must have felt that they were lucky to have any pastor at all, when so many communities in Portugal had none. Others gave no quarter: any pastor, good or bad, was fair game for them.

Father Boicinha was one who spoke truth fearlessly as he saw it. One of his first acts, and one that made him unpopular with the young people, was to preach against the inveterate dancing which commanded almost a pagan and fanatical devotion throughout the Serra da Aire. Dancing at home, yes, that was all right, he granted; but those all-night public affairs at Fátima and other villages were keeping people from going to Mass, leading them into sin, and in general becoming a scandal; and he declared that they must stop. There were many protests and murmurings, of course, especially among the girls. Maria Rosa, however, supported the Pároco, and forbade her daughters to attend any more dances.

"But dancing never was a sin till now," objected a neighbor, "and how does it happen that this new Pároco makes it one?"

"I don't know," replied Maria Rosa. "All I know is that the Prior doesn't want dancing, and my daughters aren't going to those gatherings."

Life was difficult for Maria Rosa that year. Her two eldest girls, Maria and Teresa, were married, and could no longer help the family. Her husband Antonio Abóbora seemed to be getting more and more shiftless. From time to time he had disposed of some piece of land to pay his debts, or had lost some valuable property that he had mortgaged, until there was hardly enough left for the once prosperous family to live on. To make ends meet, his wife now felt obliged to send Gloria and Caroline out to work as servants, while she herself continued to care for the house, and, whenever possible, to earn a little extra money by nursing. Lucia, of course, was the guardian of the sheep. Nearly all the farm work was devolving upon young Manuel, and it was not to his taste. Why should he like it, when his father shirked it at every opportunity?

The war offered this lad a good excuse to avoid the drudgery of spading and threshing, cutting hay and digging *batatas*. Portugal by this time was deeply involved. Every day one heard of some young man who was leaving for the front, or worse still, of this one killed, that one maimed, such a one missing. Something of the sense of uneasiness and apprehension that had become a settled despair in other countries was beginning to pervade the clear air of the Serra. But Manuel was young, strong and hopeful. And one evening he came home with the news that he had offered himself for service in the army, and would be accepted if he passed the physical examination.

From that time a mood of profound bitterness took possession of Maria Rosa. With the four oldest girls away, and her husband almost always late as he lingered in some wineshop for one more *copozinho*, the once happy family group had dwindled to four sad and silent persons. One night when the poor woman looked about the table at young Antonio, Lucia and Manuel—and now Manuel was going away!—she stared a moment at the empty places, and suddenly burst into tears. Then, with intense sadness, she said:

"My God, where has the joy of this place gone?" And putting her head on the rude table, she wept bitterly, until Manuel and his sister could not help doing likewise. "It was the saddest supper I ever remember," wrote Lucia.

Maria Rosa continued to fret and to grieve. Manuel passed

his physical examination and was accepted. Before it was time for him to leave home, his mother had become ill, and was getting worse every day. She had recourse to a doctor in a near-by village, but with no benefit. As the days passed she became so wretched that she could no longer do housework, and Gloria had to give up her employment and come home to take care of the family. Other *médicos* about the countryside were consulted. None seemed to know just what ailed Maria Rosa.

Father Boicinha, who had been noticing her debility with increasing concern, now offered to take her to Leiria, the nearest large community, to visit a surgeon who was reputed to be very skilful. One day the good priest arrived at the door in his mule cart, and Maria Rosa, with his help, climbed laboriously aboard, while one of her married daughters, Teresa, went along to take care of her. It was a long and painful journey in that crude conveyance, for the winding and rocky roads that skirted the mountainsides were not nearly as good as they are now. At last, however, they had left behind the stately old abbey church of Batalha and had come in sight of the ruins of that fourteenth-century castle, perched on a high rock far above the plain, where Saint Isabel once prayed and suffered—for she too, like Maria Rosa, had a troublesome husband. Somewhere among the white houses with red tile roofs that nestle around the base of the crag they found the noted surgeon. But his examination proved more harrowing than helpful, and Lucia's mother arrived home that night half dead from his ministrations and from the long jogging over bad roads.

It was from another surgeon at San Mamede that she learned the truth at last. He said she had a cardiac lesion, a dislocated spinal vertebra, and fallen kidneys. He prescribed a vigorous treatment of *pontas de fogo* and various medications. Poor Maria Rosa was like the woman in the Gospel who had "suffered much from many physicians."

Lucia thought a great deal those days of the Angel of Peace and what he had said. It became her greatest consolation, in fact, to remember the words, "Above all accept and endure with submission the suffering which the Lord will send you," and to ponder on their implications. Well, she was certainly seeing the fulfillment of that prophecy! But patience! She must be brave, she must accept this suffering. When she could think of nothing to do for her mother, she would go out to the well to pray and weep alone.

Sometimes Francisco and Jacinta would join her there, and add their tears and prayers to hers. It is doubtful whether they knew all that went on in the Abóbora family. Yet they must have heard enough to feel sure that something was very wrong, and their generous hearts reached out in compassion to Lucia's. Even Jacinta, young though she might be, was beginning to grasp the meaning of the mystery of suffering, and often she would say:

"My God, we offer you all these sufferings and sacrifices! It is an act of reparation for the conversion of sinners."

They were more silent and sombre than they used to be, these little shepherds, when they followed their flocks over the gorse and stubble of the Serra in the spring of 1917. Sometimes, to be sure, they would hear a familiar music played or sung by other children in a near-by field, and almost involuntarily would begin to dance, or to fling upon the fresh April wind the old refrain:

"*Ai trai-lari, lai-lai*
Trai-lari lai lai
Lai lai lai!"

But something had gone out of the joy of such singing. In the words of the old spring song, the *ah la la* was all over. How could anyone see what they had seen, and be the same?

There was something different in the air that spring. It was like the odor of death hovering upon the fragrance of the new flowers. Nearly everybody was depressed. Maria Rosa was desolate when Manuel went away. One of Jacinta's brothers also had gone to war, and was said to have been killed. Fortunately the rumor proved to be false; but Ti Marto and his family had many days of torment and suspense. One day, when Jacinta and Francisco were weeping at the thought

48

of their brother's death, Lucia proposed a dance to divert their minds; and the little ones began to dance, still wiping the tears from their faces. Yet they were often silent, all three, as they roamed over the scattered stones at Valinhos or gazed across the valley from the cave at Cabeço. They had become aware at last of a world in anguish, a humanity shackled for some obscure reason to the mystery of suffering.

Even May, the month of Mary, the month of new life and joy, weighed heavily on the world that year. On May 5, as if to voice the universal sadness and to point out the only source of hope, Pope Benedict XV lamented, in a memorable letter, "the cruel war, the suicide of Europe." After begging God to turn the hearts of rulers toward peace, and urging all to purge themselves of sin and pray for peace, he especially asked that since all graces were dispensed "by the hands of the most holy Virgin, We wish the petitions of her most afflicted children to be directed with lively confidence, more than ever in this awful hour, to the great Mother of God." He directed that the invocation "Queen of peace, pray for us," be added to the Litany of Loreto, and continued:

"To Mary, then, who is the Mother of Mercy and omnipotent by grace, let loving and devout appeal go up from every corner of the earth—from noble temples and tiniest chapels, from royal palaces and mansions of the rich as from the poorest hut—from every place wherein a faithful soul finds shelter—from blood-drenched plains and seas. Let it bear to her the anguished cry of mothers and wives, the wailing of innocent little ones, the sighs of every generous heart: that her most tender and benign solicitude may be moved and the peace we ask for be obtained for our agitated world."

It is quite improbable that Lucia and her cousins had even heard of the Pope's letter (for it was still unpublished) when they went out to the Serra five days later, the thirteenth of May, 1917. It was an uncommonly fine Sunday, and Ti Marto had hitched up his cart, early in the morning, to drive his wife Olimpia to Batalha, where they could hear Mass at the exquisite cathedral, and afterwards do some shopping in the near-by Sunday markets—what they wanted in partic-

49

ular was a young pig to raise for slaughter in the fall. So off they went, cheerily enough, leaving the children to attend Mass at Fátima. It was drawing toward noon when Jacinta and Francisco got their sheep out of the patio and on the road to the Lagoa, where as usual they met Lucia with her flock. They all proceeded across the fields to the meadows that Antonio Abóbora owned at Cova da Iria. Never was the immense sky more blue, the land more dappled with pastel colors.

Soon after they arrived at the hill north of the depression called the Cova and had got the sheep contentedly cropping the furze, they decided to make a little thicket into a "house" by closing up the opening to it with a wall; and they began to lug some of the stones that were lying all about, and to set them one upon another. While absorbed in this labor they were startled by a flash so brilliant that they took it to be lightning. Without stopping to ask how it could have come from that cloudless sky, they all dropped their stones and ran helter-skelter down the slope toward a certain holm-oak, or *carrasqueira*, about a hundred yards or more southwest of where they had been playing. They had just found shelter under its thick wide-spreading foliage when there was a second flash of light. Again frightened, the children left the tree and darted toward the east, a distance of perhaps another hundred yards. Then they stopped in amazement. For just before them, on top of a small evergreen called the *azinheira*— it was about three feet high, and its glossy leaves had prickles on them, like cactus—they saw a ball of light. And in the center of it stood a Lady.

As Lucia describes her, she was "a Lady all of white, more brilliant than the sun dispensing light, clearer and more intense than a crystal cup full of crystalline water penetrated by the rays of the most glaring sun." Her face was indescribably beautiful, "not sad, not happy, but serious"—perhaps somewhat reproachful, though benign; her hands together as in prayer at her breast, pointing up, with Rosary beads hanging down between the fingers of the right hand. Even her garments seemed made solely of the same white light; a simple tunic falling to her feet, and over it a mantle from her head to the same length, its edge made of a fiercer light that seemed to glitter like gold. Neither the hair nor the ears could be seen. The features? It was almost impossible to look steadily at the face; it dazzled, and hurt the eyes, and made one blink or look away.

The children stood, fascinated, within the radiance that surrounded her for a distance of perhaps a meter and a half.

"Don't be afraid," she said, in a low musical voice, never to be forgotten. "I won't hurt you!"

They felt no fear now, in fact, but only a great joy and peace. It was the "lightning," really, that had frightened them before. Lucia was self-possessed enough to ask a question:

"Where does Your Excellency come from?" The child used the colloquialism of the Serra: *"De onde e Vocemecê?"*

"I am from heaven."

"And what is it you want of me?"

"I come to ask you to come here for six months in succession, on the thirteenth day at this same hour. Then I will tell you who I am, and what I want. And afterwards I will return here a seventh time."

"And shall I go to heaven too?"

"Yes, you will."

"And Jacinta?"

"Also."

"And Francisco?"

"Also. But he will have to say many Rosaries!"

Heaven! Lucia suddenly remembered two girls who had died recently. They were friends of her family, and used to go to her house to learn weaving from her sister Maria.

"Is Maria da Neves now in heaven?" she asked.

"Yes, she is."

"And Amelia?"

"She will be in purgatory until the end of the world."

Purgatory! The end of the world!

The Lady was speaking again:

"Do you wish to offer yourselves to God, to endure all the suffering that He may please to send you, as an act of reparation for the sins by which He is offended, and to ask for the conversion of sinners?"

"Yes, we do."

"Then you will have much to suffer. But the grace of God will be your comfort."

As she spoke the words, *"a graça de Deus,"* the Lady opened her lovely hands, and from the palms came two streams of light so intense that it not only enveloped the children with its radiance, but seemed to penetrate their breasts and to reach the most intimate parts of their hearts and souls, "making us see ourselves in God"—these are Lucia's words—"more clearly in that light than in the best of mirrors." An irresistible impulse forced them to their knees and made them say, fervently:

"O most holy Trinity, I adore You! My God, my God, I love You in the Most Blessed Sacrament!"

The Lady waited for them to finish this. Then she said, "Say the Rosary every day, to obtain peace for the world, and the end of the war."

Immediately after this she began to rise serenely from the azinheira and to glide away toward the east "until she disappeared in the immensity of the distance." [1]

The children remained staring at the eastern sky for a long time. Even after they began to recover from the state of ecstacy which had come over them, they remained silent and pensive for a good part of the afternoon. But they were not heavy and tired as they had been after seeing the Angel of Peace. The sight of the Lady, on the contrary, had given them a delightful sense of "peace and expansive joy," of lightness and of freedom; they felt almost as if they could fly like birds. Jacinta would say from time to time:

[1] This is Lucia's phrase, at the end of her account in her Memoir IV, pp. 35, 36; 1941. It is an interesting coincidence that Monsignor Eugenio Pacelli was being consecrated Bishop at the Sistine Chapel in Rome on May 13, 1917, the very day when the children first saw the Lady of Fátima. As Pope Pius XII he took the first step to carry out the Lady's wishes in 1942.

"Ai, que Senhora tão bonita! Oh, such a pretty Lady!"

After a while they began to talk so freely that Lucia felt it necessary to caution them not to tell anybody, even their mother, what they had seen and heard. Francisco, as a matter of fact, had seen the Lady but had not heard what she said, as when he saw the Angel. When they told him all her words, he was intensely happy, especially over the promise that he was going to heaven. Folding his hands over his head, he cried:

"O my Our Lady, I will say all the Rosaries you want!"

"Ai, que Senhora tão bonita!" said Jacinta again.

"Well, I'm going to see if you tell anybody this time," remarked Lucia skeptically.

"I won't tell, no, don't worry!" answered the little girl. And Francisco also promised not to tell a soul.

Lucia still had her doubts about Jacinta. The child's face was shining with joy. She was almost bursting with it.

CHAPTER VI

When Jacinta and Francisco arrived home, they found the small house alive with people and conversation. All the family, except the boy in the army, were at home that Sunday; and an uncle by marriage, Antonio da Silva, had dropped in for supper. As the daylight began to wane, the older girls had placed a great kettle of cabbage and potato soup on the hearth fire, and were bringing loaves of tough brown bread out of a chest, when the noise of a mule cart on the cobbles outside gave notice that their parents had returned from Batalha.

Perhaps Jacinta meant only to welcome her mother when she ran into the street and saw her standing looking at the wagon, from which Ti Marto was extricating, with some difficulty but with his usual skill and quiet determination, a young, struggling and slippery pig. But at the sight of Olimpia's kindly and ready smile, the child ran to clasp her about the knees. And then out it came. The temptation was too much.

"Mother, I saw Our Lady today at Cova da Iria!"

Olimpia chuckled. "I believe you, child! Oh, yes, you are such a good saint that you see Our Lady!" And she swept by into the house.

"But I *saw* her," insisted Jacinta, following. And rapidly she told her everything almost in a breath: how they saw the lightning, and how they feared and fled, and how Francisco asked Lucia if he should throw a stone at the ball of light, and Lucia said no; and what the Lady looked like and what she said. And they must say the Rosary every day, and they were both going to heaven! Think of it, heaven!

Olimpia saw that it was not a joke; yet how could she take it seriously? "So you saw a Lady! And no one but *Our* Lady could appear to you!" She bustled around, getting something ready for the pig to eat, to prepare him for the important part he was to play in the life of the family that year.[1] Meanwhile Ti Marto had been locking the squealing animal in a shed off the corral, and had come in, weary enough and rather silent, for his supper. A moment later he was sitting on the edge of the fireplace, eating his hot dish of cabbage soup with *batatas*. Olimpia sat down beside him. Then, to divert him, she bethought her of the strange tale she had just had from her youngest daughter.

"O Jacinta! Jacinta, come tell your father what you told me about the Lady in the Cova da Iria."

Jacinta lost no time in repeating her story. Her dark eyes were brilliant, her cheeks flushed. It was evident that whatever may have happened, the child was deeply excited.

Ti Marto set down his dish gravely, and asked Francisco what he had to say about all this.

It is not clear just what the boy said; but apparently it was enough to confirm his sister's story.

Ti Marto looked from one to the other, slowly trying to make sense of it all. Olimpia still refused to take any of it seriously. "A fine little saint indeed," she repeated, "that Our Lady should appear to her!" Perhaps there was some humility in her skepticism. She and her brother Antonio Abóbora came from a rather wild family, more noted for charm and gaiety than for sanctity; even to this day she gives the impression of being a bit bewildered by what happened to her children.

"Well, if the youngsters *did* see a lady dressed in white?" put in Antonio da Silva slowly, "who could it be but *Our Lady?*"

The mind of Ti Marto moved slowly, but accurately. He had almost finished weighing and testing the two accounts, and interpreting the looks and inflections of his children. It was plain to him that they were not playing a prank on him. And as for lying—"*Ai, Jesús!*" and this he repeats even to this day, "I always found Francisco truthful, and Jacinta even more so." Finally he gave his decision.

[1] Olimpia's account to Father De Marchi, *op. cit.*, p. 64.

"From the beginning of the world Our Lady has appeared many times in various ways," he observed. "If the world is wicked, it would be much more so but for many such happenings. The power of God is great. We don't know what this is, but it will turn out to be something." It occurred to him furthermore that without some intervention of Providence the children could not have repeated such big and imposing words, for they had had little or no instruction, even in catechism. Thus Ti Marto with his shrewd common sense became the first to believe in the story of Fátima, on that Sunday evening in 1917.

Lucia knew nothing of all this until the next morning. She had gone to bed happy, without saying a word about the events of the afternoon, and had finally fallen asleep thinking of the beautiful Lady all made of white radiance; and the first she knew it was morning. She awoke early and went out to play under a fig tree near the house until it was time to take the sheep to pasture.

After some time she saw her sister Maria of the Angels coming to look for her, and was startled to hear her say, derisively:

"Oh, Lucia! I hear you have seen Our Lady at Cova da Iria!"

The child stared at her in silence.

"Is it true?" demanded Maria.

"Who told you?"

"The neighbors say that Ti Olimpia says Jacinta told her."

"And I asked her not to tell anyone!" said Lucia, on the verge of tears.

"Why?"

"Because I don't know if it was Our Lady. It was a very pretty little woman."

"And what did this little woman say to you?"

"That she wanted us to go six months in a row to Cova da Iria, and that after that she was going to say who she was and what she wanted."

"Didn't you ask her who she was?"

56

"I asked her where she came from, and she said, 'I am from heaven.'And then she kept quiet." [2]

This at least is what that excellent woman, Maria dos Anjos, recalls of the conversation after a quarter of a century. She was not being unkind to Lucia. She simply did not believe the story, and accepted her mother's theory that the child had been perverse enough to invent it. She felt she was only doing her duty when she returned to the house to tell Maria Rosa all that had been said.

Lucia, of course, was summoned promptly before her parents. Her father was inclined to dismiss the whole affair with a laugh. "Women's tales!" he said, as he set out for the greening fields. "Silly women's tales!" His wife, however, took the matter very seriously, and gave her youngest daughter a tart scolding.

"This was all I needed for my old age!" she lamented bitterly. "To think that I always brought my children up to speak the truth! And now this one brings me a whopper like this!"

It was a forlorn and miserable Lucia who went out to the patio that morning to let the sheep out of the fold. How suddenly the world had changed from joy to misery! And then she saw Francisco coming down the street, and looking very contrite. In fact, he had tears in his eyes.

"Don't cry any more," said Lucia. "And don't tell anyone what the Lady told us."

"I've already told it," replied Francisco wretchedly, blaming himself instead of Jacinta.

"What have you told?"

"I said that the Lady promised to take us to heaven. When they asked me if that was true I couldn't tell a lie! Forgive me, Lucia! I won't ever tell anyone any more!"

Somehow the discovery had spoiled their pleasure, and they were all depressed when they pastured their sheep that day. Jacinta sat pensive for a long time on a stone. Finally, Lucia said:

[2] Maria of the Angels' account to Father De Marchi, who gives the entire conversation, p. 66.

"Jacinta, go and play!"

"I don't want to play today."

"Why don't you want to play?"

"Because I am thinking that that Lady told us to say the Rosary and to make sacrifices for sinners. Now when we recite the Rosary we have to say the whole *Ave Maria* and *Padre Nostro*."

"And the sacrifices? How are you going to make them?"

Francisco had an idea. "We can give our lunches to the sheep and make the sacrifice of not eating any lunch."

From that time on he often drank from the *barreiro* where the sheep and goats took water and the women washed their clothes. Jacinta thought of a better way of disposing of their lunches, however. One day they saw some poor children from Moita, half a mile away, coming to beg at Aljustrel. "Let us give them our lunches for the conversion of sinners!" she said. And they did.

By the middle of the afternoon they were ravenously hungry, and went looking about the moor for something to eat. Francisco tried some of the acorns of an azinheira which were now green enough to be edible, and found them palatable. Jacinta decided that if they were so good it would be no sacrifice to eat them. Instead, she picked up some acorns of a different sort under a large oak and began to munch them. Yes, they were bitter, she admitted. But she would offer the bad taste for the conversion of sinners.

Every day from then on Jacinta made a lunch of these bitter acorns or of sour unripe olives.

"Don't eat those, Jacinta!" said Lucia one day. "They are very bitter."

"It is for the bitterness that I eat," said Jacinta simply. "To convert sinners."

It was not long before the children of poor families began to wait for them along the roadsides to ask for their lunches. The three always gave them cheerfully, and then ate whatever they happened to find as they roamed about the Serra. "We used to eat pine cones," Lucia remembers, "roots of bindweed, and of a little yellowish flower that grows on the root of a little ball of the size of an olive; mulberries, mushrooms, and some things that we picked from the roots of pine trees, but I don't remember what they are called." [8]

The most resolute in carrying out the Lady's wishes regarding sacrifices was Jacinta, if we are to take literally the modest recital of Lucia. One sweltry day that summer they went to a certain field that a neighbor had lent to Maria Rosa, and on the way, according to custom, gave their lunches to some of the beggar children. When they reached their destination, after a long hot walk, they were all tired, hungry and parched. There was no water about fit for human beings; even Francisco, apparently, was unable to drink from the little pool where the sheep relieved their thirst. No matter! They all offered up their pains for sinners as usual. But the sun got hotter and hotter, and as the afternoon wore on they found their resolution weakening, until Lucia suggested that they go to a house not far away and ask for a little water. When they did this, a good woman gave them a small piece of bread, which Lucia divided with her companions, and a jug of water, which they took back to the pasture. There Lucia offered it first to Francisco.

"I don't want to drink," he said.

"Why?"

"I want to suffer for the conversion of sinners."

"You drink, Jacinta."

"I want to offer a sacrifice for sinners, too."

The rest of this episode, so casually told by Lucia in her maturity, is worthy of that King who, hot from battle and served with water for which a soldier had risked his life, poured it on the ground as an offering of gratitude to the Lord God of Battles. The young shepherd girl of Aljustrel was moved by a spirit no less royal than that of the shepherd who was ancestor to the Messias and to His Mother, Our Lady of Fátima. And like David, let us note in passing, she was not without talent for narration:

"Then I poured the water into a hollow of the rock for the

[8] Memoir I, p. 13.

sheep to drink, and went to return the vessel to its mistress. The heat became more intense each moment, the grasshoppers and crickets were joining their song to that of the frogs in the near-by pond and were making an intolerable clamor. Jacinta, weak from fasting and from thirst, said with the simplicity that was natural to her:

" 'Tell the crickets and the frogs to keep quiet, it gives me such a headache!'

"Francisco said, 'Don't you want to suffer this for sinners?'

"Jacinta, pressing her head between her little hands, said, 'Yes, I do. Let them sing!' " [4]

If the children were taking the requests of the White Lady so seriously, Maria Rosa was no less constant in her determination to destroy what she considered a deception and a blot on the family honor. Stung by the neighbors' gossip, which the state of her health perhaps made her exaggerate, she felt responsible before God for making her daughter confess that she had imposed a lie upon the Marto children and deceived heaven knows how many worthy citizens. With threats and promises, with scoldings and caresses, she did all in her power to break down the serene assurance with which Lucia repeated her story. "If you don't say it was a lie," she said one day, "I will lock you up in a dark room where you will never see the light of the sun again!" Another time in exasperation she went so far as to beat her with the end of a broom. When all these measures failed, she took her to the rectory to see if the Prior could bring her to remorse and restitution. All in vain.

Lucia was beginning to understand what the Lady had meant when she said, "You will have much to suffer." Not only did her mother continue to coax and to rail, not only did her own sisters lacerate her with ridicule more cruel than they could guess, but eveyone in Aljustrel seemed to have turned against her. As she went pattering along the cobbled street, she would hear one woman say, "If she were my child—" and another remark, "A good strong dose of

[4] Memoir I, pp. 13–15.

quince tea would put an end to those visions!" Even the small children would yell, as she went by, "Hey, Lucia, is Our Lady going to walk over the roofs today?"

Yet with all this petty persecution there were consolations. One day two visiting priests stopped in to speak encouragingly to her, and to ask her to pray for the Holy Father. "Who is the Holy Father?" One of the priests explained. And every day, from then on, the children would add three Aves to their Rosary for the Pope, the successor of Saint Peter. It gave them a glow of importance to think that they could do something, so far away, to help the Vicar of Christ. Think of it, the visible head of the Church! And Francisco! What a comfort he was! He seemed not only to accept suffering, but to love it, as the saints do who follow in the footsteps of the Crucified. "Our Lady told us we would have much to suffer," he would say. "That doesn't matter to me, I will suffer everything as much as she wants!" Or when Lucia was on the verge of tears, thinking of the ill-treatment she was receiving at home and abroad, he said, "Never mind! Didn't Our Lady say we should have much to suffer?" And Lucia took heart again.

Another characteristic of the saints that Francisco began to manifest after the apparition of the Lady was the love of solitude. One May morning he left the two girls with the sheep, and climbed to the top of a high rock.

"You can't come up here!" he called down. "Leave me alone!"

It was a refreshing sunny day, and Lucia and Jacinta began to run after butterflies. By the time they wearied of this they had forgotten all about Francisco, and they thought no more of him until they realized that they were hungry, and that it must be long past the time for their *merenda*. There he was, still lying motionless on the top of the rock.

"Francisco! Francisco, don't you want to come down and eat your lunch?"

"No. You eat."

"And say the Rosary?"

"Later on."

When Lucia called him again, he said, teasingly, "You come and pray here."

The girls were not to be outdone. With much scraping of fingers and bruising of knees they managed to scramble to the top, where, breathless but triumphant, they demanded, "What have you been doing all this time?"

"I have been thinking of God, who is so sad because of so many sins," the boy answered seriously. "If only I could give Him joy!"

Some days they forgot the sinners for a little while in the zest of living with which God has endowed all children. Once they sang a variation of one of the old spring songs:

"The screech owl sings at night
And tries to frighten me.
As she disrobes the young girl
Sings in the moonlight.
         Ah la la!

The nightingale in the field
Sings all day long.
The turtle dove sings in the wood.
Even the cart squeaks a song.
         Ah la la!

The Serra is a garden
Smiling all the day,
And drops of dew are gleaming
On the mountains.
         Ah la la!"

It all sounded so good that they did it a second time. Then Francisco remembered.

"We shouldn't sing that any more," he said. "Since we saw the Angel and Our Lady I don't care about singing."

It was June now, and as the thirteenth drew near, they could hardly wait to keep their promise to the Lady to return to Cova da Iria. Maria Rosa welcomed the day also, but for a different reason. June 13 was the feast of Saint Anthony, the most popular saint in the country—and why not, when he was born in Lisboa, and prayed at Coimbra long before he wrought miracles at Padua? He belonged to Portugal, and certainly to the people of Fátima, whose church was named for him. On his feast day there would always be a Missa Cantata, a fervent sermon and a colorful procession, besides music, fire-works and feasting. And because almsgiving had been so dear to the Saint, there would be a generous distribution of what is called "Saint Anthony's bread." Special fine white loaves, much better than the dark ones that most people on the Serra have throughout the year, were baked for the poor. These were stacked upon ox-carts and sundry conveyances loaned by the most prosperous farmers and other householders, and gaudily decorated for the occasion with flowers, flags and bright-colored patchwork counterpanes. When the festive wagons, with their loads, had arrived at the church, they were lined up in the adjacent open lot behind a barrier of stakes in which there were two apertures. Through one of these the poor and the children passed to get their bread; through the other they departed in orderly fashion. Nobody went away empty-handed.

Maria Rosa knew how much her youngest daughter loved those fresh white loaves, the gaiety of the fiesta, the colors, the music, the fire-works. What a blessing that this year it would come on the very day when the little fools were planning to carry on more of their nonsense at Cova da Iria! She knew Lucia, and she and her older daughters were confident that Saint Anthony would restore her to the sanity of truth and obedience. All that June 12 they enlarged, for her benefit, upon the attractions of the next day.

Lucia said nothing. When they pressed her for an answer, she replied firmly, "I am going tomorrow to Cova da Iria. That's what the Lady wants." But her elders doubted this. "We'll see if you'll leave the feast to go to talk with that Lady!" said Maria Rosa disdainfully.

Ti Olimpia was inclined to agree with her sister-in-law. She could hardly believe, from past experience, that Jacinta and Francisco would forego all the fun at the church for an imaginary Lady. But she did not allow herself to be upset about the matter. Her husband found himself in a more embarrassing position when his little daughter begged him to go along to Cova da Iria. He did not wish to expose himself to ridicule on the one hand, or to offend his children on the other. Happily he remembered that there was to be a fair in a near-by village next day, and that he had to buy a couple of oxen. So he must miss both the feast and the apparition. Well, well! There was no doubt that Ti Marto's duty was to look after the stocking of his farm. This solution pleased his Olimpia also, and she decided to go with him.

Maria Rosa was made of no such flexible stuff. She did all in her power to discourage Lucia from returning to Cova da Iria. Doubtless she would have employed stronger measures if she had not happened to talk the matter over with the new *pároco*, Father Manuel Marques Ferreira.

"Let them go if they persist," he advised, prudently, "and see what happens. Then bring them to me and I will question them. We'll get to the bottom of this yet!"

CHAPTER VII

On the Feast of Saint Anthony the shepherds of Aljustrel take their sheep to graze much earlier than on other days, and bring them back to the inclosure at about nine o'clock, in good time to attend the Missa Cantata at ten. Lucia had her flock out of the corral before the sun had begun to redden the rim of the eastern ridge. She had probably been out in the meadows a good while, perhaps munching a piece of bread (for so the shepherd children generally eat, instead of sitting at a table) when her brother Antonio came running across the fields to tell her that there were several people at the house, looking for her.

Leaving the boy in charge of the sheep, she hurried home and found men and women from various places far and near —from Minde near Tomar, from Carrascos, from Boleiros. For the story of the May apparition had somehow spread all over the mountains. Many believed it; others were merely curious to see what would happen; and quite a number had taken the trouble to get up before dawn and walk over the hills to accompany the children to Cova da Iria. Lucia was not at all pleased. But she told her visitors that if they would wait until she returned from eight-o'clock Mass, they might follow her if they chose. Then she departed for Fátima.

They waited patiently for some two hours or more under the fig trees near the house. Naturally their presence was not very agreeable to Maria Rosa and her eldest daughters, and many acid comments were passed about the whole proceeding in general, and their folly in particular. This did not discourage the pilgrims. They waited, looked around, laughed, talked quietly until Lucia returned from Mass.

It was about eleven o'clock when the child finally left home, with the strangers fanning out on either side of her. "I felt very very bitter that day," she remembers, for the disdain and contempt of her mother and sisters had cut her to the heart. "I recalled the times that were past, and I asked myself where was the affection which my family had had for me only a little while ago." And now to be followed through the village by all these impertinent strangers, who asked her a thousand questions! She began to weep as she walked along. Her face was wet with tears when she stopped at the Marto house.

"Don't cry!" said Jacinta, when she saw the red eyes and quivering lips. "Surely these must be the sacrifices that the Angel said God was going to send us. That is why you suffer —and to make reparation to Him, and to convert sinners!"

Lucia dried her eyes, and the three, followed by the strangers, walked briskly down the main road and over the fields for half an hour or more. At Cova da Iria they found awaiting them another group of devout or curious persons from hamlets far and near. There was a woman from Loureira, a little man from Lomba de Equa, others from Boleiros, Torres Novas, Anteiro; and Maria Carreira and her daughters from Moita. There must have been at least fifty.

Maria Carreira is one of many reliable witnesses who still live near the scene; it was there, in fact, that I spoke with her in the summer of 1946, for she is the caretaker of the shrine and is known as Maria da Capelinha. A widow of seventy-five, always dressed neatly in black with a kerchief of the same color over her white hair, she looks younger than she is, for she is straight, slender, and quick in her motions. She has the serenity of one who has nothing more to ask of life; her blue-gray eyes are calm, honest, searching, intelligent. She remembers clearly how she happened to be at Cova da Iria on that Feast of Saint Anthony, 1917. She had been planning it for weeks. Two or three days after the May apparition, her husband had been working with Antonio Abóbora, the father of Lucia, weeding a garden, and he came home with a strange tale. Antonio had told him that Our Lady had appeared at Cova da Iria to his youngest daughter and to two of the children of his sister Olimpia, who was married to Ti Marto. Carreira thought it was crazy nonsense. But his wife took it seriously. Their son John was a cripple, hunch-backed, with knees that crossed and knocked together as he walked. Maria clutched at the thought that it might be true, and that Our Lady might return the following month and cure the lad.

As soon as Lucia reached the place, according to the story Maria Carreira told Father De Marchi (and confirmed to me last summer) she stopped about nine feet from an azinheira, facing east, with Jacinta on one side of her and Francisco on the other. Presently they all sat down to wait, for it was not quite noon, and the crowd, too, began to relax. Some opened their wicker baskets and drew forth loaves of bread and bottles of wine. A few offered the children bits of food, which they declined, though they did accept oranges, holding them in their hands. Jacinta began to play, until Lucia told her to stop. A girl from Boleiros commenced to read in a loud voice from a prayer book.

Maria Carreira, who had been ill, felt faint from standing. "Will Our Lady delay much longer?" she inquired.

"No, Senhora, not very long," replied Lucia, scanning the eastern sky.

They all said five decades of the Rosary. This done, the pious girl from Boleiros started the Litany of Our Lady. Lucia interrupted her, remarking that there would not be time. Then, arising from the ground, she cried,

"Jacinta, there comes Our Lady! There is the light!"

The three children then ran to the azinheira, and the crowd closed in behind them. Maria Carreira still remembers the details of the scene with some vividness: "We knelt on the bushes and the gorse. Lucia raised her hands as if in prayer and I heard her say, 'Your Excellency told me to come here, please say what you want of me.' Then we began to hear something like this, something like a very faint voice, but we could not understand what it was saying. It was like the buzzing of a bee." [1]

Some of the bystanders noticed that the light of the sun seemed dimmer during the following minutes, though the sky was cloudless. Others said that the top of the azinheira,

[1] De Marchi, *op. cit.*, p. 78.

covered with new growth, appeared to bend and curve just before Lucia spoke, as if under a weight.

In Lucia's own artless but telling account, she asked, "What does Your Excellency want of me?" substantially as in the story of Maria Carreira. The Lady replied:

"I want you to come here on the thirteenth day of the coming month, to recite five decades of the Rosary[2] every day, and to learn to read. I will tell you later what I want."

Lucia then asked for the cure of a certain sick person.

"If he is converted, he will be cured during the year," was the reply.

"I should like to ask you to take us to heaven," continued the child.

"Yes, Jacinta and Francisco I will take soon. But you remain here for some time more. Jesus wishes to make use of you to have me acknowledged and loved. He wishes to establish in the world the devotion to my Immaculate Heart."

"I stay here?" Lucia was in dismay. "Alone?"

"No, daughter. And do you suffer a great deal? Don't be discouraged. I will never forsake you. My Immaculate Heart will be your refuge and the road that will conduct you to God."

With these last words she opened her hands, as she had on the previous occasion, and again communicated to them the light that streamed in two rays from her palms, enveloping the children in its heavenly radiance.

"In it we saw ourselves as if submerged in God," wrote Lucia. "Jacinta and Francisco seemed to be in the part of this light that went up toward heaven, and I in that which spread itself over the ground. Before the palm of the right hand of Our Lady was a Heart encircled by thorns which seemed to have pierced it like nails. We understood that it was the Im-

[2] The word Our Lady used, according to Lucia, was *"terço,"* meaning "a third"—that is, five of the fifteen decades of the Rosary.

In addressing Lucia, alone, Our Lady always used the tender singular form, *"tu"*—"thou"—instead of the formal "you."

maculate Heart of Mary outraged by the sins of humanity, for which there must be reparation." [3]

The Immaculate Heart of Mary! The Angel had said something about that. "Through the infinite merits of His Most Sacred Heart and of the Immaculate Heart of Mary, I beg of You the conversion of sinners." Now the children saw both Jesus and Mary in that vision of the Most Blessed Trinity that enfolded them. Our Lady seemed neither sad nor joyful, but always "serious"; but the impression left by the Word of God, on the mind of Francisco, at any rate, was one of infinite sadness.

As this tremendous revelation faded from their view, the Lady, still surrounded by the light which emanated from her, arose without effort from the little tree, and glided swiftly toward the east until she could be seen no longer. Some of the people standing around noticed that the new leaves on the top of the azinheira were drawn in the same direction, as if the Lady's garments had been trailed across them, and it was several hours before they gradually returned to their usual position.

Lucia remained looking at the vast emptiness of the sky. Maria Carreira heard her say, *"Pronto!* Now she can't be seen any more. Now she is entering heaven. Now the doors are being shut."

The people were intensely excited. Though none of them had seen the Lady, it was evident that something extraordinary had occurred. Some began to ask questions of the children, others to dispute among themselves. Many were examining the azinheira and exclaiming over the dislocation of the new growth. A few were plucking the top leaves for relics or souvenirs, and there would probably have been nothing left of the poor bush if Lucia had not had presence of

[3] Memoir IV, pp. 37–38. The revelation of the Immaculate Heart devotion has been called "the June secret" in some accounts. Lucia has explained that Our Lady did not ask to have it kept secret. Something within them made the children keep it secret for the time being.

mind to ask them to take only the lower ones, which Our Lady had not touched. Maria Carreira was gathering some of the rosemary which grew all about, filling the air with its sharp fragrance; she was already thinking of setting up an altar or shrine on the spot.

"Let's say the Rosary!" said someone. "No, the Litany," cried another. "We have to say the Rosary on the way home." Reciting one or the other, they broke up into small groups and moved off slowly in various directions.

It was not until about four o'clock that Lucia and her companions were able to set out for Aljustrel, followed by a few of the more curious spectators, who still pestered them with questions and supplications. Some of them were inclined to be flippant.

"So Our Lady didn't say anything to you this time, Jacinta?" No reply.

"What's this, Francisco, are you still here? Didn't you go to heaven?"

"What did she say to you, Lucia? Come now, tell us."

The children resented this sort of questioning. They were still somewhat dazed from their experience; it was not easy to turn their thoughts back to everyday affairs. To some they gave laconic answers. To others none at all. Most commonly they would say, "It's a secret. I can't talk about it." Finally the last of the strangers became discouraged and took themselves off, leaving them in peace.

Francisco had many questions of his own to ask when they were alone. As on the first occasion in May, he had seen all that Jacinta and Lucia had seen, but had heard nothing that the Lady said—only the voice of his cousin. And even after they had explained everything to him, he was still puzzled about many details, especially about the reference to the Immaculate Heart. Yes, he had seen the Heart, and could not forget the rays of light from the Lady's hands, which he had felt penetrating his own breast.

"But why was Our Lady with a Heart in her hand," he persisted, "scattering on the world such a great light that is God? You were with Our Lady in the light I saw on the ground, Lucia. And Jacinta and I were going up toward the sky."

"It's this way," said Lucia. "You and Jacinta are soon going to heaven, and I stay with the Immaculate Heart of Mary for some time longer on earth."

"How many years will you stay here?"

"I don't know. Plenty."

"Was it Our Lady who said so?"

"It was. And I saw it in that light that struck us in the breast."

"That's right," put in Jacinta. "I saw that too."[4]

"I am going to heaven soon!" said Francisco. And from then on he often said it ecstatically. "Jacinta and I are going to heaven soon! Heaven! Heaven!"

The two younger children ran home full of joy, while Lucia, more thoughtful, went on her way alone to her own house.

When Jacinta and Francisco burst in, Ti Manuel and his Olimpia had just returned from the fair with two fine fat oxen, with which they were well pleased. Other members of the family had been at the festivities at Fátima. But the two youngest children became the center of attention the moment they appeared in the doorway.

"We saw the Lady again, Mother!" cried Jacinta, "and she told me that I am going to heaven soon!"

"Nonsense!" said Olimpia. "What Lady?"

"The beautiful Lady. She came again today."

"Beautiful?" repeated one of the family. "Is she as pretty as So-and-so?"

"Much, much prettier!"

"Is she as pretty as that saint in the church with so many stars on her mantle?" demanded another, referring to the image of Saint Quiteria at Saint Anthony's.

"No! Much, much prettier!"

"As pretty as Our Lady of the Rosary?"

"Much more yet!"

[4] Memoir IV, pp. 9–10.

"Well, what did she tell you this time?"

"To say the Rosary, and to go again every month till October."

"Is that all?"

Jacinta felt perhaps that she had said too much already. "The rest is a secret."

"Oh, a secret! A secret! Tell us the secret!"

But nothing could persuade either of the children to do that.

Ti Marto has often chuckled over this conversation. "All the women wanted to know what the secret was," he reminisces. "But I never asked them. A secret is a secret, and it has to be kept." [5]

Lucia meanwhile was being received by a much more skeptical and less cordial audience. Her insistence that Our Lady had appeared to her a second time made no impression on a family already convinced that she had become an unconscionable liar. It fanned the holy indignation of Maria Rosa, on the contrary, almost to the combustion point. To think that fifty persons had made fools of themselves by going to Cova da Iria, and all on account of her good-for-nothing Lucia, who was bringing her so fast to her grave!

During the next few days Maria Rosa became yet more exasperated, if possible. Almost every gossip she knew brought her evidence of the tremendous sensation her daughter had caused, even in the remotest corners of the Serra. Most of the witnesses had believed in the apparition. Hence the news had been scattered profusely in all directions and, although many still doubted, nothing else was talked of.

The last straw was when Lucia ventured to ask her mother to send her to school, since the Lady had told her to learn to read.

"School, indeed!" said Maria Rosa with withering sarcasm. "A lot it matters to Our Lady whether the likes of you can read and write!"

Fortunately perhaps for her health of mind and spirit,

[5] De Marchi, *op. cit.*, p. 84.

Maria Rosa bethought herself in good time of what the pastor, Father Ferreira, had said.

"Tomorrow," she said, "we are going again to see the Prior. And this time you are going to tell him the truth!"

CHAPTER VIII

Early next morning the two set out for Fátima, Maria Rosa stalking grimly ahead until they came to the Marto cottage. There she paused to unburden her heart to Ti Olimpia, and Lucia, weeping bitterly, had a few furtive words with Jacinta.

"Don't cry!" said the younger girl. "I will call Francisco, and while you are gone we will pray for you."

Lucia dried her tears and followed her mother up the hill to the church of Saint Anthony. Not once did Maria Rosa glance behind, not a word did she mutter. In her black dress, black kerchief and dark shawl she was as silent and ominous as an executioner. Her bare feet fell with deadly precision on the stones of the winding road. Even her sloping shoulders and dumpy form suggested iron resolution that morning.

Before going to the rectory, Maria Rosa entered the church to hear Mass. This respite was some relief to her daughter. As she knelt before the uplifted Host and Chalice, the poor child offered all her sufferings to Him who had suffered so much for men. "You will have much to suffer." How well the Lady had known! The Mass over, Lucia followed her mother out of the church and across the parched and trampled field to the house of the Pároco.

It was not until she was halfway up the flight of some fifteen or more steps, leading to the rectory porch, that Maria Rosa deigned to give any sign that she was aware of her daughter's miserable existence. Turning abruptly, she said over her shoulder:

"Don't annoy me any more! Tell the Prior now that you lied, so that on Sunday he can say in the church that it was a lie, and end the whole thing before all the people go running to Cova da Iria to pray in front of a holm oak bush!" [1]

Father Ferreira received them with grave courtesy, and

[1] Memoir II, p. 15, 1937.

asked them to sit on a bench and wait for a few moments. After a while he invited Lucia to step into his study, where he proceeded to ask her many many questions, very minute questions—"I am almost tempted to say boring questions," she added when she came to write the story twenty years later—but always with kindness and delicacy. He had already examined Jacinta and Francisco. He was comparing all the answers in his mind. And at the end he seemed convinced that the children had told the truth about what they had seen and heard. Yet his conclusion was even more alarming, in a way, than if he had convicted them of lying.

"It doesn't seem to me like a revelation from heaven," he ventured, thoughtfully. "It may be a deception of the devil, you know! We shall see. We shall see." He arose as a sign of dismissal. "We shall give our opinion later on," he added to Maria Rosa.

The devil! That was a possibility that had never occurred to Lucia or to her mother. The reading of Maria Rosa had not carried her very deeply into mystical theology. It is hardly probable that she had read the difficult pages in which Saint Teresa of Ávila recorded her torments at the hands of friends who suspected that her visions and ecstacies had been suggested by the enemy of God and man. Nor were such timid counselors necessarily to be blamed. For the Church has learned, from centuries of experience, that evil spirits can counterfeit the appearances of sanctity, and that all such manifestations must be tested thoroughly before they are accepted as coming from God. There was once a notorious impostor in Spain who deceived many holy persons by pretending to have the *stigmata* of Christ and to live on the sacred Host alone.

Lucia went home exhausted, abashed, and terrified. Nor was her anguish at all lessened by the utter abhorrence of her mother, who lost no opportunity, from then on, to belabor her with words and sometimes even with blows and kicks. The girl felt like an outcast as she glided through the house and stole out again to seek the quiet of the old well where she had once seen the Angel, and where she had shed so many tears and said so many prayers in other times of woe. And there she found Francisco and Jacinta, still praying.

Jacinta ran to embrace her and to ask how she had got on with the Senhor Prior. They listened wide-eyed, with growing indignation, as she repeated many of the Pároco's questions and his final remarks.

"It's not the devil," cried Jacinta. "No! They say the devil is very foul and ugly, and he is under the ground in hell. And that Lady is so beautiful, and we saw her go up to heaven!" [2]

Francisco was of the same opinion and nodded approval when his sister continued to encourage Lucia with:

"Look here! We don't have to be afraid of anything. That Lady will always help us. And she is *such* a friend of ours!" [3]

This was undeniable. Yet all that night Lucia lay awake, thinking of the Prior's words, and wondering, as many others have wondered, if she could have become, without knowing it, the instrument of God's enemy to bring contempt and ridicule upon everything holy. Night after night she suffered as only children can suffer when there is no older person who will understand their enormous perplexities and griefs. Every day under the heartening assurances of her young cousins the fears and doubts of solitary hours melted into the warm sunlight and the fragrance of mint and rosemary, as they all carelessly followed the sheep over the Serra. It was different when darkness skulked about her, and the same fear returned to lour by her bedside or to trouble her dreams. As the time approached for the July rendezvous with the White Lady, she was so tired and limp from this constant battering of invisible foes that she decided, at last, that the Prior must be right; and on the afternoon of July 12, she informed her two little cousins that she did not intend to go to Cova da Iria the following day.

After the first howl of dismay, there was a long earnest discussion.

[2] Memoir II, p. 18.

[3] Memoir I, p. 15.

76

"How can you think it was the devil?" asked Francisco. "Didn't you see Our Lady and Our Lord in that great light? And how can we go without you, if you are the one who has to talk?"

"I'm not going," said Lucia.

"Well, I'm going." Francisco was very positive.

"And so am I," added Jacinta, "because that Lady told us to."

Later the boy found Lucia at the threshing floor and made a final effort to persuade her.

"Look, you're going tomorrow?"

"I'm not going. I told you I'm never going any more."

"Don't you see it can't be the devil? God is already so sad over so many sins, and now if you don't go, He will be sadder."

"I tell you I'm not going!" [4]

Lucia held to this determination. Maria Rosa, who had her own ways of knowing what was happening, must have been relieved that night. And on the following morning she could hardly disguise her satisfaction when she noticed that her youngest daughter still had no intention of taking the sheep to Cova da Iria.

It was only when the time approached to turn them loose that Lucia felt a sudden desire to see Jacinta and Francisco. Running to the Marto cottage, she found them both kneeling beside a bed, weeping desolately.

"Aren't you going?" she demanded.

"We don't dare go without you!" they wailed.

"Well, I've changed my mind, and I'm going."

They arose with great joy. Francisco said they had been praying for her all night.

"*Vamos!*" Off they went by the zig-zag paths they knew so well across the two and a half miles of dusty terrain between Aljustrel and the Cova. It was the month of the Precious Blood of Our Lord; and July in that part of Portugal can be oppressively hot. As noon approached, a sultry stillness settled

[4] Memoir IV, p. 11.

over the fields where the sparse hay had already been cut and stacked in tight bundles around the trunks of the olive trees. Sweating men and boys, who had been digging the first little round potatoes from the red soil with great pronged hooks, began to steal away early for their siestas. Trees loaded with ripe plums were sagging visibly, cabbages along the roadside were drooping and wilting. Occasional sounds like the chirping of cicadas, the thwacking of flails on some farm in the resonant valley below Cabeço, or the squeaking of a cart on the glaring road, had a strange exaggerated quality that was startling. The oxen and sheep seemed almost too oppressed to thrust their noses into the muddy water of the Lagoa. A few darkly clad women, and an old man or two passed silently over the fields or down the highway under great black umbrellas. The sky was a huge blue glare of light; the dry air, unmoistened by rain for many weeks, was hard to breathe.

Yet on this particular thirteenth of July, in 1917, there was something unusual afoot in all the villages and fields of the Serra. Even before the children arrived within sight of the Cova da Iria they must have become aware of it. For all over the mountains and beyond people had been hearing, by the mysterious grapevine that disperses news so thoroughly and so fast in country places, of what had taken place on the feast of Saint Anthony. An astonishing number had made up their minds to be on hand for the next apparition. Maria Carreira had come again from Moita, bringing her crippled son, her incredulous husband, and all her daughters. Among the most fervent believers was another resident of Moita, one José Alves, who had told the Prior of Fátima to his face that his theory about diabolical intervention was all nonsense. For who had ever heard of the devil inciting people to pray?

When Ti Marto arrived (for he had decided to take the day off and see what his children were up to), the crowd was so dense that it took him a long while to elbow his way through to where Jacinta stood with Francisco and Lucia. Portuguese crowds are orderly and well behaved, as a rule, but this one troubled him a little. "The power of the world!" he reflected philosophically. He still chuckles when he remembers some of the richly dressed and adorned persons who had arrived "from who knows where," ladies in long skirts and wide-brimmed "picture" hats, gentlemen with fancy vests, very high collars and derbies. Ti Marto found them ridiculous. "*Ai, Jesús!* There were fine gentlemen who came to laugh and to make fun of people who didn't know how to read handwriting. But it was we who had the laugh on them. . . . *Ui!* Poor little wretches! They didn't have any faith at all. Then how could they believe in Our Lady?" Most of the people, however, were peasants of the Serra, the women generally barefoot, with black shawls over their heads, the men wearing their Sunday suits, and great hobnailed boots. And among them Ti Marto encountered his wife and Maria Rosa.

It may be that his Olimpia had been listening to that last tense conversation of the three children in the bedroom of her house. For no sooner had they scampered away, all their sorrow turned to relief, than she hurried to her brother's house to tell Maria Rosa what had occurred. "*Ai, Jesús!*" The heavens seemed once more to be crashing down about the tired head of Lucia's mother. After all she had been through, to think that the silly *cachopa* was going off to keep a tryst with the devil! Arming themselves with some holy candles and a supply of matches, the two women started for Cova da Iria, evidently with some notion of exorcising the evil spirit if he should turn up there again. They were too late to head off the children, if that was their intent; however, there they were, clutching their candles and ready to light them if need be. And with them were some 2,000 to 3,000 other persons, devout or curious, waiting to see what would happen.

The children, in the center of the throng, were now reciting the Rosary and gazing with expectancy toward the east. They paid no attention to a rude woman who was berating them as impostors. Jacinta and Francisco did not even see their father as he took his place beside them, ready to help them if necessary. Ti Marto was looking at Lucia. Her face had a deathlike pallor. He heard her say:

"Take off your hats! Take off your hats, for I see Our Lady already!" He saw something like a small cloud descend upon the azinheira; and suddenly, as the sunlight became dimmer, a cool fresh breeze blew over the hot Serra. Then he heard something that sounded to him, he says, "like a horse-fly in an empty water-pot"; but neither he nor Maria Carreira nor any of the rest, except the children, could distinguish any words.

By this time all the stimuli of the sensory world—the crowd, the sun, the breeze, all the trivialities of space and time—had fallen away from the three young mystics as some supernatural force descended upon and drew them up into that white radiance where once more with inexpressible joy they saw the Lady glide to the top of the little tree.

"*Vocemecê que me quere?*" asked Lucia as before. "What do you want of me?"

"I want you to come here on the thirteenth day of the coming month, and to continue to say five decades of the Rosary every day in honor of Our Lady of the Rosary to obtain the peace of the world and the end of the war. For She alone will be able to help."

Lucia said, "I wish to ask you to tell us who you are, and to perform a miracle so that everyone will believe that you have appeared to us!"

"Continue to come here every month," answered the Lady. "In October I will tell you who I am and what I wish, and will perform a miracle that everyone will have to believe."

Here Lucia thought of some requests that various people had asked her to present. "I don't remember just what they were," she wrote in 1941. But it is believed that one of them was for the cure of Maria Carreira's crippled son; and the Lady is said to have answered that she would not cure him, but would give him a means of livelihood if he would say his Rosary every day. What Lucia now recalls is her insistence on the daily use of the beads to gain graces during the year.

"Sacrifice yourselves for sinners," she repeated, "and say many times, especially when you make some sacrifice:

" 'O Jesus, it is for your love, for the conversion of sinners and in reparation for the sins committed against the Immaculate Heart of Mary.' "

As the Lady spoke the last words, she opened her lovely

hands as before, and poured down from them the revealing and penetrating radiance that had warmed the hearts of the children on the previous occasions. But this time it seemed to pass into the earth, disclosing beneath—and these are Lucia's words, written in 1941—"a sea of fire; and plunged in this fire the demons and the souls, as if they were red-hot coals, transparent and black or bronze-colored, with human forms, which floated about in the conflagration, borne by the flames which issued from it with clouds of smoke, falling on all sides as sparks fall in great conflagrations—without weight or equilibrium, among shrieks and groans of sorrow and despair which horrify and cause to shudder with fear.

"The devils were distinguished by horrible and loathsome forms of animals frightful and unknown, but transparent like black coals that have turned red-hot." [5]

The children were so frightened that they would have died, they felt, if they had not been told they were all going to heaven. After gazing in fascinated horror at the gruesome spectacle which not even Saint Teresa has described more fearfully, they raised their eyes as if in desperate appeal to the Lady who stood gazing down on them with sombre tenderness.

"You see hell, where the souls of poor sinners go," she said at length. "To save them God wishes to establish in the world the devotion to my Immaculate Heart. If they do what I will tell you, many souls will be saved, and there will be peace. The war is going to end. But if they do not stop offending God, another and worse one will begin in the reign of Pius XI.

"When you shall see a night illuminated by an unknown light, know that it is the great sign that God gives you that He is going to punish the world for its crimes by means of war, of hunger, and of persecution of the Church and of the Holy Father.

"To prevent this I come to ask the consecration of Russia to my Immaculate Heart and the Communion of reparation on

[5] Memoir IV; also III, in almost the same words.

the first Saturdays. If they listen to my requests, Russia will be converted and there will be peace. If not she will scatter her errors through the world, provoking wars and persecutions of the Church. The good will be martyrized, the Holy Father will have much to suffer, various nations will be annihilated.

"In the end my Immaculate Heart will triumph. The Holy Father will consecrate Russia to me, and it will be converted and a certain period of peace will be granted to the world.[6]

"In Portugal the dogma of the Faith will always be kept.

"Tell this to no one. Francisco, yes, you may tell him.

"When you say the Rosary, say after each mystery, 'O my Jesus, pardon us and deliver us from the fire of hell. Draw all souls to heaven, especially those in most need.' "

The Lady then told the children a final secret which has never been revealed, and which Lucia will not disclose until the Queen of Heaven herself commands her to do so. She has never told it even to her confessors.

In the long moment of silence that followed, the crowd seemed to sense the apocalyptic solemnity and tenseness of a communication on which hangs, perhaps, the fate of the entire human race. Not a sound could be heard anywhere. The children, the crowd, the wind, all were silent as death. Finally Lucia, as pale as a corpse, ventured to ask in her high thin voice:

"Do you want nothing more of me?"

[6] The exact words of Our Lady, as Lucia wrote them down in Portuguese, were these: *"Para impedir virei pedir a consagração da Rússia a meu Imaculado coração e a Comunhão reparadora nos primeiros sábados. Se atenderem a meus pedidos, a Rússia se converterá e terão paz; se não, espalhará seus êrros pelo mundo, promovendo guerras e perseguições a Igreja. Os bons serão martirizados, o Santo Padre terá muito que sofrer, varias nações serão aniquilados. Por fim o meu Imaculado Coração triunfará. O Santo Padre consagrar-me-á a Rússia que se converterá e será concedido ao mundo algum tempo de paz . . ."* Memoir III, p. 2; also IV, p. 39. In 1927 Our Lady explained further how the consecration of Russia (not "the world," as in some inaccurate accounts) should be made. See below, p. 221, and p. 222, n. 2.

"No, today I want nothing more of thee."

With a last affectionate but overpowering glance, the Lady passed as usual toward the east—so Lucia concludes the tremendous story of the third apparition—"and disappeared in the immense distance of the firmament."

As the children left off gazing eastward and stared, wan and shaken, at one another, the people began to press around them, all but suffocating and trampling them in their eagerness to ask all manner of questions.

"What did she look like?" "What did she say?" "Why do you look so sad?" "Is it the Blessed Virgin?" "Will she come again?"

"It's a secret," said Lucia. "It's a secret."

"Good or bad?"

"Good for some, for others bad."

"And you won't tell us?"

"No, sir. It's a secret and the Lady told us not to tell it."

Ti Marto picked up his daughter Jacinta, and elbowed his way to the edge of the crowd, the child clinging to his neck. Stragglers followed them, still pelting them with questions. And Lucia and Francisco kept saying:

"It's a secret. It's a secret."

Someone offered to take them home in an automobile. Ti Marto consented, and the children rode for the first time in one of the strange horseless monsters they had seen occasionally rumbling along the road from Ourem to Leiria. They were not in a mood to enjoy a new experience. But they were grateful for the ride, for all three were exhausted.

CHAPTER IX

Everybody in Portugal seemed to have heard the news from Fátima. Catholic diocesan papers began to publish short articles in which a note of prudent reserve was evident; the headline of the one in *The Ouriense* of Ourem, for example was, "Real Apparition or Supposed Illusion." More generous with its space if not with its approval, was a secular press almost wholly and openly devoted to the anti-Catholic revolution. Editors of the Jacobin tradition of 1789 flatly accused the clergy, and particularly the Jesuits, of having invented the story to regain the prestige they had lost in the Revolution of 1910. The anti-clerical *O Seculo*, chief daily of Lisboa, printed a sarcastic and distorted account on July 21, under the heading, "A Message from Heaven—Commercial Speculation?" Liberals of a more moderate tinge wrote suavely of psychosis, epilepsy and collective suggestion as possible explanations of the incredible tale from the Serra da Aire. A casual reader of the daily press might have concluded that the net result thus far had been to provoke a new and bitter attack upon the Church.

If the illiterate children of Aljustrel and their families were spared from all this, they could not escape so easily from hordes of pilgrims, devotees, relic-hunters and mere sensation-seekers that broke in more and more upon their peace. Some they were sorry for—poor wretches shattered by want or sorrow or some incurable disease, who often walked barefoot over great distances, sometimes completing the last mile on bleeding knees, to ask their prayers for some favor, some cure from the Holy Virgin. They found it more difficult to be patient with some of the rich and well-fed persons, fashionably dressed and sporting furs and jewels, who would appear suddenly in carriages or even in automobiles, some from as far as Porto or Lisboa, either to beg some boon from heaven—for not even the rich are satisfied!—or to divert themselves with a new marvel. Ti Marto remembers them well. "What questions they would ask! *Ai Jesús!* Some of them were terrible. 'Did Our Lady also have goats and sheep when she was a little girl?' 'Did Our Lady ever eat potatoes?' What questions! It was a scandal, that's what it was!" [1]

Francisco, like his father, resented the smug complacent stupidity of the nabobs, and all the inquisitions and caresses to which they subjected him. One day he turned on Jacinta, boylike, and said, "It's too bad you didn't keep quiet! Then nobody would know it. If it wasn't a lie," he added regretfully, "we could tell all the people we saw nothing, and that would be the end of it."

After a while they began to develop a certain skill in avoiding bores of the sleek and curious variety, who were so hard to shake off. They could tell them at a glance from a distance. One day they saw a group of fine ladies and gentlemen getting out of a motor car on the road from Aljustrel to Fátima. There was no doubt what they were, but it was too late to escape: the ladies had already seen them and were approaching with smiles only too familiar.

"Where do the little shepherds live? The ones that saw Our Lady?"

The children gave the most precise directions to their homes. The visitors thanked them, and went on down the hill, while the three, giggling with triumph, tumbled over the wall and ran to hide among the olive trees behind the Abóbora cottage.

"We must always do this!" said Jacinta with great satisfaction.

There were many priests among the pilgrims at this period. And most of them, despite the accusations of the anti-clerical press, were skeptical and even hostile. Priests trained in theology were well aware of the harm that fraud or delusion might do the Church, and could ask a thousand clever questions that would never occur to one of the unbelieving skeptics. The mere sight of a black soutane far down the road

[1] De Marchi, p. 104.

became a warning signal to be acted upon instantly. "When we saw a priest coming, we always escaped if we could," wrote Lucia. "When we saw ourselves in the presence of a priest, we prepared ourselves to offer to God one of our greatest sacrifices."

Fortunately there were exceptions. One of those they liked to remember afterwards was the visit of the Jesuit Father Cruz, who came all the way from Lisboa to investigate what he had heard. Four years had passed since he had said to Lucia, at her first confession, "My daughter, your soul is the temple of the Holy Spirit. Keep it always pure. . . ." And though he was prematurely old and bent almost double, he still went about, never carrying money with him, preaching and directing souls, which he seemed to read instantly with his small, shrewd benevolent eyes.[2] After questioning the children for some time, he persuaded them, as a good detective might, to take him to the exact spot where they had seen Our Lady, and to reënact for him all they had done and said.

"On the way," Lucia recalls, "we walked on each side of His Reverence, who was mounted on an ass so small that his feet almost dragged on the ground." It was a long and painful journey for him, and a tedious one, perhaps, for them, but it was worth while, for he came away convinced that they had told the truth. He taught them many ejaculatory prayers that proved useful and consoling. And from that day on he was their champion.

Unfortunately this did not effect the conversion of Lucia's family. They had been more unsympathetic than ever since the apparition of July 13. Previously her father had shrugged off the whole affair with some muttering about "women's tales." But he had passed from neutrality to open hostility on the day when he went to inspect his vegetable gardens at Cova da Iria, and saw what the crowds had done to them. Thousands of feet had packed the soil so hard that there was

[2] He is still doing this at the age of eighty-six. I met him by happy chance on a train between Lisboa and Santarem last summer. He told me he had given Lucia her first communion.

no sense cultivating it any more; horses had eaten or trampled his cabbages, beans and potato vines; all his labor had been wasted. Antonio grumbled and fumed, and drank more *copinhos* than ever.

The rest of the family also had a new weapon to brandish over the head of poor Lucia. She and her visions had brought them all to the verge of starvation. When she was hungry, her sisters would say, "Go and eat what you find growing at Cova da Iria!" Or Maria Rosa would cry, "Yes, ask that Lady to give you something to eat! You made all the people go to Cova da Iria. Get your food there."

"We didn't make them go," said loyal Jacinta from the doorway. "They went there themselves!"

But Maria Rosa felt too strongly to listen to reasoning. There were days when Lucia feared to ask her for so much as a piece of bread, and went to bed hungry.

From time to time her mother would take her to the Prior for another interrogation, hoping each time that he would find a way to break her stubborn will. At the end the good man always shook his head and said, "I don't know what to say about all this." No wonder Maria Rosa still doubted, when a man, so learned, confessed that he could make nothing of it.

It was only at Cabeço or Valinhos or on the hills near Cova da Iria that Lucia could find any peace or solace at all. And even there the discussions of the three had taken on a sombre and more thoughtful tone since the breath-taking revelations of July 13. The fires of hell, the damnation of many souls, a second world war with millions of people starving, homeless, tormented, butchered, tumbling unprepared into eternity— how could the world ever look the same to childish eyes after Divine Wisdom had disclosed to them such horrors! The two girls could think of nothing else. Francisco, for some reason, was much less shaken by the experience. Instead of brooding on the countless souls he had seen rising and falling like sparks in the flames under the taunts of fallen angels, he would fix his thoughts upon God, upon His goodness and His glory.

"How wonderful God is!" he would cry ecstatically. "There

87

is no way to say it. All you can say is, that nobody can say it! But isn't it too bad that He is so sad! If I could only console Him!"

Jacinta did not find it so easy to put out of mind the horror of eternal death. If a world war could be both incredible and painfully real, so much the more so was hell. But what does a child of seven know of the enormity of sin? She was shocked, profoundly puzzled. A few days after the apparition of July she sat for a long time on a stone, reflecting deeply while the sheep munched the withered grass and furze. Finally she said:

"That Lady said that many souls go to hell. What is hell?"

"It is a pit full of worms and a very big bonfire," replied Lucia, perhaps quoting her mother, "and people go there who commit sins and don't confess them, and they stay forever and burn."

"And never get out any more?"

"No."

"Not after many, many years?"

"No. Hell never ends. And heaven doesn't either. Whoever goes to heaven never gets out of it, and whoever goes to hell doesn't either. Don't you see that they are eternal, because they never end?"

Jacinta found this concept of endlessness at once baffling and tantalizing. She could never put it wholly out of mind. Often in the midst of some game she would stop suddenly and say:

"But look here, doesn't hell end even after many, many, *many* years?"

"No."

"And those people who have to burn there never die? Never? And they never turn into ashes? And if people pray a great deal for sinners, Our Lord will save them from that? And with sacrifices too? Poor sinners we have to pray and make many sacrifices for them!"

Then, when the thought of the burden of sin became almost unbearable, she would remember the consolation that had been granted with it.

"How good that Lady is! Yes, she has promised to take us to heaven!"

Jacinta was too unselfish to be able to dwell long or complacently on her own good fortune when there were so many others who would never share it. To her the sight of gehennah was like a gate opening upon a steep road of asceticism. "I think I would lay down a thousand lives to save one soul of the many I saw being lost," wrote Saint Teresa of Jesus after a similar experience; and the little *serrana* of Aljustrel was so stricken with the same noble pity that she acquired a thirst for penance to which Lucia could apply only the word "insatiable." Other Christians accepted hell on faith, because Christ had said repeatedly and with solemn emphasis that there is a hell, but Jacinta had *seen* it; and once she grasped the idea that God's justice is the counterpart of His mercy, and that there must be a hell if there is to be a heaven, nothing seemed important to her except to save as many souls as possible from the horrors she had glimpsed under the radiant hands of the Queen of Heaven. Nothing could be too hard, nothing too small or too great to give up.

"Eat, Jacinta."

"No, I will offer this sacrifice for poor sinners who eat too much."

"Drink, Jacinta."

"No, this is for those who drink too much."

She would say suddenly to Lucia, "I am sorry for you. Francisco and I are going to heaven, but you stay here alone. I will ask Our Lady to take you to heaven! But she wants you to stay here for a while! When you see the war, don't be afraid —in heaven I will be praying for you."

More and more, however, she brooded on the lost souls.

"Jacinta, what are you thinking of?" asked Lucia one day.

"Of that war that is going to come, and of so many people who are going to die and go to hell. What a pity there must be a war and they must go to hell because they won't stop sinning!"

Time and again this thought recurred with sickening impact. She would say, with a look of terror, "Hell! Hell! How sorry I am for the souls that are going to hell!" Then she would fall on her knees, clasp her hands and repeat over and over the prayer Our Lady had taught them to add to each decade of the Rosary:

"O my Jesus, pardon us, save us from the fire of hell, draw all souls to heaven, especially those in most need!"

One day after she had been thus long upon her knees, she called:

"Francisco! Francisco, are you going to pray with me? It is necessary to pray a great deal to save souls from hell. So many are going there! So many!" And they said the prayer again together, for those who said no prayers.

"Why doesn't Our Lady show hell to sinners?" demanded Jacinta one day. "If they saw it, they would never sin again, so they wouldn't go there. You must tell that Lady to show hell to all those people. You will see how they will be converted!" Poor Jacinta! It seemed so simple. Perhaps she had not yet heard the parable of Dives and Lazarus. "If they will not listen to Moses and the prophets, neither would they believe were one to rise from the dead."[3] She was silent for a moment. Then she said:

"Why didn't you tell that Lady that she ought to show hell to those people?"

"I forgot."

"So did I," said the younger child sadly.

"What sins are they that those people do," she asked one day, "to have to go to hell?"

"I don't know." Lucia, after all, was not much older than her cousin. "Perhaps the sin of not going to Mass on Sunday, of stealing, of saying wicked words, cursing people, swearing."[4]

"And only for one word they can go to hell?"

"Well, it's a sin! Let them keep quiet and go to Mass."

[3] St. Luke XVI, 31.

[4] Lucia's impression is that most souls are lost through "sins of the flesh." She believes that Our Lady revealed this to Jacinta in 1920. —III, p. 5.

"Oh, if I could only show them hell!" She reflected a few moments, then said, "If Our Lady lets you, tell all the people what hell is, so that they will commit no more sins and not go there."

Another time she said, in horror, as if she still saw the vision before her, "So many people falling into hell! So many people in hell!"

"Don't be afraid!" Lucia tried to reassure her. "You are going to heaven."

"Yes, yes, I'm going. But I want all those people to go there too!"

Jacinta's round cheeks were beginning to look drawn and hollow, her black eyes to glow like those that peer into other worlds than ours. And like many other friends of God, she had already begun, in August, to have prophetic visions. Some of the most gruesome scenes of the Second World War passed through the mind of this child of seven almost a quarter of a century before they were enacted upon the roads of France or Holland, or in the ruins of London or of Frankfort.

One hot day when they had been sitting on the rocks at Cabeço, lazily watching the listless sheep below, she suddenly prostrated herself and uttered the prayer the angel had taught them:

"My God, I believe, I adore, I hope, and I love you! I beg pardon of You for those who do not believe, do not adore, do not hope, and do not love You!"

A profound silence followed. Then the little girl said to Lucia:

"Don't you see such a long street, so many roads and fields full of people weeping with hunger, and they have nothing to eat? And the Holy Father in a church before the Immaculate Heart of Mary, praying? And so many people praying with him?"

Possibly this referred to the consecration of the world to the Immaculate Heart by Pope Pius XII in 1942. But there was much more about the Pope, or a Pope, in the visions of Jacinta, and she was so disturbed that she wanted to tell everybody, so that all good Christians would pray unceasingly for him.

"Can I say that I saw the Holy Father and all those people?" she asked.

"No," answered Lucia. "Don't you see that that makes part of the secret? And that then it will be discovered?"

"All right. I won't say anything, then."

Nevertheless, Jacinta continued to worry constantly about this future Pope. One very hot afternoon, when even the sheep were nodding in their shelter, the three children were sitting under the olive trees on the stone slabs that covered the well behind the house of Antonio Abóbora. Francisco became restless and began to look for some wild honey among the flowers that grew in a little bramble thicket near by. Lucia was soon doing likewise. Jacinta remained sitting on the edge of the well, staring into space. Presently they heard her say:

"Don't you see the Holy Father?"

"No."

"I don't know how it is, I see the Holy Father in a very large house, on his knees before a table, with his hands over his face, crying. In front of the house there are many people, and some are throwing stones at him, others are cursing him and saying very foul words to him. Poor little Holy Father! We must pray a lot for him!"

Who was this Vicar of Christ that Jacinta saw stoned by a mob? There is a story in Portugal that Lucia has reason to believe that it may be Pope Pius XII. She assured me that Jacinta did not indicate any particular Pope—"just *a* Pope." But he was a very real one to her.

Going to the Marto house one day, Lucia found her sitting alone, still and very pensive, gazing at nothing. "What are you thinking of, Jacinta?"

"Of the war that is going to come. So many people are going to die. And almost all of them are going to hell. Many houses are going to be knocked down, and many fathers will be dead. Look, I am going to heaven, and when, some night you see that light that that Lady told us would come before it, you go there also."

"Don't you see that nobody can run away and go to heaven?"

"It is true, you can't. But don't be afraid. In heaven I must pray a great deal for you! And for the Holy Father. And for Portugal, so the war won't come here. And for all the priests."

In her simplicity Jacinta would say, "I wish I could see the Holy Father. Why doesn't he come here, if so many other people can come?"

Lucia explained how far Rome was, and what a busy man the Pope must be. With a world war going on, and a devotion to the Immaculate Heart to establish, and Russia to be converted so that the world might have peace, it was quite possible that he had not even heard of Aljustrel.

Jacinta took seriously the apostolate that had come to her. Persons who spoke with her found themselves turning a little more to prayer. Ti Marto and his wife had somewhat neglected the Rosary. Jacinta told them Our Lady wanted every family to say it together every day. After some insistence on her part they resumed the old custom, and began to like it. It was hard to resist Jacinta, she was so earnest, so persistent. Yet most days she seemed as light-hearted as ever as she followed the sheep in the August sunshine. Sometimes she would dance and play games while they grazed. Or as she went about picking blue flowers or chasing white butterflies, she would make up little songs to some of the brief prayers that Father Cruz had taught her. Passers-by would hear something like "Jesus, I love you! Immaculate Heart of Mary, save the poor sinners!" floating over the moors in a clear high voice that seemed to summon from another world melodies never before heard in this one.

There was a certain brooding sadness, though, under her gaiety, as if she knew what lay at the end of the road she had taken. Perhaps it was one of the first and surest signs of the validity of the spiritual experiences of these three shepherd children that the world, which had persecuted Christ and His saints, was already resentful of their work, and ready to avenge itself upon them in one way or another. The anticlerical press continued to jibe and grumble. In fact its indignation had reached the point where rhetoric flowers into rank political action. A few days before the thirteenth of August, when people all over Portugal were wondering whether there would be another apparition at Cova da Iria, Ti Marto and Antonio Abóbora received formal notices from the Administrator of the Council of Ourem, head of the district to which Fátima and Aljustrel belonged, ordering them to present their children, the ones who had disturbed the public peace so notoriously, at the town hall of that city for trial, at the hour of twelve noon on Saturday, August 11, 1917.

CHAPTER X

The Administrator of Ourem at that time was Arturo de Oliveira Santos, by trade a blacksmith, by temperament both an idealist and a materialist. If his idealism had prevailed, if he had been able to place his zeal, his imagination and his tenacity of purpose at the service of the Church, he might conceivably have become a bishop, a missionary, even a saint. For some obscure reason he had chosen early in life to follow his own impulse and his own interest. Yet there was something in his nature that found it impossible to love the naked and searing form of materialism; like most human beings he had to veil that terrible figure with some rags of principle before he could take it to his heart. The draperies were supplied him gladly by the leaders of that Revolution which for centuries has been maneuvering to place the Church of Christ in the state of siege in which she now stands in Europe. Thus inevitably he became a devout and tireless member of what might be called the Mystical Body of This World. "Mystical?" Yes. For the invisible head of a kingdom devoted to uprooting the work of Christ must obviously be the disfranchised spirit of revolt of whom He said, "The prince of this world cometh, and in Me he hath not anything," and of whose followers He remarked ironically, "The children of this world are wiser in their generation than the children of light."

As one of those wise children of the flesh, Arturo had logically set out, as a young iron worker, to cultivate all persons and institutions that might help him reap the fruits of the choice he had made. At twenty-six he joined the Grand Orient lodge at Leiria, under the very shadow of that Gothic ruin where Saint Isabel had wept and prayed. He became indoctrinated with the esoteric lore of a syncretistic and naturalistic religion which had been the chief opponent of the Catholic Church in modern times, and which already boasted that, by planning and carrying out the Portuguese revolution of 1910, it had taken a long step toward the total elimination of Christianity in the Iberian Peninsula. In 1911 the Grand Orient chief, Magahaes Lima, was able to predict that in a few years no young man would wish to study for the priesthood, and Affonso Costa could assure all his brethren, and some delegates from the French lodges, that one more generation would see the finish of "Catholicism, the principal cause of the sad condition into which our country has fallen." Indeed there was much evidence to support the prediction if not the accusation. In 1911 the new masters of Portugal seized Church property, scattered, imprisoned and exiled hundreds of priests and nuns, and gave the Cardinal Patriarch of Lisboa five days to leave that city, never to return. Refugee priests and religious fled to France and elsewhere. Some knelt at Lourdes and begged the Mother of God to help their unhappy country, once proud to call itself her land, now a spectacle of anarchy and unbelief, with a new revolution every month.

Arturo de Oliveira Santos owed his success in life, such as it was, to the miseries of the Church. Perhaps he had not intended this. His wife seems to have been a Catholic of sorts, and all his children had been baptized—though their names, "*Democracia*," "*Republica*," "*Libertade*," and so on, smelled more of the lodge than of the sacristy. Perhaps in a dim corner of his mind there smouldered a vague hope of sending for a priest if he should ever find the world slipping from under him and eternity yawning beneath. But all was going his way when he moved his smithy, which he called appropriately the Forge of Progress, to Ourem. And having mastered the art of easy smiling and vigorous handshaking, the brisk and expansive affability so highly esteemed in a world given to salutations in the marketplace and the first seats at banquets, he had little difficulty in founding a new lodge there. By 1917, when he was but thirty-three years old, he was its President; and thanks to the mysterious brotherly bond of those who walk through the shady labyrinth of degrees and initiations to sunny places of honor, he was also President of the town Administration and of the Chamber, and Deputy Judge of

Commerce—in short, he had become a sort of republican czar of the whole district, including Fátima and Aljustrel. Fewer and fewer went to Mass and to the sacraments; there were more divorces, not so many children; and when he arrested six priests and held them incommunicado for eight days, the leading Catholic laymen in the Council and the Chamber were so busy making profitable compromises that they did not have time to protest loudly enough to be heard. To the blacksmith and his friends the fight for progress and enlightenment, as they preferred to describe their conflict with the Church, was all but won.

What a challenge it must have been to the vigilance and zeal of such a man to hear that two or three thousand of his people had gone to Cova da Iria to hear a couple of children converse with an invisible woman, and that other thousands everywhere were talking of a new apparition of the Virgin! To such idealists it was axiomatic that Mary belonged to the Middle Ages, and had no place in modern life. She was part of the supernatural order on whose grave so many earnest liberals and radicals had laid the stone of unbelief. It was not to be tolerated that she should arise from that darkness into the light of the twentieth century. The whole Masonic press resounded with a clarion call against what liberal editors called "an invasion of mysticism," "a revival of reaction and superstition," "a wanton act of aggression on the part of the clergy." Moved to indignation by these and similar protests, the Administrator of Ourem decided to take a firm stand. Hence the order to the parents of the children to present them for trial.

The two fathers reacted characteristically.

"There's no sense in taking such young children before a court of that kind," said Ti Marto. "Besides, it's three leagues, and that's too far for them to walk. And they don't know how to ride on a beast. I'm not going to do it. And I'll go over and tell the Administrator why." Olimpia agreed that he was perfectly right.

His brother-in-law, Antonio, was more complacent. "They can arrange things to suit themselves over there," he grumbled. "I don't know what it's all about." [1] He was inclined to agree with his wife Maria Rosa that if Lucia was lying, it would be a good thing to have her taught a lesson; while if by any chance she was telling the truth—though they both doubted this—Our Lady would take care of her.

Lucia heard these discussions and thought bitterly, "How different my father is from my uncle and aunt! They put themselves in danger to defend their children, but my parents turn me over with the greatest indifference, that they may do with me what they will. But patience!" she argued with herself. "I expect to have to suffer more for Thy love, O my God, and it is for the conversion of sinners!" [2]

On the morning of Saturday, August 11, her father set her on the back of a burro, and they started up the hill. Stopping on the way, they found Ti Marto getting himself a bite to eat, as unconcerned as ever; and he repeated, with emphasis, that he had no intention of taking his young children before a court, for it was all nonsense. However, he would go and speak for them, and if Antonio was in a hurry, let him go ahead, and he would meet him at Ourem. One of Ti Marto's material advantages over his brother-in-law was the ownership of a horse.

Lucia meanwhile had slipped off the burro and had gone to look for Jacinta, whom she told, weeping, what had happened. "Never mind," said the little girl, though she was evidently frightened. "If they kill you, you just tell them that I am like you, and Francisco even more so, and that we want to die too. And now I will go with Francisco to the well to pray very hard for you." [3]

They embraced again, tearfully, and parted. Lucia's father put her back on the burro. He walked stolidly along beside her, staff in hand. The small beast lurched and swung on the hot glaring road. Now and then Antonio would give him a

[1] Memoir I, p. 16.

[2] Memoir II, p. 21.

[3] Memoir I, p. 16.

sharp command or a blow on the flank to expedite his pace. The Administrator was expecting them at twelve o'clock! The poor *burrito* did his best; but something had to be sacrificed to speed, and Lucia fell off three times in the course of the long journey. The road went uphill and downhill, circling around many a bald slope irregularly criss-crossed with stone walls or bristling with stunted pines. It seemed to Lucia that they would never get there—yet it would be too soon! She was bruised, aching, disheveled and unhappy when at last they arrived in the ancient Moorish town.

Ourem lies sprawled along both sides of the main road, under a terraced and cultivated hill crowned with the noble ruins of an old castle thrust like a dark threat against a cobalt sky. Antonio led the jouncing *burrito* over the cobblestones of the main street. He knew where the Administration building was. It was closed, however; not a soul was stirring anywhere about; the heat was suffocating. He prodded the beast along to the marketplace, hoping to find someone to direct him. There he saw the slight figure of a man who had just dismounted from a horse. It was his brother-in-law.

"Well, is everything settled?" asked Ti Marto jovially.

Settled! Antonio retorted somewhat hotly and profanely that they had found the place shut and nobody there.

Ti Marto suggested that, as it was high noon, they had better find something to eat before visiting the Administrator. They did so, and returned at their leisure to the public building. They found it still silent and unoccupied. Then a man came along who told them that the Administration had moved to another house on another street. A few minutes later they were standing in the presence of the local *cacique* and several of his henchmen.

The dark nervous eyes of Arturo de Oliveira Santos took in the three dusty figures.

"And the boy?" he asked abruptly.

"What boy?" So the Administrator did not know that there were three children! Ti Marto played for time. He finally remembered that he had a son, but pretended that he had not understood that the great man wanted to see him.

"Besides, Senhor Administrator," he added, "it is three leagues from here to our country, and children can't stand walking so far, and they're not safe on a horse or a burro, for they're not used to it."

So at least he now remembers the conversation. "And I had a good mind to tell him something more: 'Two children of that age in court!' But I kept quiet." [4]

Santos angrily berated him for his negligence, and Antonio for being late. Then he turned brusquely to Lucia. Had she seen a lady at Cova da Iria? Who did she think it was? Was it true that the lady had told her a secret? Well, then, Lucia must tell the secret, and promise never to return to Cova da Iria.

Lucia looked straight ahead and said nothing.

"Will you tell me the secret?" he asked again.

"No."

The Administrator glared at Antonio, who, sheepish and sleepy as usual, had been standing with his hat in his hand, waiting. "You there, do they believe these things over in Fátima?"

"Oh, no, sir!" said Lucia's father. "All this is just women's tales."

"And you, what do you say?" The Administrator was looking at Ti Marto.

"I am here at your command," replied the father of Jacinta and Francisco, "and my children say the same things I do."

"Then you think it is true?"

"Yes, sir, I believe what they say."

All the bystanders laughed heartily at this. Ti Marto regarded them with unruffled composure. He was not afraid of these small politicians. As for Santos, it was clear to him by this time that nothing was to be gained by questioning these two clodhoppers and their stolid *cachopa*, and he made a gesture of dismissal, whereat one of his underlings told them all to be off.

The Administrator followed them to the door and said pointedly to Lucia:

[4] De Marchi, *op. cit.*, p. 110.

"If you don't tell that secret, it will cost you your life!" [5]

The frightened child glanced back at the dark frowning face in the doorway. He looked as if he meant it.

It was late in the day when they got back to Aljustrel. Antonio probably betook himself to the nearest tavern to recuperate from the ordeal. Lucia slipped away from the reproachful questions and censorious eyes of her mother and sisters to seek a few minutes of peace at the old well. Francisco and Jacinta were kneeling there on the stone slabs. Jacinta had kept her promise; they had been there since morning.

"Ai, Lucia!" she cried, running to embrace her. "Your sister told us they had killed you!"

One of the older girls had gone out to draw some water, and perhaps had dropped the remark as a jest. Francisco and his sister had taken it seriously. Yet here was Lucia alive and free! They all laughed and gamboled as the cool wind freshened the parched fields, and the lamps of the angels began faintly to glitter.

The next day, August 12, was Sunday, but not a very quiet one at Aljustrel. In every village of the Serra, in fact, there was tense expectation regarding what might happen on Monday, and pilgrims were already on the march, whole families of peasants with their wicker lunch baskets and earthenware water bottles, some with blankets wrapped around their necks or packed on their shoulders, to sleep in on the dry grass under the stars. All day these poor wayfarers, and with them a scattering of more prosperous ones in carriages and automobiles, kept arriving at Aljustrel to visit the houses of Ti Marto and Antonio Abóbora, to ask questions, to take photographs, to tell the favors they wanted from Our Lady on the morrow. Jobs, love, money, cures, conversions, promotions—all the desires of the human heart were poured out upon the three bewildered children. Maria Rosa was almost beside herself. The insolence of these strangers! And the iniquity of a girl who would cause such a commotion with her lying tongue! At one stage of the confusion Lucia was tempted to accept the invita-

[5] So ends Ti Marto's account to Father De Marchi, pp. 110–111.

tion of an aunt from Cascais, who offered to smuggle them all to her house and keep them there until the excitement had blown over. But they had promised Our Lady to be at Cova da Iria August 13, and at Cova da Iria they would be.

Toward evening the Abóbora cottage was completely surrounded by a noisy crowd. "In the hands of those people," wrote Lucia, "we were like a ball in the hands of a little girl. Each one pulled us in his direction and asked his question, without ever giving us time to answer anybody." In the midst of all this, who should appear but three policemen from Ourem, to summon them to the house of Ti Marto, where the Administrator in person was waiting, and to drop more than one dark hint that death might be the penalty for further silence on their part.

"Never mind," whispered Jacinta, tightening her pretty lips. "If they kill us, so much the better, for then we will see Jesus and Our Lady."

In the interrogation which followed, Santos demanded the secret and their promise not to return to Cova da Iria. When the children refused on the ground that they could not disobey the Lady, he took another tack and suggested, with unexpected affability, that after all the man to look into matters of this sort was the Senhor Prior, Father Ferreira. He wanted to know whether the parents of the little ones would have any objection to their going to the rectory next morning before keeping their rendezvous at Cova da Iria. Fátima, after all, was on the way to the place of the apparition. It would take only a few minutes to see the Fároco. With this he took his leave, amid general relief.

Early the next morning Ti Marto went out to do some hoeing in a field near his house. The task finished, he returned and began to wash the thick red soil off his hands, in preparation for his breakfast. As he was doing this he noticed that his wife had come into the house, and was making stealthy gestures to indicate that he was wanted outside.

"All right, all right," said Ti Marto, continuing to scrub his great calloused hands.

Olimpia's motions became more frantic.

"What's the hurry?" asked her husband. "I'm coming." And

in leisurely fashion he began to dry his hands. Before he could finish, the door darkened, and looking up, he saw the Administrator of Ourem glaring at him.

"Ah, so it's you, Senhor Administrator?"

"It's true. I also want to go to the miracle."

Ti Marto's heart gave a thump. There was something wrong here, for all the geniality of the reply, and he noticed that Santos looked nervous, and kept glancing about the cottage, now here, now there, as he went on, rapidly:

"Let's all go together. I will take the little ones with me in the wagon. See and believe like Saint Thomas! Where are the children, by the way? Time is getting on. You'd better have them called."

"It isn't necessary to invite them," answered the other drily. "They know when they have to fetch the cattle and get ready to go."

Just then the children came in, and the Administrator, all smiles and benignity, invited them to ride with him to Cova da Iria.

"No, thank you, Senhor," said Francisco.

"We can walk all right," added Jacinta.

"We'll get there earlier this way, and you won't be bothered by people on the road."

"Don't put yourself out, Senhor Administrator." It was Ti Marto speaking. "They can get there all right."

"Besides," continued the official, "we'll have more time to stop at Fátima, at the house of the Prior. He wants to ask them some questions, you know!"

As none of them could think of an answer to that, the children, with many misgivings, piled into the wagon, Francisco sitting in front with the Administrator, the two girls behind, while Ti Marto and Antonio followed on foot. It was only a minute or two to the church at the top of the hill. Arriving there, Santos dismounted, and going up the rectory steps, shouted:

"First!"

"First what?" demanded Ti Marto, who had managed to keep up with the wagon.

"Lucia!" called the Administrator peremptorily.

"Go ahead, Lucia," said her uncle, and the child got out of the wagon and entered the rectory.

"You can stay there for now," added Santos to the younger children.

The Prior was waiting in his study. It seems plain enough that he had changed from a cautious and kindly reserve to something like hostility. Perhaps he had been disturbed by the growing notoriety of the affair and the opposition of the public authorities, and wanted to spare the Church from further persecution at a time when she was harassed and straitened enough.

"Who taught you to say the things that you are going about saying?" he inquired.

"That Lady whom I saw at Cova da Iria."

The Prior's face was severe.

"Anyone who goes around spreading such wicked lies as the lies you tell will be judged, and will go to hell if it isn't true. More and more many people are being deceived by you."

"If anyone who lies goes to hell, I will not go to hell," said the ten-year-old girl, looking him in the eyes, "for I don't lie and I tell only what I have seen and what the Lady has said to me. And as for the crowd that goes there, they only go because they want to. We don't call anybody."

"Is it true that that Lady confided a secret to you?"

"Yes, Senhor Prior."

"Tell it, then."

"I can't tell it. But if Your Reverence wants to know it, I will ask the Lady, and if she gives me permission, I will tell you."

"Come," interrupted the Administrator at this point, "these are supernatural matters. Let us be going." [6]

With that he led Lucia outside, and brusquely ordered her into the wagon. As the child obeyed, Santos jumped in after her, seized the reins and cracked the whip.

Ti Marto and Antonio Abóbora, wondering what was afoot

[6] De Marchi gives this conversation, from the Canonical Process, op. cit., p. 114, n. 1.

now, saw the beast turn sharply and bolt down the road, not toward Cova da Iria, but in the opposite direction.

"You're going the wrong way!" cried Lucia.

"It's all right," Santos assured her cheerfully. "We'll stop and see the Prior at Ourem a moment. Then I'll take you to Cova da Iria by automobile. You'll be there in time!" and he threw some blankets or mantles over the three children, to hide them from the pilgrims who, in growing numbers, were trudging along the road toward Cova da Iria.

When the wagon passed out of sight in a cloud of fine white dust, Ti Marto and his brother-in-law turned and followed the people who were straggling along the highway toward the west. Santos had said he would drive the children to Cova da Iria, and Ti Marto may have assumed, with characteristic calm, that for some reason to be explained in due course the Administrator had decided to go by another road. When the two men reached the scene half an hour later, they were astonished to find more than 6,000 persons gathered there. Some had come walking barefoot for three or four days, from distant villages, at enormous inconvenience, to present their petitions to Our Lady; others had arrived on mules, burros, horses, bicycles; a few in carriages, and some in automobiles. All were asking where the children were, for it was close upon noon.

Some of them were frightened and ill at ease. They had been told that there was a small extinct volcanic crater near Cova da Iria, as in fact there was, and that it was all a trick of the devil to get these good people in one place, and then have it open up and swallow them in its fiery depths. Others scoffed at this fear. Maria Carreira of Moita, for one, was not going to let such a threat keep her from attending an apparition of Our Lady. In fact she had arranged a table with flowers on it as a sort of altar or repository, and had supervised the erection of a rustic arch, with some crosses tied to it, and two hanging lamps to mark the spot at night. It seems incredible, but Maria Rosa is said to have contributed something toward these lamps; and her oldest daughter was helping to arrange the arch and the table.

But where were the children?

About twelve o'clock some of those around the azinheira began saying the Rosary, and gradually the whole throng joined in. Then a faint murmuring sound was heard, followed by what seemed to be a rumble of thunder—some thought in the road, others in the little tree, still others in the far horizon. Here and there a frightened cry was heard: "We are all going to die!" and a few ran away. Most of them stood silent and rather fearful. Presently they saw a flash of light, and then, far over their heads to the east, something like a little cloud, frail, white, transparent, filmy, that floated slowly down until it came to rest above the azinheira. A moment later it rose again and melted away into the blue sky.

As the people stared at one another and all about in wonder and surprise, many noticed a strange fact, to which Maria Carreira and others testify even to this day: their faces were richly tinted with the various colors of the rainbow, and even their garments were red, yellow, blue, orange, and so on, while the foliage of the trees and bushes seemed like brilliant flowers instead of leaves, and the dry earth itself was checkered with different gorgeous hues. "There is no doubt Our Lady had come," says Maria Carreira, "but she didn't find the children." And where were the little rascals? The question was on all lips again.

Thus far Ti Marto and Antonio had said nothing about the odd conduct of the Administrator. And now they saw some people arriving with news that he had taken his prisoners first to the Prior, and then to his own house at Ourem.

So the Administrator was the one who had spoiled the apparition, and disappointed the Mother of God! And the Prior! The crowd at once leaped to the conclusion that the two had conspired together to frustrate them; and as the implications of this suspicion dawned upon the tired minds of those who had walked so many miles to be there, or had given up a day's work and a day's pay to do honor to Our Lady, all the various emotions of reverence, fear, expectation, affection, hope, and curiosity became fused by the subtle alchemy of mob emotion into one tense vibration of human anger. The whole assembly, as if congealed by indignation into a monster with one mind and six thousand heads, burst into a shout of rage that made the hot air tingle, and was heard as far away as Aljustrel, more than two miles distant. Well for the Administrator, well for the Prior, that they were not at Cova da Iria that moment; Father Ferreira, at least, was convinced, as he wrote in a letter denying the charge of collusion, that he would have been murdered on the spot.

Bitter voices began to wrangle and expostulate throughout the mass. Some cried, "Down with the Administrator!" Another yelled, "Down with the Prior!" For a moment it looked as if not even distance would save the two from the hands of this self-appointed court of hangmen, for such a mob is; and hundreds of the men, still roaring their grievance, began to move as mobs move, with a terrible purposeful unity, with glazed eyes that see nothing but blood, and hands that grope for the necks of victims.

"To Fátima and settle with the Prior!"

"To Ourem and have it out with the Administrator!" shouted another.

"And the Regidor!" added a third.

They might at least have got to Fátima, if not Ourem, had they not come face to face with a little man of courage and presence of mind, who raised his hand and spoke with an air of command.

"Boys, take it easy!" he cried. "Don't hurt anyone! Whoever deserves punishment will receive it. All this is by the power of the One above!"

This is Ti Marto's recollection of what he said that day. And after a moment of hesitation the mob wavered, stopped, and began to break up into groups.

Ti Marto makes very little of this. He was more concerned about his children, and how he could get them out of the hands of their captor.

"And I went home," he concludes, "and found my wife weeping." [7]

[7] De Marchi, p. 117.

CHAPTER XI

If Ti Olimpia had reason to weep, the Administrator of
Ourem was highly pleased with the success of his bold plan
to kidnap her children. It gave him a certain sardonic pleasure to think of all the silly pious people waiting at Cova da
Iria for a show in which the principal actors would not appear. And what a joke on the Prior! Now his parishioners
would believe that he was in league with the forces of progress and enlightenment! He would never be able to explain
that away. Best of all, Santos had the three disturbers of the
peace locked up in a room in his house, and before they got
out they were going to tell him the secret, and reveal who
or what was at the bottom of the whole ridiculous piece of
medievalism. He would leave them alone for a while, and let
terror do its work.

He was not wrong in calculating that the children would
be frightened. When the clocks of Ourem began, one after
another, to announce the hour of twelve with long and solemn strokes, they exchanged looks of utter consternation. It
was the moment when they had promised to meet the Lady
at Cova da Iria.

Francisco was the first to recover. "Perhaps Our Lady is going to appear to us here!" he said hopefully. Perhaps! They
waited for some sign, a flash of light, a movement, a heavenly
voice. But nothing happened. The noonday hour passed, and
there was no word from her. Jacinta began to cry. Francisco
said, almost tearfully:

"Our Lady must be sad because we didn't go to Cova da
Iria, and she won't appear to us any more." He glanced im-
ploringly at Lucia. "Will she?"

"I don't know." The older girl was stolid and composed
again. "I think she will."

"Oh, I want so much to see her!"

After that, as Lucia remembers, he was quite *animado*,

quite the little man taking care of his sister and his cousin. It was Jacinta who burst into tears when the last hope of a visit from Our Lady forsook them.

"Our parents will never see us again!" she wailed. "They will never hear any more about us!"

"Don't cry, Jacinta," said her brother. "Let's offer this to Jesus for poor sinners, as that Lady told us to do." And raising his eyes to heaven, he made his offering: "My Jesus, it is for Your love and for the conversion of sinners!"

"And for the Holy Father too!" sobbed Jacinta, wiping her tears. "And in reparation for the sins against the Immaculate Heart of Mary," she added almost choking. After that the little girl kept a brave mien until nightfall, when the darkness made her think of her mother.

The next morning at ten o'clock the Administrator came to conduct them to the town hall, where he put them through another long and tiresome examination. The result was the same as before: they insisted that they had seen a beautiful Lady, all of white radiance, and that she had told them a secret. And they refused to tell this secret even when he threatened them with life imprisonment, torture and death. At noon they were so exhausted that it was a relief to return to the Administrator's house, especially when they discovered that Senhora Santos had prepared a good luncheon for them; for the Administrator's wife, like Pilate's, had more compassion and insight, and seems to have treated the young prisoners with a great deal of motherly kindness. Her husband, on the other hand, was resolved not to let them go without obtaining some sort of confession that would put an end to the unfortunate epidemic of mysticism they had brought upon the district. He told them sternly that since good treatment and tolerance had had no effect, he was going to throw them into jail. And this he proceeded to do.

The town *cadea* was not a very fragrant or attractive place. Its cells were dark, acrid with old and disreputable odors, full of harsh discordant echoes, and shut in by iron bars from the world of free men. Most of the malefactors, probably pickpockets, cutpurses, drunkards, brawlers, the riff-raff of the taverns and the marketplace, were herded together in a common room. Without ceremony the three children were thrust among them. They shrank away, and went instinctively toward a barred window at one end of the room. Jacinta looked out upon the marketplace of Ourem, and burst into tears.

Lucia put her arms about her. "Why are you crying, Jacinta?"

"Because we are going to die without ever seeing our parents again. I want to see my mother!"

Francisco said, "If we never see our mother again, patience! Let us offer it for the conversion of sinners. The worst will be if Our Lady never comes back any more. That's what bothers me. But I am going to offer that, too, for the conversion of sinners." Yet even after this brave speech, the boy was tormented from time to time by the fear that the Lady might never return, and had to be reassured.

All that Lucia has recorded about the prisoners is that there were several, and that one of them was a thief, appropriately enough a sort of good thief in his way. She leaves us to imagine the others: perhaps one of those mangy beggars, so common in Portugal, wrapped in layer after layer of filthy rags infested with fleas and smelling of the red soil on which they had slept so often; perhaps a drunkard reeking with cheap *vinho*; perhaps a pimp, a cutpurse, even a murderer; lost and forgotten men with bloated unshaven faces, weak or defiant mouths, heavy sensual or crafty eyes, hopeless expressions and movements, the rag-tag and bob-tail of the Serra, the offscouring of Portugal and the world. I wish I had thought to ask Sister Mary Lucia of the Sorrows to describe these poor fellows. The contrast they offered to the three innocents with their clean and spiritual eyes must have been more than accidental. There must have been something fitting and inevitable about it, like the publicans and wine-bibbers who walked with Christ, the two thieves with whom He died.

The mere sight of this company was such that whenever the two girls allowed themselves to think about it they began to weep all over again. "I want to see my mother!" moaned Jacinta. "I want my mother!"

Francisco quieted her, as before, asking, "Then don't you want to offer this sacrifice for the conversion of sinners, for the Holy Father, and in reparation for the sins committed against the Immaculate Heart of Mary?"

"Yes, I do, I do."

The boy knelt on the floor, and as the girls followed his example, he repeated his offering:

"O my Jesus, it is for Your love, for the conversion of sinners, for the Holy Father, and in reparation for the sins committed against the Immaculate Heart of Mary!"

Sights and sounds so unfamiliar in that place could hardly fail to attract attention from the other prisoners, and they began one after another to gather about the kneeling group. Presently they were asking questions, good-humored and sympathetic enough; and on learning who the children were and why they were there, they offered various bits of consolation and advice.

"The easiest way for you to get out," said one, "would be to tell the Administrator the secret, since he wants to know it so much."

"But the Lady doesn't want us to tell it!"

"What is it to you whether that Lady likes it or not?"

"I would rather die!" answered Jacinta sharply, and the other two were of the same mind.

"Let us say the Rosary." The three brought forth their beads. Jacinta took from around her neck a chain with a medal on which there was an image of Our Lady. Handing this to a tall prisoner, she asked him if he would please hang it on a nail high up on the wall. He did so good-humoredly. All the men watched, with curiosity and some amusement, as the three knelt on the floor, and earnestly fixing their dark eyes upon the medal, began to recite their *Terço*.

"I believe in God . . . Our Father, Who art in Heaven . . . Hail, Mary, full of grace . . ."

The sight of the upturned faces and the sound of their high voices repeating the words so familiar in Portugal was more than hardened reprobates could resist, and presently some of the men were on their knees joining in the responses, while even those who remained standing were mumbling phrases that they had not spoken in many years. Francisco paused and said, "When people pray they can't keep their hats on." A poor fellow threw his *chapeu* on the floor; the boy picked it up, laid it on a bench, and went on with the prayer. What memories of childhood, of decent women half forgotten, of broken hopes and dreams unrealized must have passed through some of those unkempt bowed heads that August afternoon! At the end there was a moment of awkward silence as all shuffled to their feet. Jacinta went to the barred window and looked out. She was sobbing again.

"Jacinta!" said Lucia, following her. "Don't you want to offer this sacrifice to Our Lord?"

"Yes, but when I remember my mother I can't help crying."

This made the prisoners uncomfortable. They had all taken a great fancy to Jacinta. One of them bethought him of a harmonica he had concealed somewhere about his person. Drawing it out, no doubt giving it the preliminary caresses with which harmonica players warm up their instruments, he pursed his lips and blew his best. Some of the others began to sing. Soon they were all feeling very jolly, for music can unlock or close the gates of sorrow. Jacinta's eyes were dry now, perhaps they even sparkled a little with interest when one of the prisoners asked if they knew how to dance.

"We know how to dance the fandango."

"And the vira, too!"

Lucia records that "Jacinta was thereupon the partner of a poor thief who found her so small that he ended by dancing with her around his neck." [1] Soon everyone was in hilarious motion. The room shook with the shuffling and thumping of hob-nailed boots, the hoarse singing of voices off-key, the in-and-out wheezing wail of the harmonica.

This grotesque scene was interrupted by a noise outside, and the sudden opening of a door. A policeman entered.

[1] She adds that "Our Lady had compassion on his soul and he was converted."—Memoir I, 1936, p. 18.

"Follow me," he said to the three children. They did so, and found themselves presently in the office of the Senhor Administrator.

Santos made a final demand for the secret. When the only answer was a defiant silence, he assumed the look of a man at the end of his patience, and said coldly:

"Very well. I have tried to save you. But since you will not obey the government, you shall be boiled alive in a cauldron of hot oil."

He shouted a command. A door opened to reveal a guard with an incredibly horrible leering face; he must have been chosen for the part he was to play. A conversation something like this followed:

"Is the oil good and hot?"

"Yes, Senhor Administrator."

"Boiling?"

"*Sim, Senhor.*"

"*Vamos!* Take this one and throw her in."

He pointed to Jacinta. The guard seized her and carried her away before she could say a word of farewell.

So it had come at last! Lucia began to pray fervently. Francisco said an *Ave Maria* that his sister would have the courage to die rather than betray the secret. Neither doubted that she was already in her last agony, and that they too had but a few more minutes to live. They were resolved to die with her. Death was not as terrible to them as it would have been to other children.

"What do we care if they kill us?" murmured Francisco. "We'll go right to heaven."

The door opened and the ugly guard returned. "She's *fried,*" he said with ghoulish satisfaction. "Now for the next one!"

With that he laid hold of Francisco and dragged him off. Lucia was left alone with the Administrator.

"It will be you next," he remarked. "You'd better tell me the secret, Lucia."

"I would rather die."

"Very well. You shall."

The guard returned, and led her away. He took her through a corridor, and into another room. And there she saw Jacinta and Francisco, both unharmed, and speechless with joy and surprise. For they had been told that she was being fried in oil. The play was over, the tragedy had turned into a farce.

Santos hated to admit, even then, that three children had defeated his purpose. He kept them at his house that night, in the same room as before. Next morning he took them to the town hall for one more inquisition. When that failed, he admitted that it was no use, and ordered them sent back to Fátima. It was Wednesday, August 15, 1917, the feast of the Assumption of Our Lady.

When Manuel Pedro Marto and his Olimpia went to Fátima that morning, they were a sad and harassed couple. During two nightmarish days and nights they had had no idea where their two youngest children were. Apparently they believed a rumor to the effect that the Administrator, after taking them to Ourem, had secretly transferred them to some place of incarceration at Santarem, a larger and more anti-clerical center of bigotry; and this may be why the record reveals no effort on the part of the courageous Ti Marto to obtain their release. It also sheds no flattering light upon the state of civil liberties under a Republic which had expended so much oratory upon the alleged tyranny of the decayed monarchy, but had done nothing of importance to improve the status of the proletariat. Ti Marto did not consider himself a poor man. He owned property worth from $4,000 to $5,000 in United States money; this with his labor satisfied his wants, which were few and simple. Yet he was at a loss how to proceed against an official who had wronged him in the most criminal way. Lawyers and litigation, to be sure, are luxuries that peasants can seldom afford, even when they pride themselves, as he does, on not being paupers. Ti Marto turned in his humble way to God and asked Him to straighten all this out. Olimpia said her Rosary. On the feast of Assumption they went to Mass as usual.

Everyone at Saint Anthony's church was talking about the kidnapping, but none had any suggestion to make as to getting the children back, or any information about where they were, until Ti Marto's stepson Antonio brought word, after Mass, that they had been seen at Ourem playing on the veranda of the Administrator's house. That was news with a vengeance; but before he could think about going there, he heard someone else say they were in Fátima, on the porch of the rectory. And there, sure enough, they were, with one of the underlings of the Administrator. Presently Ti Marto had Jacinta in his arms, his tears falling on her face. Francisco and Lucia clung to him, asking for his blessing.

"Well, here are your children," said the official from Ourem, as if announcing a great favor.

It was well for him that before Ti Marto could reply, a hullaballoo arose from the churchyard near by, where the people had lingered to gossip after Mass. The air was full of clenched fists, clubs, and angry words. Father Ferreira appeared in the side door of the church, very indignant. He had been making his thanksgiving after Mass at a prie-dieu before the altar, when the noise had startled him, and seeing Ti Marto on the rectory porch, he suspected him of being responsible.

"Senhor Marto, you are doing me a great injustice here!" he exclaimed.

The father of Jacinta and Francisco did not know what to reply. But after the priest had gone back into the church, he addressed the mob:

"Boys, behave yourselves! Some of you are shouting against the Prior, some against the Administrator, some against the Regidor. Nobody is to blame here. The fault is one of unbelief, and all has been permitted by the power of the One above!"

The Prior, who was listening at the church window, thrust his head out and cried:

"He speaks very well! Senhor Manuel speaks very well!"

Just then the Administrator appeared in his wagon, on his way home (not from Mass, but from the market), and concluding, as the Prior had, that Ti Marto was inciting the mob to vengeance, he shouted, "Stop that, Senhor Marto!"

"All right, all right! There's nothing new about it." Ti Marto steadily watched his enemy approach. He saw something else that the Blacksmith had not noticed. Some of the young men in the crowd had caught sight of him, and armed with clubs and staves, they were advancing upon him from the rear. Santos addressed the father of Jacinta and Francisco almost jovially:

"Senhor Marto, come and have a glass of wine with me!"

"No thank you, much obliged."

Then, according to Marto's account, he saw the young fellows with bludgeons closing in about the Administrator. Something had to be done at once if bloodshed was to be prevented. Ti Marto quickly stepped up to the side of Santos and said:

"With regard to your invitation, perhaps I will accept it."

Agreeably surprised, and wholly unaware of the danger he was in, the Administrator took his arm, and they crossed the churchyard and the highway toward a little wine shop near the gate of the cemetery.

"You can ask the children if I treated them badly," began the Blacksmith, a little uncomfortable perhaps under the searching brown eyes of his companion.

"Yes, yes, Senhor Administrator! No doubt about it. The crowd has more questions to ask about that than I have."

Santos looked back and saw the young men with their bludgeons, glaring at him and still undecided whether to attack him or no. But the intervention of Ti Marto had been effective, and the Administrator, at the door of the little shop, was already calling for bread, cheese and wine. He began talking volubly as they seated themselves at a table. Among other things he tried to convince his guest that the children had told him the secret.

"Yes, yes!" said the farmer with his slow canny grin. "They don't tell their father or their mother, but they tell the Senhor Administrator! I can well believe it."

He drank a glass of wine and excused himself. As they

left the shop the Administrator offered him a lift as far as the Post Office. The people along the roadside were saying, "Ti Marto said too much and the Blacksmith has arrested him."[2]

Meanwhile Lucia and her cousins, followed by a few curious stragglers, had gone to the scene of the apparitions, two miles away (and they did this, as Ti Marto remembers, before they went home) to say the Rosary before the tree. Poor azinheira! It had only a few leaves left, for people had been carrying away the upper foliage and even some of the branches as relics and souvenirs. Near it stood the table, with two candlesticks and some flowers, that Maria Carreira had placed there on the thirteenth of August.

The good woman from Moita had little realized what a responsibility she was taking upon herself. Many small coins had been cast upon the table; but when it was knocked over during the confusion over the discovery of the kidnapping, they were scattered on the ground. Loud voices appraised her of the fact. "Woman, pick up that money! Keep track of it! See you don't lose any of it!" Everyone took it for granted that she was the official custodian of the shrine. So on hands and knees she crawled this way and that, picking up all she could find; and when she had them all gathered on the table, the total came to 1340 reis.[3]

On Tuesday, the fourteenth, Maria Carreira took this treasure in a bag to the home of Ti Marto. He refused to accept it, saying sarcastically, "Don't tempt me, woman, for I am already tempted."

Next she offered it to Lucia. And she remembers that the child said:

"God defend me! I don't want it either!"

The good soul then took it to the Prior of Fátima. Father Ferreira by this time was heartily sick of the whole affair of Cova da Iria, which had so disturbed his tranquility and

[2] So ends another of Marto's recollections in De Marchi, *op. cit.*, pp. 127–129.

[3] Less than two dollars.

that of his parish, and he shrank away as if the money were accurst.

"And then the mustard stuck in *my* nose too," Maria recalls, with great dignity, "and I said, 'Well! *I* don't want it either, and I'm going to put it right back where I got it.'"

The Prior raised his hand in protest, "Don't do that, woman! Keep it, or deliver it to someone who will keep it until we see what is to be done about all this!"

Maria Carreira took the money home and hid it. Yet there was no peace in its possession. Everyone wanted to know what she intended to do with it. If one of her daughters had a new pair of shoes, eyebrows were raised significantly. One day a self-appointed committee of four men called upon her to demand the hoard, saying they were going to build a chapel on the site of the apparitions. "Not a *reis* shall you have," exclaimed Maria. Afterwards she was afraid she had been wrong. Perhaps Our Lady wanted these men to make a shrine. She hurried to Fátima to offer the money once more to the Prior. No, he would have none of it.

Finally, she remembered that the owner of the land on which the money had been cast was Lucia's father. If anyone ought to have something to say about the disposal of it, it was he; and his consent would certainly be necessary if a chapel was ever to be built. She was afraid of Antonio Abóbora. People had told her what he had said about her: "If I meet that woman from Moita in the Cova, the thing won't stop there!" and some had warned her to avoid him, especially in his cups. Perhaps the best time to talk with him would be just after Mass. On August 19, the Sunday after the arrest of the children, she got up her courage and went, not without some qualms, to his house in Aljustrel. And sure enough, she found him "without a drop on him."

"I am told that Senhor Antonio is much offended," she began, "because I go to his land in Cova da Iria for flowers, and so on. And I would like to ask his permission to continue to go there."

"Take as many flowers as you want," he replied, unexpectedly genial. "What I won't stand for is building a tabernacle on my property. Some people have already asked me, but I won't have it."

Maria thanked him and took her leave. She thought it better not to mention the money. But she had another idea. She sought out Lucia again and begged her to ask Our Lady, the next time she saw her, what to do with the treasure. The child said she would, on the thirteenth of September.

That same Sunday morning (August 19) Lucia and Francisco and his brother John took their sheep out to graze on the Serra. She was in a happy mood. It was good to be free on a warm clear day, like those birds that darted by in flashes of brilliant blue, or the white butterflies that flitted more drowsily now, or even the cicadas that sang a little wearily in the trees. So the three strolled, played, talked, and said their prayers, until, about four o'clock in the afternoon, they found themselves in a hollow called Valinhos, on the northern slope of Cabeço and about halfway between the cave and Aljustrel. The narrow wagon road bent sharply there, under some large olive trees, and the ancient stone wall on one side had fallen down, leaving an opening into a barren and rocky pasture. Beyond this were several other olive trees, and a few dark scrubby pines and azinheiras.

Suddenly Lucia became aware of some subtle change in the atmosphere. It was not a gathering storm, it was more like the mysterious intensity she had always felt before any supernatural visitation. She looked at Francisco and knew that she was right. Yes, the Lady was coming. And Jacinta was not there.

They begged John to run and fetch her while they watched the sheep. When they offered him two *vintens* or pennies he finally consented, and lumbered off toward Aljustrel. Their eyes followed him anxiously.

A few minutes later there was a flash of light, exactly like those that had always heralded the approach of the Lady. They saw Jacinta running toward them, frantically. Now she was with them, panting, questioning.

The olive trees were a shimmer of pale silver in the slanting light of afternoon. This might have been a corner of that hill country of Judea where Mary went in haste to meet her cousin. But far more brilliant than the sheen on the olives was the radiance that now assembled at the breach in the wall just over a small azinheira, very much like the one at Cova da Iria. And there in the midst of the unearthly glow was the lovely familiar figure, looking tenderly down at the young apostles who had suffered so much for love of her.

"*Que é que Vocemecê me quere?*" asked Lucia almost mechanically. "What is it that you want of me?"

"I want you to continue to go to Cova da Iria on the thirteenth day and to continue to recite the Rosary every day. In the last month I will perform the miracle so that all shall believe."

Lucia remembered the promise she had made to Maria Carreira.

"What do you want me to do with the money that the crowd left in the Cova da Iria?"

"Make two pedestals; one, carry it, you with Jacinta and two other girls dressed in white, and the other let Francisco carry with three other boys. The money on the pedestals is for the feast of the Lady of the Rosary, and that which is left over is for the support of the chapel which they are going to have built."

"I want to ask you to cure some sick people."

"Yes, some I will cure during the year."

The Lady paused, and then continued, very earnestly:

"Pray, pray a great deal, and make sacrifices for sinners, for many souls go to hell because they have no one to sacrifice and pray for them."

With that she receded toward the east and vanished.[4]

The children remained for a long while in a state of exalted joy, joy twice as sweet after so many troubles and disappointments. It was the ninth day since Lucia had been taken to Ourem by her father for the first talk with the Administrator.

[4] This is Lucia's recollection of the conversation, Memoir IV, p. 40.

What a novena! It had gone on from trial to trial, until the issue seemed almost hopeless, only to end in glory and thanksgiving.

When they finally became capable of motion, they cut off the branches of the shrub on which the Lady had stood, and took them home. Ti Marto still remembers a fragrance that he can only call *magnifico*. Even Maria Rosa had to admit that there was a singularly sweet something that she had never before noticed. Clearly she was weakening a bit. But she still maintained that it was all nonsense about the Mother of God appearing to the likes of her Lucia.

CHAPTER XII

The three children were standing on the narrow street of Aljustrel discussing their adventures, when Lucia noticed, almost under her bare brown feet, a heavy piece of rope. She picked it up idly. "Ouch!" The shaggy coil had scratched her arm. This gave her an idea. "Look! This hurts! We can make a girdle of it and offer this sacrifice to God." Dividing it forthwith, each one wore a piece of it wrapped around the body, next to the skin. Day and night they hugged this improvised hair shirt, even though it pricked, chafed and itched until they could hardly tolerate it another moment; even though it troubled their rest at night, and sometimes would not allow them to sleep at all. What was health compared to saving souls from hell? And what was comfort to the joys of an eternal heaven?

It hurt Jacinta more than a hair shirt to hear people cursing or using foul language. On one such occasion she covered her face with her hands and said, "O my God, these people don't know that for saying such things they can go to hell. Pardon them, my Jesus, and convert them." Then she would say the prayer the Lady had told them to add to the Rosary.

There were many objective signs that these penances were pleasing to God, and that Jacinta in particular was advancing on the road to sainthood. She had become more patient, more long-suffering, more affectionate; she had many visions of things that later came to pass; and in Lucia's opinion she must have received, by this time, the gift of infused wisdom. One day she said three *Aves* for a wretched woman with a terrible disease, and all the symptoms vanished.

There was another woman in Aljustrel who never lost an opportunity to revile the three children as liars and imposters. Instead of getting angry, Jacinta said, "We must ask Our Lady to convert this woman. She has so many sins which she does not confess that she will go to hell!" They offered some penances for her. And never again did she give them an unkind word.

It would have been hard for the children to say which caused them more annoyance, the hordes of the devout, or professedly devout, who darkened their doors daily and made the lives of their families miserable, or the opposition, which incongruously included most of the clergy and many sincere Catholics along with Carbonari, Radicals and Liberals of all shades of unbelief. There was this at least to be said for the scoffers: they did not come knocking at Lucia's door at all hours, asking for a piece of her kerchief as a relic, or wanting to touch her hair, or insisting that when she saw Our Lady she remember all the symptoms of Cousin Quiteria's kidney trouble, or the numerous qualifications of Brother Antonio for a better position than the one he held. And the diatribes of the anti-clerical press gave no annoyance in Aljustrel, because no one read them.

Yet now and then the opposition made some special effort to be troublesome. There was a certain journalist named José do Vale, who edited an anarchist paper called *O Mundo* (*The World*). He was also a tireless pamphleteer with a distinguished gift for excoriation and invective which his enemies attributed to a habit of getting drunk before sitting down to write. His indignation over the scandal at Cova da Iria was already boiling over into pamphlets that were peddled in Torres Novas, Ourem and other towns of the Serra.

Had this been all, the humble Christians of the Serra might have been content to console themselves with the words, "If the world hates you, know that it has hated Me before it hated you. If you were of the world, the world would love its own; but because you are not of the world, but I chose you out of the world, therefore the world hates you." But the editor of *The World* did not stop with denunciations of priests, Jesuits, tricksters and superstitious ignoramuses. He summoned all liberals, all friends of progress and enlightenment to hold a meeting on the following Sunday at Fátima just after the parish Mass, to consider what measures should be taken to unmask and punish the authors and comedians of the farce at Cova da Iria.

On learning this, the Prior of Fátima quietly had the word passed among his parishioners that Mass that Sunday would be at the Chapel of Our Lady of Ortiga, two miles away. When a considerable number of fervent unbelievers assembled at Saint Anthony's they found almost no one on hand except a few of their own, including the Administrator of Ourem, the Regidor Francisco da Silva, and José do Vale himself. Disappointed but undaunted, they decided to proceed to Cova da Iria.

The Catholics of Lomba d'Egua and Moita had expected this, and a certain peasant who had a whole herd of burros had tied them to azinheira trees near the scene of the apparitions. As the liberals approached, he rubbed on the nose of each "a certain liquid" guaranteed to make any burro bray his loudest. Now, the bray of that dwarfed animal even under the most favorable circumstances is one of the most disturbing, not to say excruciating, sounds in all the range of audible creation. On a dark night in a lonely place it acquires a power to evoke blood-curdling suggestions, such as groans of dying men on a rainy battlefield, the yowling of gigantic alley cats, the curses and reproaches of lost souls in pain. It was no conciliatory or complimentary sort of music, then, that greeted the forces of enlightenment as they struggled up the hill from the highway. And as a final insult to climax this injury, they found waiting for them, near the azinheira where Our Lady had appeared, a pile of straw and feed. The farmers of Moita had spread it about as if to welcome a delegation of asses.

To make sure that the subtle point would not be missed, a group of people from Moita, including the indomitable Maria Carreira, were waiting on the next rise to explain it with loud and lusty scorn. This enraged some of the newcomers so much that they began to shout back some highly uncomplimentary things about Catholics and the Church. The faithful countered this with:

"Viva Jesus e Maria! Viva Jesus e Maria!"

This drew another taunt from the invaders. The shouts echoed back and forth through the clear air of Cova da Iria. The Catholics would cry:

"*O burros, o burros, o bestas!*" "Burros! Beasts!"

And the Freethinkers would retort:

"*Botas da serra! Botas da serra!*" "Clodhoppers! Mountain clodhoppers!"

The appearance of some policemen put an end to this in good time. But the incident had revealed how tensely the inhabitants of the highlands, both believers and non-believers, were waiting for the thirteenth day when, according to the three children, the Lady had promised to return to Cova da Iria. On the twelfth of September the roads were full of pilgrims, and by evening the houses of the Martos and Abóboras were surrounded by them, as on the previous occasion. Most of these people slept in the fields. At sunrise on the thirteenth there were thousands of them at Aljustrel and Cova da Iria, reciting the Rosary or the Litany of Our Lady.

By the time the three children were ready to start for the place of the apparitions, the main highway was so jammed that it was impossible to move. "All wanted to see and talk with us," wrote Lucia. "There was no human respect in that crowd! Many of them, and even gentlemen and noblemen, broke through the press and knelt before us, asking us to present their necessities to Our Lady. Others, unable to get near, would shout:

" 'For the love of God, ask Our Lady to cure my son, who is lame!'

" 'Ask her to cure mine, who is blind!'

" 'And mine who is deaf!'

" 'And to bring my sons home from the war!'

" 'And my husband!'

" 'And to convert a sinner for me!'

" 'To give me health, for I have tuberculosis!'

"And so on. In that place appeared all the miseries of poor humanity," continued Lucia, "and some shouted even from the tops of trees and walls where they had climbed to see us pass. Saying 'Yes' to some, giving a hand to others to help them get up out of the dust of the earth, we managed to move along, thanks to some gentlemen who went ahead opening a passage for us through the multitudes.

"When now I read in the New Testament such enchanting scenes of the passage of Our Lord through Palestine, I remember these that Our Lady made me a witness of when I was so young, on those poor roads and streets from Aljustrel to Fátima and to Cova da Iria, and I give thanks to God, offering Him the faith of our good Portuguese multitude; and I think, 'If these people so humbled themselves before three poor children only because they had been granted mercifully the grace to speak with the Mother of God, what would they not do if they saw before them Jesus Christ Himself? . . . Finally we arrived at Cova da Iria, near the *carrasqueira*, and I began to say the Rosary with the crowd."

Ay, what a crowd! It was larger than ever, and composed of pilgrims from all parts of Portugal. And besides the usual barefoot peasants, the rich and the poor, the workers, the ladies and gentlemen from many villages and towns, there were some thirty young seminarians and five or six priests. One of the latter was the Reverend Monsignor João Quaresma. Another was the Reverend Father Manuel Pereira da Silva, then a curate at Leiria, who went to the scene (so he told me) chiefly out of curiosity, with no preconceptions either way. These priests, with the Prior of Santa Catalina and Monsignor Manuel do Carmo Gois, had left Leiria early that fine September morning in a squeaky carriage drawn by a decrepit old horse. When they finally arrived after a rough journey, they secured a place of vantage on a piece of high ground overlooking the vast natural amphitheatre, already dark and seething with human forms.

"At midday a complete silence, save for the whisper of prayers, fell over the crowd," wrote Monsignor João Quaresma fifteen years later. "Suddenly there were shouts of rejoicing . . . voices praising Our Lady. Arms went up to point at something above. 'Look, don't you see?' . . . 'Yes, now I see!' . . . There was not a cloud in the azure sky. I too raised my eyes and tried to scrutinize the amplitude of the sky, to see what more fortunate eyes had first looked upon. . . . To my great astonishment I saw clearly and distinctly a luminous globe that moved from the east toward the west, slowly and majestically gliding down across the distance. My friend also looked and had the good fortune to enjoy the same unexpected and enchanting apparition. . . . Suddenly the globe with its extraordinary light vanished before our eyes. . . .

" 'What do you think of that globe?' I asked of my friend, who seemed to be enthusiastic over what we had seen.

" 'That it was Our Lady,' he replied without hesitation. It was my conviction also. The little shepherds looked on the Mother of God herself; to us was granted the grace to see the carriage which had transported her from heaven to the barren inhospitable heath of the Serra da Aire.

"We must say that all those who were near us observed what we did. For on all sides were heard manifestations of joy and greetings to Our Lady. Many, however, saw nothing.

"We felt that we were very fortunate. How enthusiastically my colleague went about from group to group in the Cova da Iria and afterwards on the highway outside, finding out what they had seen. The persons interrogated were of various social classes; all unanimously affirmed the reality of the phenomena which we ourselves had witnessed." [1]

Meanwhile the Lady had revealed herself to the three children, and Lucia and Jacinta had heard her lovely voice in the briefest of all their conversations.

"Continue to say the Rosary," she said, "to bring about the end of the war. In October Our Lord will come also, and Our Lady of the Sorrows of Carmel, and Saint Joseph with the Child Jesus, to bless the world. God is content with your sacrifices, but does not wish you to sleep with the rope—wear it only during the day."

Lucia said, "They have begged me to ask you many things: the cure of some sick persons . . . of a deaf mute."

"Yes," answered the Lady, "some I will cure, others not. In

[1] Letter of October 13, 1932, in De Marchi, pp. 147–148.

October I will perform the miracle so that all will believe."

And she disappeared in the same manner as before.

So ended the fifth apparition, as Lucia records it.[2] Short though it was, it left the children confirmed in their faith and greatly consoled. How relieved they were to give up wearing the rough rope next to their tender bodies at night! What pleased Francisco more than this, though, was her promise that in the following month he would see Our Lord.

"*Ai que bom!*" he cried. "Only one more month, and I love Him so!"

One of the priests at Cova da Iria on September 13 was the Reverend Doctor Manuel Nunes Formigão, canon of the cathedral at Lisboa and professor at the Seminary of Santarem. Noted throughout Portugal for his integrity and learning, he had been asked by the Administrator of the Patriarchate in Lisboa to investigate the strange occurrences, of which conflicting reports had traveled as far as the capital. Standing in the road about two hundred meters from the azinheira, he had noticed the peculiar dimming of the sun's light in a cloudless sky, but had discounted this as a possible natural phenomenon due to the altitude of the Serra, almost half a mile above sea level. He had not noticed the luminous globe reported by Monsignor Quaresma and others, but the fact that they were so positive about it convinced him that they must have seen something extraordinary, and stimulated his curiosity to get at the bottom of the whole affair. For this purpose he returned to Fátima on Thursday, September 29, and went to Aljustrel to ask questions. Both Maria Rosa and Olimpia received him with all respect, and sent out messengers to find the children. Lucia was at Cova da Iria, the others playing about the village. Jacinta was the first to arrive.

The little girl seemed frightened and embarrassed, in the opinion of Dr. Formigão, but answered readily, and seemed no longer ill at ease after her brother made his appearance. Francisco came in carelessly with his hat on. When Jacinta motioned him to take it off, he paid no attention to her, but sat

[2] Memoir IV, p. 41.

down on a stool and looked attentively at the inquisitor. When questioned he answered calmly and with no sign of embarrassment. The visitor decided to interrogate him first, and sent Jacinta out to play on the street with some other girls until he had finished. Then he recalled Jacinta and questioned her separately.

By that time Lucia had come in from Cova da Iria. She was the most natural and composed of the three, as Dr. Formigão reported when he published his first account of the conversations in 1921. He remarked too that she was a robust, healthy, normal-looking girl, with no indications of vanity, and no pathological traits whatever. Poor Maria Rosa hovered about like an anxious mother bird, worried and lamenting as usual. The sharp eye of Dr. Formigão noticed a leak in the roof.

All three of the examinations (which have been printed verbatim in the books of Dr. Formigão, Father De Marchi and Father Fonseca) give the impression, to this reader at least, that the children were truthfully reporting what they had actually seen and heard. The few slight discrepancies offer no real difficulties. Jacinta, for example, said without hesitation, as the others did, that the Lady held her rosary in her right hand. When the question was repeated with some insistence, she became confused, trying to imagine which of her own hands corresponded to the one in which the Lady had held the beads. Again, Francisco said he could not see her ears because they were covered with her mantle; Jacinta agreed. But Lucia was under the impression that she had seen small dazzling earrings. At first, too, she said that she had seen a bright gold border on the Lady's gown; later she was of the opinion that this was simply a more intense edging of the light of which all the vision, including the garments, seemed to be made. This sort of divergence is to be expected in all human testimony.

Lucia's examination is the longest and most detailed of the three. Possibly the priest had heard one of the vague rumors about the Angel in 1915 or 1916, for almost at the outset he remarked:

"They say that the Lady appeared to you last year also? What is true about this?"

"She never appeared to me last year," replied Lucia quietly, "or before May of this year, nor have I said so to anyone, for it was not true."

"Did she show herself desirous that many persons should be present on the thirteenth day of each month during the apparitions at Cova da Iria?"

"She said nothing about that."

"Is it certain that she revealed a secret to you, forbidding you to tell anyone what it was?"

"It is certain."

"Did she say this only to you or to your companions?"

"To all three."

"Can you not reveal it at least to your confessor?"

Lucia was silent. She seemed somewhat perplexed.

"They say," continued the investigator, "that to free yourself from the importunities of the Senhor Administrator the day when you were arrested, you told him, as if it were the secret, a thing that was not, thus deceiving him, and boasting afterwards of having beaten him at this game. Is it true?"

"It is not. The Senhor Administrator really wanted me to reveal the secret, but as I could not tell it to anyone, I kept silent, in spite of his insisting much that I comply with his wishes. What I did was to tell all that the Lady had told me, short of the secret. And perhaps on this account the Senhor Administrator thought that I had also revealed the secret. I did not try to deceive."

"The Lady commanded you to learn to read?"

"Yes, the second time she appeared."

"But if she said that she would take you to heaven in the month of the coming October, what good would it be for you to learn to read?"

"That is not true. The Lady never said that she would take me to heaven in October, and I never said that she had told me such a thing."

Later in the questioning he asked:

"Why did you lower your eyes sometimes and stop looking at the Lady?"

"It was because at times she blinded me."

"Did she teach you some prayer?"

"Yes, and she wanted us to recite it after each mystery of the Rosary."

"Do you know this prayer by heart?"

"I do."

"Say it."

"O my Jesus, pardon us, save us from the fire of hell, draw all souls to heaven, especially those in most need." [3]

Thus ended the first interrogation of which a record was made. Dr. Formigão admitted that the children had made a favorable impression upon him. Yet, after thinking the whole matter over at the Seminary of Santarem, he prepared another series of questions of a more searching and fundamental sort, framed to expose the subtle deceits, if any, of subconscious or satanic agencies. On October 10 he boarded a train for Chão da Maçãs, and there engaged a horse and two-wheeled buggy in which he was driven to Vila Nova de Ourem. It was eleven o'clock at night when he reached a tiny hamlet called Montelo, about two miles from Fátima. There he found a pen name, "the Visconde de Montelo," and a lodging for the night with a family named Gonçalves, who were able to give him full dossiers on the Marto and Abóbora families.

Everyone agreed that Ti Marto was the most solid and trustworthy citizen of the mountains—indeed, he was incapable of deceiving anyone; and he and his wife Olimpia were universally respected as good Catholics who practiced what they professed. Maria Rosa was devout, honest and hard-working. Her husband Antonio was indifferent to religion and liked wine too well, but there was no malice in him. Neither family was

[3] This is only a partial abstract of the testimony first published in 1921 in *Os episodios maravilhosos de Fátima*, by the Visconde de Montelo (the pen name of Dr. Formigão). Later works of his on the same subject appeared in 1923, 1927, 1929, 1930 and 1936.

poor according to the standards of the Serra. Neither had done anything to capitalize on the apparitions—quite the contrary; they had discouraged the cult which had put them to so much annoyance, and this was especially true of the Abóboras. The children, too, were all well liked. Most people had disbelieved them in May and June, but were now inclined to accept their story, since so many had seen the cloud over the tree on August 13, and had noted the other strange phenomena in August and September. With all this background now established in his mind, Dr. Formigão proceeded on October 11 to Aljustrel, and again visited the home of Antonio Abóbora.

While Lucia was being sought, the investigator noticed that the leak in the roof was still unrepaired, and asked some questions of Maria Rosa. He was especially curious to know whether she had ever read to Lucia the fairly well-known story of the apparition of Our Lady to two shepherd children, Maximin and Melanie, at La Salette in southern France on September 19, 1846. There were certain resemblances between that episode and the ones at Fátima. At La Salette Our Lady had told the children a secret, which they revealed to no one but Pope Pius IX; and she had given them a warning of great calamities if the people of France did not stop offending God. The similarity was not necessarily conclusive, yet it might be significant. Father Formigão was curious to know whether Lucia had been much impressed by the French account. Maria Rosa thought not; the child had never mentioned it again, so far as she could recollect.

When the girl appeared, she was questioned at some length in the presence of four witnesses.

"What did the Lady say she would do to make the crowd believe she had appeared?" asked Dr. Formigão.

"She said she was going to perform a miracle."

"When did she say that?"

"She said it a few times—once on the occasion of the first apparition, and when I asked her the question."

"Aren't you afraid that the crowd will do you some harm if nothing extraordinary is seen on that day?"

"I haven't any fear," replied Lucia.

"Did you ever see the Lady bless herself, pray, or finger the beads?"

"No. . . ."

"Did she tell you to pray for the conversion of sinners?"

"No. She told me to pray to the Lady of the Rosary so that the war would end." Lucia explained later that the Lady had asked for sacrifices rather than prayers for the conversion of sinners.

"Did you see the signs other persons say were seen, such as a star and roses displayed on the garment of the Lady, and so on?"

"I saw no star or other signs."

"Can you read?"

"No, I can't."

"Are you going to learn to read?"

"No, I'm not."

"How then will you obey the order the Lady has given you in this regard?"

Lucia was silent. As she later explained, she did not wish to accuse or embarrass Maria Rosa.

Finally the priest said:

"You have heard your mother read the book called *Short Mission* where the story is told of the apparition of Our Lady to a boy and a girl?"

"Yes, I have."

"Did you often think of that story and speak of it to other girls?"

"I didn't think of that story, nor did I tell it to anyone."

Dr. Formigão then reëxamined Jacinta.

"Did you also hear the secret, or was it told only to Lucia?"

"I heard it too."

"When did you hear it?"

"The second time, on the day of Saint Anthony."

"Is this secret so that you will be rich?"

"No!"

"Is it so that you will be good and happy?"

"Yes, it is for the good of all three."

"Is it that you will go to heaven?"

"No."

"Can't you reveal the secret?"

"No."

"Why?"

"Because the Lady said we were not to tell the secret to anyone."

"If the crowd knew the secret, would they be sad?"

"Yes, they would."

Now it was Francisco's turn.

"How old are you?"

"I am nine years old."

"Did you only see Our Lady or did you also hear what she said?"

"I only saw her, I heard nothing of what she said."

"Was there some light around her head?"

"Yes, there was."

"Could you see her face well?"

"I could see, but only a little, because of the light."

"Were there some ornaments on her dress?"

"There were some edgings of gold."

"Of what color is the crucifix?"

"It is white."

"And the chain of the rosary?"

"That also is white."

"Would the crowd be sad if they knew the secret?"

"They would."

Doctor Formigão believed that all three had told him the truth, whatever the final explanation might be. He was inclined to think that the test of whether or not they had been deluded in some way would be the "miracle" promised by the Lady for October 13. He went away resolving to let nothing keep him from being at Cova da Iria on the day after the morrow.

Another priest who examined the children about that time was Father Poças, Prior of Porto de Mos. It is Ti Marto who remembers how brusquely this self-appointed inquisitor said to Lucia:

"Look here, girl, now you are going to tell me that all this is lies and witchcraft. If you don't say so, I will say it and have it said everywhere. . . . Everybody will believe me . . . and you shall not escape!"

Lucia made no reply. The Prior was furious, or he pretended that he was. But in the end, after he had made every effort to break down her calm reticence, after he had even accused Ti Marto of being an accomplice in a gigantic fraud, he admitted that he believed they were speaking the truth.

Yet when the attitude of a priest could be so distrustful and so menacing, it is no wonder that Maria Rosa was almost at her wits' end with fear and weariness. She was convinced that Lucia was about to be exposed and punished at last. Indeed, all the Abóboras but Lucia were in a state of something like panic when that twelfth of October dawned over Aljustrel. Was it not bad enough, reasoned Maria Rosa and her husband, that their child had begun the deception in the first place; worse, that she had stubbornly carried it on all these months; but worst of all, that she had had the incredible effrontery to promise the whole world a miracle, no less, at a definite hour on a definite day, the thirteenth of October! And what would cheated people say and do when the miracle did not occur? Undoubtedly they would turn in anger on Lucia and tear her to pieces. Many of the villagers were making similar predictions. One woman said that Lucia Abóbora ought to be burned before she caused the destruction of them all.

Maria Rosa made a last pathetic appeal to her daughter. "It is better for us to go and tell everything," she said. "People say we are going to die tomorrow in the Cova da Iria. If the Lady does not make the miracle, the crowd will kill us."

"I am not afraid, Mother," replied Lucia. "I am sure the Lady will do everything she has promised."

"We had better go to confession, to be prepared for death."

"If you want me to go with you to confession, I will, but not for that reason."

Maria Rosa turned away, almost distracted.

That afternoon the sky became overclouded, and a fine

cold mist began to fall over the gloomy autumnal expanse of the Serra da Aire. Shepherds in Aljustrel locked the beasts up early, for it was plain that thick weather was brewing in the northeast.

CHAPTER XIII

What a night! It was as if the devil, somewhere in the ice and snow that could never slake the burning of his pain, had resolved to destroy with one blow all that remained of the Europe which had so long been his battleground against the Thing he hated most. Somewhere in the dark misery of Siberia, he was permitted, heaven knows why, to disturb the equilibrium of the air, setting in motion a cold and cutting blast that shrieked across the continent to the western sea. It may have passed howling over a cabin in Finland where a little lynx-eyed man who called himself Lenin was waiting to enter St. Petersburg (he had lately sown the seeds of revolution there), and to begin, in a very few weeks, the transformation and destruction of all that world which owed what was best and noblest in it to the teachings of Christ. It screamed in mockery over vast armaments moving stealthily through Germany to prepare for the "peace through victory" drive of 1918. It scourged poor wretches of both armies into the cover of slimy dugouts all along the western front, and plastered with mud the Italian fugitives from Caporetto. It seemed to echo and enlarge the despair that was settling over the vineyards of war-wearied France, where Haig stood, as he said, with his back to the wall. Finally it dashed itself against the Pyrenees, and then, as if it had gathered up all the hatreds and discontents of disobedient men and all the rebellious powers of a corrupted nature in its mad career from the Baltic to Cape Saint Vincent, it let them all loose on the little country that has never been permanently conquered, the land where she who treads upon the serpent's head has long been honored, the *terra da Santa Maria*.

Darkness fell swiftly, with blacker clouds scudding from the northeast, and huge shapeless masses of fog drifting along the mountain sides and down the river valleys to the ocean. As the drizzle thickened to a fine, cold, slanting rain, the wind, whipped to a gale, bent under it the waving and moaning plumes of the pine forests near Leiria; it ripped the square sails of ancient windmills on the gray heights of the Serra da Aire; it scattered pale glistening leaves of poplars and aspens across the swollen Tagus; it flattened the plucked and reddened vineyards of Braga and the withered gardens of Moita and Fátima; it went roaring across hundreds of miles of narrow beaches until the frothy Atlantic bellowed back in anger, and cast up vengeful floods into village streets. The rain fell steadily, pitilessly.

Yet there were thousands of human beings and many beasts on the roads of the little Republic that night. For faith is stronger than doubt, and love is hardier than hate. Devout Catholics in every village had heard by this time that Our Lady had promised to return to Cova da Iria to perform a miracle on October 13. Rain or shine, that was all they needed to know. Peasant families slung their wicker baskets and earthen water jugs over their shoulders, or packed them in panniers on the backs of burros, and started out under the lowering skies. Fathers and mothers carried sick or lame children in their arms for incredible distances. Fishermen left their nets and boats on the beaches of the Vieira and took to the oozy roads. Farmhands from Monte Real, sailors from ships in the harbors of Porto or Algarve, factory workers from Lisboa, *serranas* from Minde or Soublio, ladies and gentlemen, scrubwomen, waiters, young and old, rich and poor, all sorts of people (but most of them humble, most of them barefoot, most of them workers and their families)were plodding through the mud under the pelting rain that night, like a great scattered army converging upon Fátima, hoping to find there some favor of health or conversion, forgiveness of sin, consolation for sorrow, the beginning of a better life, the blessing of the Mother of God.

It made no difference to these devotees if saturated trousers or skirts sloshed around their tired legs as their bare feet plowed the mud or spattered the puddles of bad roads. Laughter was heard among groups of several families as they walked along together. Fragments of old hymns would echo back from the wet cliffs, or come floating down out of the darkness of a lonely road. *"Ave, Ave, Ave Maria!"* Not for nothing had the ancestors of these people sung the *Salve Regina* on the decks of galleons in the Indian Ocean or whalers in the China Sea. It might have been a useful lesson for some of the politicians at Lisboa if they could have heard those songs.

They were not left wholly uninformed, however. Avelino de Almeida, managing editor of *O Seculo*, the largest newspaper in Lisboa, who was on his way to cover the story at Cova da Iria, describes some of the pilgrims he met near Chão de Maças, before the rain began to fall:

"Nearly all, men and women, have bare feet, the women carrying their footgear in bags on their heads, the men leaning on great staves and carefully grasping umbrellas also. One would say they were all oblivious to what was going on about them, with a great lack of interest in the journey and in other travelers, as if lost in a dream, reciting their Rosary in a sad rhythmic chant. A woman says the first part of the *Hail, Mary*; her companions in chorus say the second part of the prayer. With sure and rhythmical steps they tread the dusty road which runs between the pine woods and the olive groves, so that they may arrive before night at the place of the apparition, where, under the serene and cold light of the stars, they hope they can sleep, keeping the first places near the blessed azinheira so that today they can see better."

It was not devotion that took the editor of *O Seculo* to Fátima. Almeida was a Freemason who made no secret of his dislike for priests, sacraments, creeds and dogmas. He was covering the story because it had been too much talked about to be ignored, and he was one of the best newspaper men in Portugal. His dispatch, published in *O Seculo* on the morning of October 13, reveals him as a kindly, cynical gentleman in the Newmanian sense, one who did not believe but had no wish to hurt or ridicule those who did:

"Thousands of persons are hastening to a wild expanse of country near Ourem to see and hear the Virgin Mary. Let pious souls be not offended and pure believing hearts be not afraid; we have no intention of being a scandal for those who sincerely hold to their faith and whom the miraculous still attracts, seduces, bewitches, consoles and fortifies, as has been the case for thousands of years, and most certainly will be for other thousands of years! . . . This is only a short newspaper article on an event which is not new in the history of Catholicism. . . . Some regard it as a message from heaven and a grace; others see in it a sign and proof that the spirit of superstition and fanaticism has planted deep roots that it is difficult or even impossible to destroy.

"Times of great calamities have always revived and renewed religious ideas and have favored them. And war, which strikes everywhere, offers them the most favorable and fertile soil for growth. We see that confirmed in the life of the trenches and even in the spiritual atmosphere of the belligerent countries."

After some pointed observations about the speculators who doubtless were waiting to profit by the credulity of the masses, he gave a fair summary of the events at Fátima, and recalled previous apparitions of the Holy Virgin at Lourdes, La Salette, and other places. Then he continued more ironically:

"The miracle takes place between noon and one o'clock, according to those who have been there. But not all have the chance to see the holy figure. The number of the elect seems very small. Despite their efforts, many see nothing. This is why those who find themselves near the children are contented with hearing them speak with an invisible partner. Others, on the contrary, see in a divinely solemn moment the stars shining in the firmament, even though the sun be at the zenith. They hear a subterranean groaning which announces the presence of the Lady. They claim that the temperature falls and they compare the impressions of that moment with those they have experienced during an eclipse of the sun. . . .

"According to what the children say, the figure of the Virgin appears on an azinheira, surrounded on all sides by a nuage. . . . The suggestion of the masses, brought there by the supernatural and captivated by a superhuman force, is so powerful that eyes fill with tears, faces become as pale as corpses, men and women throw themselves on their knees, chant songs and recite the Rosary together.

"We do not know if there have already been blind persons who have recovered their sight, paralytics who have regained the use of their limbs, hardened sinners who are turned back from the straight ways of sin to plunge into the purifying water of penance.

"But that matters little. The news of the apparitions has spread from Algarve to the Minho. Since the Day of the Ascension the pilgrims have flocked there by thousands on the thirteenth of each month, from near and far. The means of transportation do not suffice.

"The clergy of the place and the neighborhood maintain, as regards the events, a prudent reserve, at least in appearance. It is the custom of the Church. It proclaims loudly that in such circumstances doubt means nothing, for doubts also come from the devil. But secretly it rejoices over the great concourse of pilgrims who since May have become more and more numerous.

"And there are even people who dream of a great and magnificent church, always full, of large hotels near by with every modern comfort, of shops well stocked with a thousand and one different objects of piety and souvenirs of Our Lady of Fátima, and of a railway which will take us to the future miraculous sanctuary with more convenience than the buses in which, for the moment, the mass of the faithful and of the curious now achieve this right. . . ."

While the author of these pessimistic observations was making his way to Ourem, and then with deepening discomfort to Cova da Iria, the Abóbora and Marto families, after a restless night listening to the rain pelting on the tiles, were rising in the cheerless dawn. Indeed, the east was hardly streaked with dismal gray when the first dripping pilgrims came knocking at their doors. Soon there were dozens and scores of them, and they not only surrounded the two cottages, clamoring for a glimpse of the children, but were cheerfully forcing their way inside without waiting to be invited. Ti Olimpia was furious at the casual way they shed puddles of water and red mud from the fields all over her floors. Ti Marto still twits her on how she fluttered about, trying to get the children ready and at the same time to answer the questions of a jostling mob. It was too much when these strangers began to make themselves comfortable on her beds and chests.

"Get out of here, all of you!" she cried.

The people paid no attention. A few more pushed their way in.

"Leave them alone, woman," advised her husband. "When the house is full, no more will be able to get in."

A neighbor plucked him by the sleeve and said in his ear:

"Ti Marto, you'd better not go to Cova da Iria. They might beat you up. The little ones, no. They are babies, no one is going to hurt them. You are the one in danger of being mussed up."

"I'm going openly," returned the other, "and I'm not afraid of anybody. I have no doubt everything will be all right."

Olimpia did not share this confidence. She was praying fervently to Our Lady to protect her and her family that day, and she still wonders how her children could have remained so calm and unafraid in the midst of all that confusion.

"If they hurt us," said Jacinta, "we are going to heaven. But those that hurt us, poor people, are going to hell."

One of the intruders in the house of Ti Marto was a Baroness from Pombalinho, who insisted on presenting two ornate dresses, a blue one for Lucia, a white one for Jacinta. The girls declined these, preferring their own white Communion attire. Finally, after infinite confusion, they managed to get a bite to eat and to squirm out of the house.

At the last moment Maria Rosa put on her shawl and said she would accompany them. "I know they are going to kill you," she said tearfully to Lucia. "Very well, then, if you must go, I will go and die with you."

It was a long and slow journey. The highroad was crowded all the way from Fátima to Cova da Iria. Men and women were kneeling in the thick slime on both sides, imploring their prayers. Hands reached out to touch them. Wet burros brushed against them. Umbrellas threatened to poke out their eyes. But what a sight when at last they arrived near the scene of the apparitions! Fully 70,000 men, women and children, people of all ages and conditions, were standing patiently in the rain waiting for them—a dark mass under innumerable black umbrellas, dripping sombreros, soaked blankets. They were packed so densely between the highway and the azinheira that the children were able to get through only with the help of a chauffeur, who seized Jacinta and mounted her on his shoulder, crying, "Make way for the children who saw Our Lady!"

Ti Marto followed with Lucia and Francisco. When they reached the place of the apparitions, he was surprised to find his wife already there. He had forgotten her in his anxiety for Jacinta. "My Olimpia turned up from another direction, I don't know from where," he confesses.

At all events there she was close to the stump of the azinheira, which Maria Carreira had lovingly draped, along with her alms table, under garlands of flowers. The crowd lurched and swayed this way and that, ducked umbrellas, huddled together for warmth, scanned the leaden eastern sky. Loud voices were repeating the Rosary in various rhythmical cadences. A priest who had been praying all night in the rain and mud was reading his breviary and from time to time nervously fingering his watch. Presently he turned to the children and asked at what hour Our Lady was going to arrive.

"At midday," replied Lucia.

He glanced at his watch again, and said, disapprovingly: "It is midday already. Our Lady is not a liar. We shall see."

Nearly all the people now were saying the Rosary. "*Avé, Maria, cheia de graça . . . Santa Maria, Mãi de Deus, rogai por nos pecadores . . .*"

"Put down your umbrellas!" cried Lucia—why she never knew—and one after another they obeyed, although the rain was still falling. "Put down your umbrellas!" said one after another. They all stood patiently in the rain.

A few minutes more passed. The priest looked at his watch again.

"Midday is past," he said with gloomy finality. "Away with all this! It is all an illusion."

He began to push the three children with his hands, if we may trust the memory of Maria Carreira.[1] But Lucia, almost in tears, refused to budge, saying.

"Whoever wants to go, can go, but I'm not going. Our Lady told us to come. We saw her other times and we're going to see her now."

Disappointed murmurs and grumblings began to be heard among the bystanders. Then of a sudden Lucia looked toward the east and cried:

"Jacinta, kneel down, for now I see Our Lady there. I can see the flash!"

"Watch out, daughter!" It was the shrill voice of Maria Rosa. "Don't let yourself be deceived!"

Lucia did not hear the warning. Those near her noticed that her face had become flushed and transparently beautiful. She was gazing rapturously now at the Lady herself, who stood in a flood of white light on the flowers that Maria Carreira had draped on the stump of the azinheira. Jacinta and Francisco, on either side of her, stared likewise, both radiant, both quite oblivious of the multitude around them.

"What do you want of me?" Lucia was kneeling with the others. The fine rain fell on her upturned face.

"I want to tell you to have them build a chapel here in my honor. I am the Lady of the Rosary. Let them continue to say the Rosary every day. The war is going to end, and the soldiers will soon return to their homes."

"I have many things to ask of you," said Lucia. "The cure of some sick persons, the conversion of some sinners. . . ."

"Some yes, others no. It is necessary that they amend their lives, and ask pardon for their sins."

Her face became graver as she continued, "Let them offend Our Lord God no more, for He is already much offended."

With this the Lady of the Rosary opened her white hands as always, and it seemed to Lucia that the light emerging from

[1] De Marchi, p. 175.

144

them ascended to where the sun ought to be, directly over-head, and it was brighter than any sunlight. Perhaps it was at this moment that the crowd saw the clouds separate like two vast curtains rolled apart, and the sun appear between them in the clear blue, like a disk of white fire. Certainly many heard Lucia cry, "Look at the sun!" but she said this in ecstacy and has no recollection of it. For she was wholly absorbed in something she saw where the sun must have been.

As Our Lady disappeared in the very radiance that came from her outstretched hands, there stood out in the zenith above three tableaus which symbolized, one after another, the Joyous, the Sorrowful and the Glorious mysteries of the Rosary. The first was a distinct representation of the Holy Family: Our Lady herself in her traditional dress of white with a blue mantle, and Saint Joseph beside her holding the Child Jesus on his arm—Saint Joseph in white, the Infant in bright red.

Lucia was heard to say, "Saint Joseph is going to bless us!" All three of the children saw this first vision, and saw the Saint make the sign of the cross three times over the crowd. The holy Child did likewise.

The next vision, seen by Lucia alone, was one of Our Lady of Sorrows in the sombre garb assigned to her by tradition, the Mater Dolorosa of Good Friday, but without the sword in her breast; and beside her stood her divine Son grieving as when he met her on the way to Calvary. Lucia saw only the upper part of His figure. He looked pityingly on the crowd for whom He had died, and raised His hand to make the sign of the cross over them.

Our Lady then appeared in a third vision of glory, as Our Lady of Mount Carmel, crowned as queen of heaven and of the world, her infant Son upon her knee.

The crowd saw nothing of all this: at least there seems to be no solid verification of the claim that a few saw the Lady. What they all did see, however, was something stupendous, unheard of, almost apocalyptic. The sun stood forth in the clear zenith like a great silver disk which, though bright as any sun they had ever seen, they could look straight at without blinking, and with a unique and delightful satisfaction. This lasted but a moment. While they gazed, the huge ball began to "dance"—that was the word all the beholders applied to it. Now it was whirling rapidly like a gigantic fire-wheel. After doing this for some time, it stopped. Then it rotated again, with dizzy, sickening speed. Finally there appeared on the rim a border of crimson, which flung across the sky, as from a hellish vortex, blood-red streamers of flame, reflecting to the earth, to the trees and shrubs, to the upturned faces and the clothes all sorts of brilliant colors in succession: green, red, orange, blue, violet, the whole spectrum in fact. Madly gyrating in this manner three times, the fiery orb seemed to tremble, to shudder, and then to plunge precipitately, in a mighty zigzag, toward the crowd.

A fearful cry broke from the lips of thousands of terrified persons as they fell upon their knees, thinking the end of the world had come. Some said that the air became warmer at that instant; they would not have been surprised if everything about them had burst into flames, enveloping and consuming them.

"*Ai Jesús,* we are all going to die here!"

"Save us, Jesus! Our Lady, save us!"

"Oh, my God, I am sorry—" And one began the Act of Contrition.

Some who had come to jeer fell on their faces and broke into sobs and abject prayers.

The Marques do Cruz said, "Oh my God, how great is Thy power!"

This had lasted about ten minutes, perhaps. Then all saw the sun begin to climb, in the same zigzag manner, to where it had appeared before. It became tranquil, then dazzling. No one could look at it any longer. It was the sun of every day.

The people stared at one another in joy and amazement. "Miracle! Miracle! The children were right! Our Lady made the miracle! Blessed be God! Blessed be Our Lady!" The shouts were taken up all over the Cova da Iria. Some were laughing, others weeping with joy. Many were making the discovery that their drenched clothes had in some unexplained manner become perfectly dry.

Avelino de Almeida reported the event in *O Seculo* of October 17 as "a spectacle unique and incredible if one had not been a witness of it. . . . One can see the immense crowd turn toward the sun, which reveals itself free of the clouds in full noon. The great star of day makes one think of a silver plaque, and it is possible to look straight at it without the least discomfort. It does not burn, it does not blind. It might be like an eclipse. But now bursts forth a colossal clamor, and we hear the nearest spectators crying, 'Miracle, miracle! Marvel, marvel!'

"Before the astonished eyes of the people, whose attitude carries us back to biblical times and who, full of terror, heads uncovered, gaze into the blue of the sky, the sun has trembled, and the sun has made some brusque movements, unprecedented and outside of all cosmic laws—the sun has 'danced,' according to the typical expression of the peasants. . . . An old man whose stature and face, at once gentle and energetic, recall those of Paul Deroulède, turns toward the sun and recites the *Credo* with loud cries from beginning to end. I ask his name. It is Senhor João Maria Amado de Melo Ramalho da Cunha Vasconcelos. I see him afterwards addressing those about him who have kept their hats on, begging them vehemently to uncover before so extraordinary a demonstration of the existence of God. Similar scenes are repeated in all places. . . .

"The people ask one another if they have seen anything and what they have seen. The greatest number avow that they have seen the trembling and dancing of the sun. Others, however, declare that they have seen the smiling face of the Virgin herself; swear that the sun turned around on itself like a wheel of fireworks; that it fell, almost to the point of burning the earth with its rays. . . . Another tells that he has seen it change color successively. . . .

"Almost three o'clock. The sky is limpid and the sun follows its course with its habitual brilliancy so that no one dares to look at it directly. And the shepherds? . . . Lucia, the one who speaks to the Virgin, announces with theatrical motions, on the neck of a man who carries her from group to group, that the war is going to end and that the soldiers are coming home. Such news, however, does not increase the joy of those who hear her. The celestial Sign, that is everything. Much curiosity, nevertheless, to see the two little girls with their garlands of roses; some try to kiss the hand of the 'little saints'; and one of the two, Jacinta, is much nearer to fainting than to dancing. But what all aspired for—the Sign in the Sky—has sufficed to satisfy them, to enroot them in their Breton-like faith. . . .

"Their dispersion follows rapidly and without incidents, without the shadow of disorder, without the need of any intervention of police patrols. The pilgrims who leave first, in haste to be on their way, are those who arrived first with their shoes on their heads or hung on their staves. They are going, their souls full of joy, to spread the good news in the villages that were not wholly depopulated to come here. And the priests? Some have shown themselves on the scene, standing rather with the curious spectators than in the company of pilgrims avid for celestial favors. Perhaps now and then one does not manage to conceal the satisfaction which appears so often on the faces of those who triumph. . . . It remains for those competent to pronounce on the *danse macabre* of the sun, which today, at Fátima, has made hosannas burst from the breasts of the faithful and naturally has impressed—so witnesses worthy of belief assure me—even freethinkers and other persons not at all interested in religious matters who have come to this once famous countryside."

All over Portugal, in fact, the anti-clerical press was compelled to bear witness of the same sort. There was general agreement on the essentials. As Dr. Domingos Pinto Coelho wrote in *O Ordem*, "The sun, sometimes surrounded with crimson flames, at other times aureoled with yellow and red, at still other times seemed to revolve with a very rapid movement of rotation, still again seeming to detach itself from the sky, to approach the earth and to radiate strong heat."

Theories of mass hypnotism or suggestion were discarded

148

when it became known that reliable witnesses not in the crowd had seen the miracle many miles away. The poet Affonso Lopes Vieira saw it from his house at S. Pedro de Moel, forty kilometers from Fátima. Father Inacio Lourenco told later how he had seen it from Alburita, eighteen or nineteen kilometers away, when he was a boy of nine. He and some fellow students heard people shouting in the street near by. Running out of the school with his teacher, Dona Delfina Pereira Lopes, he saw with amazement the spinning and falling of the sun. "It was like a globe of snow revolving on itself," he wrote. "Then suddenly it seemed to come down in a zigzag, threatening to fall on the earth. Terrified, I ran to shelter myself in the midst of the people. All were weeping, expecting from one moment to the next the end of the world.

"Near us was an unbeliever without religion, who had spent the morning mocking the blockheads who had made all that journey to Fátima to go and stare at a girl. I looked at him. He stood as if paralyzed, thunderstruck, his eyes fixed on the sun. Then I saw him tremble from head to foot, and raising his hands to heaven, he fell on his knees in the mire, shouting, 'Nossa Senhora! Nossa Senhora!'

"Meanwhile the people continued to scream and cry out, begging God to pardon their sins. . . . Afterwards we ran to the chapels of the town, which were filled in a few moments.

"During those long minutes of the solar phenomenon objects all about us reflected all the colors of the rainbow. As we looked at one another, one seemed blue, another yellow, another vermilion. . . . All these strange phenomena increased the terror of the crowd. After about ten minutes the sun returned to its place in the same way it had descended, still pale and without splendor . . ."

Plenty of witnesses are still living in the neighborhood. I spoke with many of them last summer, including Ti Marto and his Olimpia, Maria Carreira, two of the sisters of Lucia (Mary of the Angels and Gloria) and several others of the country folk, all of whom told the same story with evident sincerity; and as they mentioned the falling of the sun there was always a trace of terror in their voices. The Reverend Father Manuel Pereira da Silva gave me substantially the same details. "When I saw the sun fall zigzag," he said, "I fell on my knees. I thought the end of the world had come."

The fact has been established beyond any doubt. How is it to be explained?

As early as May, 1917, Jacinta and Lucia had told people that the Lady they saw had promised a miracle on October 13, at the hour of noon, as a sign of their sincerity. They had repeated this at various times, and had never altered their story even under threats and persecution which must have been terrifying to such children at the ages of ten, nine, and seven. On the very day and hour they had foretold, some 70,000 persons testified that they had the unique experience of seeing the sun spin round and seem to fall. Such widespread testimony serves to confirm that the children actually had seen the Mother of Christ, and that He had given to the simple souls at Cova da Iria the sign in the sky for which the Pharisees had begged Him in mock reverence, and which He had refused to grant their unbelieving and adulterous hearts.

The Administrator of Ourem still denies that anything miraculous happened. I suspect he would have denied it even if he had been there. Or like the Pharisees who denied the Resurrection after they had seen Christ dying on the cross, he would have made up some rationalistic explanation to save himself the humiliation of believing.

He was removed from office following the coup d'etât of Sidonio Païs some two months after the miracle. The last heard of him was that he was injured in Tomar by the premature explosion of a bomb he was making to throw at certain members of the new government.

CHAPTER XIV

Lucia has drawn the mantle of a charitable silence over the reactions of her family to the events of October 13. There must have been apologies and acts of reparation, furtive, perhaps, on the part of Antonio, honest and flatfooted on that of Maria Rosa. But on that day the wan and spiritless girl had no time to enjoy her triumph. Mobs of pilgrims followed her about all afternoon. They were still milling about the street and passing in and out of the houses of the Abóboras and the Martos when Dr. Formigão arrived in Aljustrel at seven o'clock in the evening. He wanted to talk with the three children before anyone else did, and before they could compare notes. Thanks to his authority as a priest he dispersed the strangers in short order, and then summoned the three principals to the house of Ti Marto, where he questioned them separately.

All three had seen Our Lady stand on the stump of the tree. Lucia and Jacinta were agreed as to what she said. Francisco had seen her but had not heard her speak. All three had seen the sun turn. All had seen, near the sun, the vision of the Holy Family. Only Lucia had seen the two succeeding tableaus of Our Lady of Sorrows and Our Lady of Mount Carmel. All agreed as to the colors of the garments and other details. There were some discrepancies. Was the Infant Jesus large? No, very little, replied each one separately. But Lucia believed he was on the arm of Saint Joseph, while both Jacinta and Francisco saw him standing beside him—on the right side, said Jacinta, and he did not come up to the waist of Saint Joseph. To Lucia he seemed about one year old. To Jacinta and Francisco he was about the age of a baby of the neighborhood, Deolinda de Jose das Neves, who was two years old.

The divergence regarding the position of the Child is the only important one, and I confess I do not know how to explain it. In all such visions there is a subjective element, and it may be that they present different details to different persons.

Dr. Formigão made one more attempt to learn the secret from Francisco.

"Which was brighter, the figure of the Virgin or the sun?" he asked.

"The figure of the Virgin was brighter."

"Did you hear what she said?"

"I heard nothing."

"Who told you the secret? The Lady?"

"No, it was Lucia."

"Can you tell it to me?"

"I cannot."

"You don't want to speak, because you are afraid of Lucia, you are afraid she will strike you, isn't it true?"

"Oh, no!"

"Then, why can't you tell it to me? . . . Would it be a sin, perhaps?"

"I believe that it would be a sin to reveal the secret."

"Is the secret for the good of your soul, and Lucia's and Jacinta's?"

"Yes."

"Is it also for the good of the soul of the Senhor Prior?"

"I don't know."

"Would the people be sad if they happened to learn it?"

"Yes."

The children were so pale from fatigue and dazed from excitement that Dr. Formigão shortened his examination, fearing they would be ill if they were not given some rest. When he returned October 19, they were still so exhausted that they answered mechanically, like sleepwalkers. Lucia's memory was vague on recent events, though accurate about those in the past. The questioner was convinced that all three had answered honestly. He had seen the miracle of the sun. He went away believing also in the apparitions; and from then on he was a defender of the children even in the face of a persistent persecution, all the more difficult to understand when the prime movers in it happened to be not Carbonari or Masons, but fellow Catholics, fellow priests.

As for the liberal opposition, the first stupefied silence of the Carbonari lasted but a few days. "What are we about?" said the children of this world on another occasion. "For this Man is working many miracles. If we let Him go on like this everybody will believe in Him!" Within a week the Grand Orient lodge of Santarem had recovered sufficiently to plan not merely a defense but a counter-attack. On the night of October 23 several of the brethren, including one known as Cemetery Frank, went to Ourem, where they were reinforced by certain henchmen of the Administrator Santos. All then repaired by automobile to Cova da Iria with the intention of destroying what remained of the azinheira tree, and thus killing the cult by robbing it of a rallying point and chief relic. Some carried lanterns, others axes and hatchets.

A few strokes close to the roots, and a small tree was lying flat on the ground. Near by were other paraphernalia of devotion: the table of Maria Carreira with flowers and coins on it, and a picture of Our Lady; the rustic arch that pilgrims had built of two upright poles, with one hanging between to support a couple of lanterns and some crosses. All these the raiding party confiscated and carried off to Santarem. They placed them on exhibition as medieval monstrosities in a house near the seminary, charging a modest fee to inspect them, and offering the proceeds to the manager of the Misericordia, who, however, declined. The next evening they bore the entire exhibit in procession through the streets, singing blasphemous litanies to the accompaniment of drums.

The Liberal and Masonic *O Seculo* of Lisboa published these and other details, with a hearty condemnation of the whole desecration, remarking that it was especially shameful at a time when Catholic processions were forbidden. Other anti-clericals were less tolerant. When a group of educated Catholics of Santarem published an indignant protest, the Portuguese Federation of Free Thinkers retorted with one of the most curious documents in Portuguese history, a Manifesto addressed to all liberals against "the shameful spectacle staged as a ridiculous comedy at Fátima," which they ascribed to an ecclesiastical plot to unite Church and State and restore diplomatic relations with the Vatican. In his fervor the writer went so far as to declare that miracles ought to be punished like transgressions against city ordinances, since they were violations of the laws of nature. He was particularly incensed because the miracle of the sun was invented and perpetrated on the anniversary of the Freethinker Francisco Ferrer. Demanding prompt public action against all those guilty of dragging such medievalism into the light of the twentieth century, he concluded with:

"LONG LIVE THE REPUBLIC!
DOWN WITH REACTION!
LONG LIVE LIBERTY!"

On the morning of October 24 the news of the ravishing of the shrine passed rapidly from mouth to mouth through the grapevine of the Serra. There were cries of anger in Moita, in Fátima, in Aljustrel. Maria Carreira was one of the faithful who hurried to Cova da Iria to see what had happened. *Ai!* the worst had happened. The table, the arch, the lanterns, all had disappeared. Yet not the worst! For the marauders had chopped down the wrong tree. And there, a few feet from the uprooted one, stood the brave little azinheira on which Our Lady had appeared, its upper leaves sadly shorn, but the trunk and lower branches still standing in the sun for all to see. Maria Carreira gave thanks to God.

The net result of the outrage was to increase rather than discourage the devotion to Our Lady of Fátima. The number of pilgrims gradually increased. There were sure to be many of them on Sundays and on the thirteenth of each month from May to October, sometimes in a veritable procession from Leiria, Ourem, or Chão de Maçás. Even during the week it was a rare day that did not bring at least a few. The barefoot poor still predominated; many were sick, lame, brokenhearted, all hopeful that if they could but touch the bark of the azinheira, the Queen of Heaven would have pity on them. One cold winter morning Maria Carreira found a man who had slept all night on the ground near the tree, after walking eleven leagues. "I am glad I came," he said. "I feel very happy in this place."

Along with the devout poor came a few more prosperous persons, sometimes from as far as Lisboa or Porto. Almost every day one would appear at the Martos' or Abóboras' and ask for a few words with the children. At first Olimpia used to send out to the meadows for Jacinta and Francisco, but this got to be such a nuisance that she finally lost patience, and decided to turn the flock over to her son João. The two were greatly disappointed, for it meant giving up, in great measure, the company of Lucia. But before long she too ceased to be a shepherdess.

Maria Rosa and her husband were too human to have been transformed into angels by the stupefying experience they had shared on October 13. Miracle or no miracle, Antonio bitterly resented the fact that the vast crowd had increased, if possible, the destruction of his farm property in the Cova. Nothing would ever grow there now, especially with pilgrims coming to camp out or walk about daily. It was no small sacrifice for a farmer of Aljustrel to lose fifty sacks or more of potatoes a year, not to mention his beans, spinach and other vegetables. Maria Rosa remained irascible to the end, for it was her temperament. But she was too honest to deny that Lucia had been right, and too devout, having made the admission, to refuse to do all in her power to carry out the wishes of the Mother of God. If Our Lady wanted the *cachopa* to learn to read, there was nothing more to be said. Since the time of the monarchy there had been a small day school for boys at Fátima, near the church. Recently, by a happy coincidence, one had been started there for girls. Maria Rosa entered Lucia, and prevailed upon her sister-in-law to send Jacinta also.

CHAPTER XV

Francisco was left alone now, but he was never lonely.
He was never without a calm sense of the presence of God.
He never tired of seeing the rising and the setting of the
sun. He could go with the girls on holidays to say the Rosary
at Cova da Iria or the Angel's prayer at Cabeço, scampering
over walls and ditches at the first glimpse of anyone who
looked like a curious pilgrim.

Sometimes he was caught before he could escape. One day
a whole group of such persons surprised him, with his sister
and his cousin, at a bend of the road. They at once recognized and surrounded the three. One set Jacinta on top of a
wall, so that all might see and hear her better. Another tried
to do likewise with Francisco. More nimble, he fled to the
top of another old wall near by, whence, looking back in
triumph, he saw a poorly clad woman and her young son
kneeling and holding out their arms to him in supplication.
The mother begged him to ask Our Lady to heal her husband, who was ill, and not to let him be sent to the war.
Francisco knelt on top of the wall and began to say his Rosary.
The strangers all joined in.

"Afterwards they accompanied us to Cova da Iria," wrote
Lucia, "and said another Rosary on the way. The poor woman
promised to return and thank Our Lady. She did, various
times, and brought her husband, who was restored to health.
They were of the parish of San Mamede, and we called
them the Casaleiros." [1]

Most strangers bored Francisco. What silly questions! One
of the favorites was the one inflicted on small boys everywhere
in the world: What are you going to be when you grow up?
Such a query, for him, entailed too much explanation. There
were those two stuffy *senhoras*, for example.

[1] Memoir IV, p. 25.

"Do you want to be a carpenter?"

"No, ma'am."

"Ah, you want to be a soldier, then?"

"No, ma'am."

"A doctor, isn't that it?"

"Oh, no!"

"I know what you would like to be—a priest!"

"No."

"What! To say Mass? . . . to hear confessions? . . . to pray in the church? Isn't that it?"

"No, *senhora*. I don't want to be a *padre*."

"Then what *do* you want to be?"

"I don't want to be anything."

"You don't want to be anything? !"

"No. I want to die and go to heaven." [2]

Francisco had no ambition to go to school with Jacinta and Lucia. What was the use, if he was going to heaven so soon? But he liked to walk with them as far as Saint Anthony's Church in Fátima. Then he would say:

"Look, you go to school and I will stay here in the church near the hidden Jesus. It isn't worth the trouble for me to learn to read. I'm leaving here soon for heaven. When you come back, call me."

The church was being repaired, and the Sacred Host had been moved from the main altar to a small one on the left side, near the entrance. "And there I found him when I returned," said Lucia. He used to spend whole days on his knees looking at the tabernacle where his Lord was waiting for someone to come and visit Him. It is likely enough that in this way, without direction, Francisco learned to practice mental prayer. He may well have become a fairly advanced contemplative, he may possibly have had ecstacies. He had learned from the Master Himself the lesson that Saint Teresa teaches in her *Way of Perfection*: that lofty prayer demands love, solitude, detachment, freedom from all self-seeking or sensuality.

[2] Another of Ti Marto's recollections, in De Marchi, p. 211.

Yet he never paraded his piety, but concealed it, even from Jacinta. One day after school when the girls lost sight of him on the Serra, they found him lying prostrate and motionless behind a stone wall.

"Why don't you come and pray with us?"

"I'd rather pray alone, to think, and to console Our Lord. He is so sad."

"Francisco, which do you like better, to console Our Lord or to convert sinners so that their souls won't go to hell any more?"

This was a more profound theological question than Lucia may have realized, but he answered without hesitation:

"I'd rather console Our Lord."

"Don't you remember then how sad Our Lady was the last month when she said not to offend Our Lord, because He was much offended already?"

"I want to console Our Lord first and then convert the sinners so that they won't offend any more."

One day he was missing so long that Jacinta thought he was lost. "Francisco! Francisco!" No answer. Finally they discovered him, prostrate and motionless, behind a pile of rocks. Still no answer. He hardly stirred even when they shook him, and when he finally got up, he seemed hardly to know where he was. He explained that he had been saying the prayer of the Angel, and then had remained there thinking.

"And didn't you hear Jacinta calling you?"

"I? No, I heard nothing."

Francisco's prayer was not a form of self-indulgence, like that of the pseudo-mystics. There was nothing in it of what Saint John of the Cross calls "spiritual gluttony." Rather, it flowered radiantly into good works for the benefit of others. He would go out and gather up the sheep and goats of a certain poor old woman who had trouble managing them. He obtained notable cures and conversions. He could never resist any honest appeal. Just as he had once offered a boy two *vintens* to release a captive bird, and had run all the way to Aljustrel and back to fetch the money, so now he would spare himself no trouble to free some struggling soul from sin or pain. One day on the way to school Lucia met her sister Teresa, recently married, who had come from Lomba, where she now lived, with a request for prayers. The son of a woman there had been arrested and falsely accused of a grave crime for which he might be exiled or imprisoned for many years. After Teresa had passed along to her mother's house, Lucia told the others what she had said. Francisco was visibly moved. When they reached Fátima he said:

"Look, while you two are at school I will stay with the hidden Jesus and ask for this grace."

When school was over the girls found him kneeling before the *Santissimo*. "Did you tell Our Lady about that?" asked Lucia.

"Yes, and you can tell your sister Teresa that the boy will be home again in a few days."

So it came to pass; and the woman of Lomba was at Cova da Iria on the thirteenth of the next month, giving thanks for her son's release.

For such favors Francisco paid the price that all the mystics pay. His great desire, next to heaven, was to receive the hidden Jesus in Holy Eucharist. This became almost a burning pain when he saw his sister Jacinta going to her First Communion. They had begun preparing for it together the previous summer. Ti Marto remembers it well; it was soon after the Prior had questioned them about the apparitions. "Senhor Prior," he said, "here are my two children, ready for their first confession. Now you can ask them all the questions you want!" Afterwards he took them to be examined for their First Communion, but Father Ferreira thought they had better wait another year. Jacinta finally passed in May, 1918; but Francisco failed again when he became confused about some point in the *Credo*. This time he went home crying. It was hard enough for a boy of ten to fail, but harder still to sit with the grown-ups on a fragrant spring day and watch his younger sister go up without him. But the pain of separation is familiar to the lovers of God, and Francisco bore it bravely as he bent once more to his prayers. "It is for your love, O my Jesus!"

It is plain from Lucia's memoirs that she recognized a certain spiritual leadership in this boy who was her junior. Just before Lent in 1918 some of her friends asked her to organize one of the *festas* of Carnival Week, leading up to the frivolities of Mardi Gras. It was the custom for a group of boys and girls to meet at a certain place, bringing oil, bread or meat from home, and then to feast and dance till late at night. José Carreira and his wife offered the use of their house for what promised to be the best party of the year. Girls were coming from Moita, Fátima, Silva dos Currais, Lomba, Pederneia, Cura da Pedra, Cosa Velha, all over the Serra. "I refused at first, but, carried away by a cowardly condescension, I gave in to their insistent demands." Yet Lucia's conscience troubled her, and she told her cousins.

Francisco's dark eyes looked her sternly through and through. "And you are going back to these kitchen parties and games? Have you forgotten that you promised never to go back to them?"

"I don't want to go, but you can see that they keep asking me, and I don't know what to do."

"Do you know what you are going to do? All the people know that Our Lady appeared to you. Just say that for that you have promised not to dance any more, and so you are not going. Then we can escape these days to the cave of Cabeço, and nobody will meet us."

On the day of the party they were all at Cova da Iria, saying the Rosary.

Lucia's godfather, Anastacio, one of the few in Aljustrel who did not have to work for a living, had a rather worldly wife named Teresa. One Sunday afternoon she saw the children passing, and cried, "Come here, my little impostors, come here! I haven't seen you in a long time!" She gave them some sweets, and then asked them to sing a certain popular song, a rather lusty pagan one, commencing:

"Greetings to the girl
With the new sun's fragrance! . ."

When they had finished, all the company laughed and

wanted it repeated. But Francisco said, "Let's not sing this any more. Our Lord certainly doesn't like us to sing such things." So they declined and took their leave. Lucia believed that in disappointing her godfather's wife she probably lost a good inheritance; "but the good God had destined me for another heritage much more precious."

It was October, 1918, and the war was about to end, as Our Lady had promised. But the great epidemic of influenza, one of the concomitant scourges of the almost universal punishment of man's apostasy, was laying low millions of persons throughout the world; and toward the end of October it made its first appearance in Aljustrel. All of the Abóbora family except Lucia were stricken. In Ti Marto's house, he alone was left to nurse the rest. Francisco, the first to be put to bed, had a severe case, ending with bronchial pneumonia.

It was heartbreaking for his father and mother to see him welcome the illness as the beginning of the journey that the Lady had promised him. He became so weak that he could hardly move, yet he never complained. "If we gave him a little milk," Olimpia remembers, "he took the milk. If we gave him an egg, he ate the egg. Poor little lad! He took the bitter medicines without making a face. This gave us hope that he would get well. But what do you think? He was always telling us that it was no use, that Our Lady was coming to take him to heaven." His only sorrow was that he was no longer able to make his daily visit to the hidden Jesus in the church at Fátima.

Jacinta became ill a few days after Francisco. One day Lucia found her strangely elated. "Look, Lucia!" she said. "Our Lady came to see us here, and she said that she is coming very soon to take Francisco to heaven. And she asked me if I still wanted to convert more sinners and I said yes.

"Our Lady wants me to go to two hospitals. But not to be cured. It is to suffer more for the love of God, for the conversion of sinners and in reparation for the offenses committed against the Immaculate Heart of Mary.

"She said that you were not going," she continued, as Lucia, perhaps, began to look hopeful. "She said my mother is going to take me, and then I will stay there alone."

Ti Marto and his wife heard this sort of talk with a chill of fear. For this was no ordinary sickness, this bronchial influenza. Every day one heard of some neighbor who had died; every day the church bell at Fátima announced another sad rendezvous in the cemetery across the way. In many Portuguese towns that winter the tolling of funeral bells had to be forbidden, to prevent a state of panic. But Ti Marto had lived through too many troubles to allow himself to get hysterical whenever a hearse went by. He had never doubted that Jacinta had seen Our Lady at Cova da Iria, but he was not the man to call in the undertaker just because a little girl had a dream or a vision.

Sure enough, the fever of Francisco began to go down day by day, his pulse to grow stronger. Toward Christmas he was able to get up, though pale and weak, and go about a little. At the beginning of the new year he seemed almost himself again. In January he went to the cave at Cabeço to say the Angel's prayer. One day he would pray at Cova da Iria, another at Valinhos. Once, although his head ached, he walked to Fátima to kneel for quite a while before the altar, consoling the hidden Jesus for the world's neglect.

When pilgrims came he tried to answer their questions patiently. This was not always easy. One afternoon he returned rather tired from Valinhos to find the house full of people who had spread rosaries, crucifixes, medals and other objects on a table, and were waiting for him to bless them. "I can't bless them, and neither can you," he said with some severity. "The priests bless them." The visitors departed in haste, shouting insults at him over their shoulders.

Before the end of January he was ill again, with a low fever. Ti Marto as usual tried to put a good face on the matter. "Never mind, Francisco, you are going to get well, just as you did before. You are going to be a strong man, you will see."

"No," replied the boy. "Our Lady is coming very soon now."

His godmother Teresa was one of those who attempted to make him take what she considered a more hopeful view. She promised him a speedy recovery, for she was going to offer his weight in wheat to give the poor, and Our Lady would never refuse to grant such a request.

"It's not worth your trouble," said the boy calmly. "Our Lady will not grant you this grace."

A few days after this he became much worse, and had to return to his bed. It was that single iron bed still to be seen there, with its patchwork quilt, its ornate colored metal back, and its two brass knobs. It filled up the space between three plain walls. Overhead, toward the right, there was a small window, showing nothing but a bit of sky. As Francisco laid his hot and aching head on the pillow, he was convinced that he would never get up again. And from that time on he became steadily worse.

Jacinta was ill most of this time in another room. She would listen until she felt sure that both her parents were out of the house. Then she would slip out of bed and steal into Francisco's room to perch beside him and talk, until this was discovered and forbidden. Toward evening Lucia would stop in on her way home from school. Ti Olimpia would smile broadly. She knew what this meant to the invalids.

Lucia would say, "Well, Jacinta, have you made many sacrifices today?"

"Yes, a lot," answered the little girl. She lowered her voice. "My mother was out and I wanted to go many times to visit Francisco, and I didn't do it."

Lucia went to the boy's room. He was flushed, his eyes much too large and bright.

"Do you suffer much, Francisco?"

"*Bastante*. But it doesn't matter. I suffer to console Our Lord, and in a little while I shall be with Him."

"When you do go, don't forget to ask Our Lady to take me there soon, also."

"I won't ask that. You know very well that she doesn't want you there yet."

One afternoon Lucia brought some other girls, schoolmates. When they had gone, Francisco looked seriously at her and said:

"Don't walk with them, because you can learn to commit sins."

"But they leave school when I do."

"When you leave, spend a little while at the feet of the hidden Jesus, and then come home alone."[8]

His fever was somewhat higher, and it was plain that he was growing weaker. One day when Lucia was alone with him, he took a piece of rope from under the bedclothes and handed it to her.

"Take it before my mother finds it. I'm not strong enough to hide it any more." It was the one they had found on the road and had made into a sort of hair-shirt.

By the first of April Francisco was so weak that he could hardly move his lips in prayer. It grieved him not to be able to say his Rosary. "I'm not strong enough, Mother," he said. "When I say the Hail Marys my head gets all mixed up."

"Just say it in your heart then." Olimpia laid an anxious hand on his brow. "Our Lady hears it just the same and is just as pleased."

He smiled at her contentedly.

It was spring again, and sometimes the distant sad song of a nightingale would come floating in through the tiny window on the sweet air of the Serra. Francisco said he wanted to see Lucia. She came running over.

"Look, Lucia, I am very sick, and I am going to heaven very soon."

Lucia tried to seem casual. "Then look here, don't forget to pray much for sinners, for the Holy Father, for me and for Jacinta."

"Yes, I will. But look—ask Jacinta these things afterwards. I'm afraid I'll forget them when I go to Our Lord. And first I want to console Him. . . . Look, Lucia I want to go to confession."

On the night of April 2 he was so much worse that his parents promised to send to the rectory the first thing in the

[8] Memoir IV, p. 20.

morning to ask the Prior to come and hear his confession and give him Viaticum.

In the early dawn Francisco whispered to his sister Teresa that he wanted to see Lucia at once. The girl ran down to the Abóbora house, woke her cousin, and said:

"Lucia, come quickly! Francisco is very sick and says he wants to tell you something!"

Lucia dressed hastily and hurried to his bedside. She asked his mother, his brother John and two of his sisters to leave the room, since it was some secret that Francisco wanted to tell her. They did so, and the boy said:

"It is that I am going to confess so that I can receive Communion and then die. I want you to tell me if you have seen me commit any sin and ask Jacinta if she has seen me commit any."

Lucia thought hard. "Sometimes you disobeyed your mother—when she told you to stop staying in the house, and you hid."

"It is true. I did that. Now go ask Jacinta if she remembers anything else."

Jacinta thought very hard. "Look, tell him that before Our Lady appeared to us, he stole a *tostão*[4] from his father to buy the hand-organ from José Marto of Casa Velha, and that when the boys of Aljustrel threw stones at those of Boleiros he also threw some."

Lucia hurried back with this message to Francisco. "I've already confessed those," he murmured. "But I'll tell them again. Perhaps it is for these sins that I did that Our Lord is so sad. But even if I don't die I will never do them again. I am sorry now." And putting his hands together he said, "O my Jesus, pardon us, save us from the fire of hell, draw all souls to heaven, especially those in most need!" Then turning to Lucia he added, "Look, you too ask Our Lord to pardon me my sins."

"I will, don't worry. If Our Lord hadn't forgiven you, Our Lady wouldn't have told Jacinta the other day that she was

[4] A small coin worth 100 *reis*—about nine cents in U. S. money.

coming soon to take you to heaven. Now I am going to Mass, and there I will pray to the hidden Jesus for you."

"Look—ask Him also that the Senhor Prior may give me Holy Communion."

"Why, yes!"

When Lucia returned from Mass, Jacinta had got up and was sitting on the edge of her brother's bed. Francisco said at once:

"Did you ask the hidden Jesus to have the Senhor Prior give me Holy Communion?"

"I did."

"Afterwards in heaven I will pray for you."

"Do! Yet the other day you said you would not!"

"That was to take you to heaven soon. But if you wish I will pray, and then Our Lady will do as you wish."

"I do wish. You pray."

This is what Lucia remembers of the conversation. "I left him then and went about my daily duties of work and school. When I returned at nightfall, he was radiant with joy. He had confessed and the Senhor Prior had promised him to bring Holy Communion the following day."

The next morning, April 3, was a lovely one. Francisco lay very tranquil, waiting for the priest. After a while his eyes opened. He had heard the tinkling of the little bell that the acolyte was ringing to let people know that the Senhor Prior had the Sacred Host with him. He tried to sit up, but he was too weak, and his godmother Teresa told him he could receive his First Communion just as well lying down. Meanwhile Olimpia had lighted the holy candles and had set them on a small table by the bed.

Now the priest was in the room holding the hidden Jesus before him, and saying three times, *"Domine, non sum dignus. . . ."* Francisco was almost in heaven.

When Jacinta went afterwards to see him—she was allowed to that day—he told her all about it. "Today I am happier than you, for I have within my breast the hidden Jesus. I am going to heaven, but there I will pray a great deal to Our Lord and Our Lady that they bring you there too, soon."

Jacinta stayed with him nearly all day, sometimes saying the Rosary for him when he was unable to say it himself, sometimes just sitting on the edge of the bed and looking at him. Lucia came after school as usual. Francisco said to her:

"Certainly in heaven I am going to pray hard for your wishes—who knows but Our Lady may take you also very soon?"

Lucia had changed her mind. "Don't do that, no. Just imagine yourself at the feet of Our Lord and Our Lady who are so good."

"All right." Then a terrible thought came to him. "But perhaps she won't remember me!"

"Perhaps she won't remember you! ! ! Patience!"

Francisco smiled.

He looked so ethereal that Lucia doubted whether she would see him again. "Goodby, Francisco," she said softly. "If you go to heaven tonight, don't forget me there, do you hear?"

"I won't forget you, no. Don't worry."

He seized her right hand with unexpected strength and pressed it hard for a long moment, looking deeply into her eyes; and both were blinded by tears. "Do you want anything else?" It sounded stupid, but it was all she could think of.

"No," he replied in a low voice.

Ti Olimpia came in to send Lucia home. "Then goodby, Francisco, till heaven. Goodby till heaven." Lucia was still weeping as she went out. She could stand no more.

All night the boy lay quietly thinking of the hidden Jesus he had received and would soon see face to face. He was thirsty, but was unable to drink the milk his mother offered; he could take only a few drops of water. "I'm all right," he would say, "don't give me anything."

Once he called her and said, "Look, mother, what a pretty light there, near the door! . . .

"Now I don't see it any more."

In the morning he asked her blessing and pardon for any trouble he had caused her in his life. At ten o'clock his life passed almost imperceptibly. There was still a faint smile on his lips when Jacinta and Lucia came to look at him.

The next day, April 5, 1919, some men in green capes, members of the Misericordia, went slowly up the cobbled road to Fátima with an acolyte carrying a crucifix. Four boys in white walked after them with a small coffin. Ti Marto and Olimpia followed, and a few others. They laid the remains of Francisco in a small grave near the cemetery gate. All said the Rosary.

Jacinta was too ill to be there. Lucia went up afterwards alone and placed a little cross on the grave.

CHAPTER XVI

Jacinta was moved into the bed where Francisco had died. It was nearer the front door, and she could see and hear people better. Perhaps Olimpia thought this would help her get over her grief. For although Jacinta knew where Francisco was and who had taken him, she missed him terribly.

The person who helped her most in those gloomy spring days was Lucia. Every day she would stop in, cheerful and matter-of-fact, on her way home from school. On holidays or Sundays she would bring flowers from the Serra, and as she arranged them on the table, would tell Jacinta where she had found them. "These are from Cova da Iria. I found this at Valinhos. This grew by the Lagoa." The best were from the slope of Cabeço—violets, wild roses, peonies and daisies in turn, all the flowers that the little girl would have picked if she had been well.

Lucia brought diverting accounts of the chapel that some of the devout were building near the azinheira at Cova da Iria. Everybody wanted to give orders, and no one wanted to take them; hence there were some warm and amusing arguments, in which we may be sure Maria Carreira put in her two cents' worth when the mustard of zealous resentment stuck in her sharp nose. No priest was there to arbitrate, and it took some time to find one who would bless the hermitage.[1]

Jacinta was amused, then pensive:

"I will never see Cova da Iria or Valinhos again," she said.

"Yes, you will, Jacinta. Courage!"

"No. Our Lady told me that my mother would take me to a hospital in a dark building and that I would not get well."

It was true that pleurisy took a long time to heal. Yet it seemed that sick people could help others even while they lay helpless themselves. There was Lucia's Aunt Victoria, for

[1] Maria Carreira, in De Marchi, p. 205.

instance, whose brilliant but erratic son was missing for weeks, until Jacinta began asking Our Lady to send him home. Then after a few days he suddenly returned, with a strange story suggesting something like bilocation on the part of the young invalid. Having spent all his money, he had resorted to theft, had been arrested, and had been thrown into jail at Torres Novas. One night he managed to escape. He fled to the mountains and hid himself in a pine forest. Frightened during a violent thunderstorm, he fell on his knees in the rain and asked God's forgiveness and a safe return home. Presently a little girl came out of the darkness and took him by the hand, and he saw that it was Jacinta. She led him down the mountain to the road that runs from Alqueidao to Reguengo; then, making a sign that he should continue that way, she vanished. At dawn he came to a bridge that he recognized as being near Boleiros, not far from his home in Fátima. When Lucia questioned Jacinta, the child could never explain but said she had prayed a great deal for the young man.[2]

When the warm weather brought no improvement in Jacinta's condition, the doctor said she would never recover unless she went to a hospital for an operation, for she had purulent pleurisy as a result of the bronchial pneumonia; and one morning in July (1919) Ti Marto placed her on the back of a burro and took her to Ourem. The hospital there was a large white, rather cheerful building, and the ward where Jacinta was put to bed was bright and airy. This could hardly be the dark place where Our Lady had said her mother would take her.

Olimpia went to see her there, however, and found her cheerful and uncomplaining, even when some delicacies that a visitor had brought had vanished from the top drawer of the medicine cabinet. "It was that glutton of a nurse," said Olimpia. But Jacinta did not care.

Lucia visited her only once. That was the summer when her father died (July 31, 1919); she records the event briefly in her memoirs without comment or emotion. Yet it seems likely

[2] Memoir IV, p. 45.

enough that all his family missed Antonio, for if he was not the best husband and father in the world, he was not the worst, and it was only "when he had a drop on him," as Maria Carreira observed, that he was inclined to be ill-tempered. Certainly Maria Rosa grieved for him, and her health rapidly failed after his death. She began to have alarming attacks of weakness and shortness of breath which the physician attributed to her old heart ailment.

After one of these seizures Maria of the Angels said to her youngest sister, "Look here, Lucia, you haven't any father now, and if your mother dies you will be an orphan. If it is true that you saw Our Lady, ask her to cure your mother."

The child arose without a word, went to her room, put on a heavy woolen dress, for it was cold and rainy, and went to Cova da Iria, to prostrate herself in the mud before the azinheira. When she returned after a few hours, she brought a handful of red earth, and told Gloria to make a tea of it. She had promised Our Lady, she said, that if her mother was cured they would all go on their knees from the highway to the place of the apparitions for nine days in succession, and give food to nine poor girls. It is Maria of the Angels who tells this curious story to Father De Marchi:[8]

"Gloria prepared the tea and I gave it to mother.

" 'What tea is this?' she asked.

" 'It is of violet blossoms,' we said. And she drank all of it."

There were no more heart attacks, though certain other infirmities continued; and faithful to Lucia's promise, she and all her sisters went to Cova da Iria for nine evenings after supper, painfully hobbling down the stony slope on their knees while Maria Rosa followed on foot, giving thanks to God.

Lucia was unable to obtain any such favor for her little friend in the hospital at Ourem. An incision had been made and a drain inserted; yet after two months Jacinta was no better—in fact she was worse than ever. It was costing Ti Marto 1,200 reis, or about $1.35 every day, and he had spent all he

[8] Op. cit., p. 218.

could afford. At the end of August he hitched up the burrita again, and brought the invalid home.

Ai, Jesús! Olimpia hardly knew her child, she was so thin, pale, transparent, emaciated. There was a great open wound in her chest that had to be dressed every day. Dr. Formigão, who saw her in October, described her as a living skeleton, her arms nothing but bones, her face all eyes, her cheeks wasted by fever.

The good theologian was one of the 600 persons who went to Fátima on the thirteenth of October that year, to celebrate the second anniversary of the great miracle. That was the day when the pilgrims were startled by twenty-one terrific explosions, one after another, near the azinheira. But it was not an attack by the enemy, as many feared. It was only a workman from Porto-de-Mos who had fired a salvo of twenty-one bombs in honor of Our Lady, to show her his gratitude for a favor unexpectedly granted him.

There was no doubt that the peasants had taken the Fátima devotion to their hearts. One small indication of this was the growth of the fund of small coins left by the tree. By the summer of 1918 the total was 357,000 *reis* or about $500. This continued to be a torment to Maria Carreira, the unofficial custodian of the shrine by common consent, all the more so when people began to malign her, insinuating that she was feathering her own nest. In vain she tried to get the Prior to accept the money, and in vain he wrote the Patriarchate for instructions. At one time the Administrator of Ourem summoned Maria's husband to Ourem to give an accounting. After the death of Antonio, Maria Rosa sent her sons, as owners of the land at Cova da Iria, to demand that Maria da Capelhina turn the fund over to a commission. Fortunately an appeal for arbitration was made to the Vicar of Olival, Father Faustino Ferreira, who arranged a friendly agreement until the money could be delivered to some diocesan authority. After that Maria Rosa and Maria Carreira became bosom friends. Another happy result was that Lucia found in the Vicar of Olival a loyal friend and wise director.

It seemed to a few thoughtful men like him that the devotion at Cova da Iria was already bringing blessings upon Portugal and on the world. Not only had the war ended, but diplomatic relations between Lisboa and the Holy See had been resumed in July, 1918. And in December, 1919, Pope Benedict XV appealed to all Portuguese Catholics to submit to the Republic as the lawfully constituted authority, and to accept offices if they were offered; while the beatification of Nuno Alvares, the victor of Albujarrota, contributed much to the growth of good feeling. Nevertheless the Government continued to persecute the Church in many ways; and it never relented in its efforts to stamp out the devotion at Fátima. Perhaps this partly explains why His Eminence, Cardinal Mendes Belo, Patriarch of Lisboa, threatened to excommunicate any priest who spoke in favor of the apparitions. A strong and able man, he was inclined to think in terms of power, of public opinion, of prudent expediency. He may have felt that when relations between Church and State were improving, it would be unwise to allow a new and untested devotion to disturb them.

Under these circumstances it took courage for Dr. Formigão to befriend Jacinta. Unfortunately he was able to do no more at this time than suggest that she ought to be sent to some really good sanitarium. Neither he nor Ti Marto had the means of accomplishing this, and he returned to Santarem feeling unhappy and helpless.

During the warm days of autumn, however, Jacinta began to improve. She was able to leave her bed, then to go outdoors, and finally to attend Mass at Fátima on Sunday. Once or twice she went as far as Cova da Iria. When her parents learned of this they put a stop to it, and none too soon. For with the first blast of cold weather she became feverish again, and had to go back to bed. This troubled her little so long as she was able to get up and say her Rosary, kneeling in contemplation with her head on the floor, as the Angel had done. But it gradually became more difficult.

"When I am alone I get out of bed to say the prayers of the Angel," she confided to Lucia. "But now I can't put my head on the floor any more, because I fall. So I pray only on my knees."

When Father Faustino Ferreira heard this from Lucia, he told Jacinta that she must say all her prayers lying down in bed.

"And Our Lord will be content?" she asked anxiously.

"Yes, Our Lord wants you to do what the Vicar orders."

"All right. I won't get up any more."

Even in bed Jacinta continued to do penance for some of those hale and hearty sinners whom she had never seen. When thirsty she would go without a drink. She would refuse some grapes for which her mouth watered. Or she would lie awake wanting to get up and pray, and offering up the desire as a penance rather than disobey her mother; and this conflict would keep her awake all night. It was only to Lucia that she revealed what a terrible pain she had in her chest. But it was to honor the Immaculate Heart of Mary.

"Tell all the people that God gives them graces through her," she said. "If I could only put in the heart of everybody that light that I have here in my breast to burn me and make me love the heart of Jesus and the heart of Mary so much! . . . I don't know how it is, I feel Our Lord inside of me, I understand what He says, and I don't see or hear Him! But it is so good to be with Him. . . . Look, do you know what? Our Lord is sad because Our Lady told us not to offend Him any more because He is much offended, and nobody pays any attention. They keep right on doing the same sins."

When Lucia came after Mass, Jacinta would say, "Did you receive?"

"Yes."

"Come over here near me, because you have in your heart the hidden Jesus. Oh, I wish I could go to Communion!"

Yet three times during the year Jacinta saw her "little Mother of Heaven" standing by her bed, encouraging her. The last of these visions was late in December, 1919.

"Our Lady came to see me last night," she reported joyfully. "She told me that I am going to Lisboa, to another hospital.

She said that after I suffer a great deal I will die. I will die all alone. But she told me not to be afraid, for she will come and find me and take me to heaven."

A little later, as certain implications became clear, Jacinta began to cry, her bony hand clinging to her friend's arm. "I'll never see you again, Lucia!"

"I'll come to see you in the hospital."

"No, you won't come to see me. Look, pray for me, a lot, for I die alone."

One day when Lucia brought her a stamp with an image of the Mother of Sorrows on it, she looked at it thoughtfully a moment, and then cried, in anguish:

"Oh, my little Mother of Heaven, do I really have to die alone?"

There was something heartbreaking in this, suggesting the awful cry in the Garden, "Father, if it be possible . . ." Lucia too was weeping as she clasped her in her arms and groped for words of consolation.

"What do you care if you die alone, Jacinta, if Our Lady is coming to take you?"

"It's true, I don't care. But I don't know how it is, sometimes I forget that she is coming to take me."

Olimpia had to get most of her information about her child's inner life from Lucia. "What did Jacinta say to you today?" she would whisper at the door. "Ask Jacinta what she is thinking of when she has her hands over her face so long without moving. I asked her, but she smiled and did not answer."

When Lucia put the question, Jacinta replied, "I am thinking of Our Lord and Our Lady and of (here she whispered part of the secret). I like to think of them."

This was little satisfaction to Olimpia, since the secret remained untold. "The life of these girls is an enigma," she complained to Maria Rosa.

"It certainly is," agreed Lucia's mother tartly. "When they are alone they talk in a corner and nobody can catch a word of what they say, no matter how much they listen, and then when anyone comes, they lower their heads and don't say a word. I can't understand this mystery."

No one but Lucia took Jacinta's talk about a hospital in Lisboa seriously. Peasants could seldom afford hospitals, and Lisboa was ninety miles away. It sounded like a delirious dream until one day in January, 1920, when they saw an automobile stop in front of the Marto cottage. The visitor was Dr. Formigão, and he had with him a lady and gentleman whom he had interested in Jacinta's case, and who had come all the way from Lisboa to see her—Dr. Enrico Lisboa, a noted specialist in ophthalmology, and his wife. A brief examination convinced Dr. Lisboa that the child would soon die if she were not sent to a good hospital. With his connections in the capital he could easily arrange this. He and some of his friends, including the Baron of Alvaiázere, would take care of all the expenses.

Ti Marto and his wife objected that their daughter had been worse after one hospital treatment, and that in any case it was useless to attempt to prolong her life if Our Lady, as they believed, had promised to come for her soon.

"The will of Our Lady," replied the physician gravely, "is superior to all human considerations. But the only way to make sure that Our Lady does in fact wish to take her is to exhaust all scientific means of preserving her life."

It was decided, then, that Ti Olimpia should take her to Lisboa as soon as the necessary arrangements could be made. Jacinta was not surprised. She had been expecting something like this. And for some reason she became notably better as the time for her departure drew near. One fine January day, her mother and a neighbor took her on the back of a burrita to Cova da Iria for a farewell visit. At the Lagoa she asked to get down, and they all said the Rosary. Then she picked some wild flowers, which she carried to the place of the apparitions and laid in the little chapel as an offering to Our Lady. She knelt by the azinheira to say a last prayer. When the two women helped her to her feet again, she looked about at the sky and the moor, and remarked:

"Mother, when Our Lady went away she passed over those

trees, and then she entered heaven so quickly that I thought they must have pinched her feet in the door." [4]

Next morning she said goodby to her father and to her best friend. "It cut me to the heart," wrote Lucia. "I held her a long time in my arms. She said to me, crying, 'We shall never meet again. Pray for me a lot till I go to heaven, and afterwards I'll pray a lot for you. Never tell anybody the secret even if they kill you. Love Jesus and the Immaculate Heart of Mary a great deal and make many sacrifices for sinners.'"

"Goodby, Jacinta."

"Goodby, Lucia."

Olimpia and her oldest son Antonio took Jacinta to Chão de Maçás, where they boarded a train for Lisboa, arriving four or five hours later at the noisy and dusty station called Rossio. None of them had ever been in the big city before. Olimpia carried a white handkerchief in her right hand, which she fluttered from time to time, and Jacinta had one in her left hand. These were the signals agreed upon so that certain ladies, friends of the Baron of Alvaiázere, might recognize them. But no ladies appeared.

Antonio, who could read, went to make some inquiries. When he failed to return, his mother feared he was lost, and went about the station crying, "Antonio! Antonio!"

After what seemed an interminable time Antonio sauntered back. A moment later three well-dressed ladies introduced themselves as the friends of the Baron.

The first thing to be done was to find lodgings for the wayfarers, for none of the ladies had room for them at home. So they all went about the city, applying at various houses where there might be accommodations. Olimpia was tired, Jacinta almost dead when, after many refusals, a good woman agreed to take them in. They remained with her for a week.

At the end of that time a place had been found for Jacinta in the Asilo in the Rua da Estrêla, next to the Church of Our Lady of Miracles. Dona Maria da Purificacão Godinho, the

_____

[4] Olimpia told this to Father De Marchi, *op. cit.*, p. 244.

head of this institution, was a Franciscan nun who went about dressed as a laywoman—since religious garb was forbidden under the Republic—collecting alms with which she managed to house, clothe, feed and educate from twenty to twenty-five orphan girls. She had a particular devotion to Our Lady, and having heard of her appearances at Fátima, was praying to be allowed to go there and see the children so favored, when someone interrupted to tell her that Jacinta was in Lisboa. From that moment she took the child to her motherly heart, made her at home in the orphanage, and had her sit every day in a sunny window looking out on the Garden of the Estrêla, where there was always something interesting to see.

Jacinta was happy. She liked living in a convent. It seemed heavenly to think that the hidden Lord was there all the time, and that she could visit Him every day and receive Him at Mass every morning. She could never understand how visitors could laugh and gossip in the chapel, and she asked Mother Godinho to remind them to have more respect for the One Who was there. When the reproof had little effect, she said positively, "Then the Cardinal will have to be told about it. Our Lady doesn't want people to talk in the church."

Mother Godinho believed that she had a saint under her roof. "She speaks with such authority!" she said. She noticed that Jacinta had little to do with the other girls, except now and then to give one of them some motherly advice on truthfulness or obedience. Often the nun would sit with her by the window and draw her into conversation. Afterwards she would write down some of the more striking things she said.

"Wars," remarked Jacinta, "are nothing but punishments for the sins of the world.

"Our Lady can no longer hold up the arm of her beloved Son over the world. It is necessary to do penance. If people reform, Our Lord will save the world. But if they do not reform, He is going to punish it.

"Our Lord is profoundly indignant with the sins and crimes that are committed in Portugal. For this, a terrible cataclysm of the social order threatens our country and principally the city of Lisboa. There will break loose there, as it appears, a civil war of anarchist or communist character, accompanied by sacks, assassinations, fires and devastations of all kinds. The capital will be converted into a veritable image of hell. On the occasion when the outraged divine justice inflicts so frightful a punishment, all who can should flee from this city. This punishment now predicted should be announced little by little and with due discretion.[5]

"Dear little Our Lady! *Ai!* I am so sorry for Our Lady! She is so sad.

"Pray much, my little mother, for sinners. Pray much for priests. Pray much for religious. Priests should occupy themselves with the affairs of the Church. Priests should be pure, very pure. The disobedience of priests and religious to their superiors and to the Holy Father offends Our Lord very greatly.

"My little mother, pray for those who govern. Alas for those who persecute the religion of Our Lord! If the Government leaves the Church in peace and gives liberty to the holy Faith, it will be blessed by God.

"My little mother, do not walk in the midst of luxury. Flee from riches. Be very friendly to holy poverty and to silence. Have great charity even for the wicked. Speak ill of no one and flee from those who do. Be very patient, for patience carries us to heaven. Mortification and sacrifices please Our Lord a great deal.

"Confession is a sacrament of mercy. For this reason it is necessary to approach the confessional with confidence and joy. Without confession there is no salvation.

"The Mother of God wants more virgin souls, which bind themselves to her by the vow of chastity.

"I should like to go into the convent. But I should like much more to go to heaven.

"To be a religious it is necessary to be very pure in soul and body."

[5] This obviously is the diction of Mother Godinho, though the substance no doubt was Jacinta's.

Here Mother Godinho asked, "And do you know what it means to be pure?"

"I do. I do. To be pure in body is to keep chastity. To be pure in soul is not to commit sins, not to look at what one should not see, not to steal, never to lie, always to tell the truth whatever it costs us.

"Those who do not keep the promises they make to Our Lady will never be happy in their affairs.

"Doctors don't have light to cure the sick because they don't have love of God."

"Who taught you all these things?" asked Mother Godinho.

"It was Our Lady. But some I think of myself. I like very much to think."

Jacinta's mother visited her more than once at the Asilo before returning to Aljustrel. Mother Godinho made her feel at home, and drew her out, with a woman's curiosity, about each member of her family. She was particularly interested in Teresa, who was then fifteen, and in Florinda, who was sixteen. "Wouldn't you be pleased if they had religious vocations?" she asked.

"God deliver me!" exclaimed Olimpia.

Jacinta did not hear this conversation. But afterwards she said to Mother Godinho, "Our Lady wants my sisters to be nuns. My mother doesn't want them to be, but for this Our Lady will take them to heaven before long."

It was on Mother Godinho's feast day, February 2 (feast of the Purification of Our Lady, 1920) that she took Jacinta to the Hospital of Dona Stefania. It was a rather dark and depressing place, and one of the child's first disappointments, after she had been placed in Bed 38 of the children's ward on the ground floor, was that there was no chapel, no home for the hidden Jesus. Then there was a long and careful examination by Dr. Castro Freire, the chief surgeon, a noted pediatrician. And his conclusion, after confirming the diagnosis of purulent pleurisy, was that an operation must be performed as soon as she got a little stronger.

"It won't do any good," said Jacinta. "Our Lady came to tell me that I am going to die soon."

One day she looked up and saw her father standing in the doorway. He had come all the way from Aljustrel to see her; but he had to hurry back in a few hours, because some of his other children were sick, and Olimpia needed his help. Perhaps it was by him that Jacinta sent word to Lucia that Our Lady had visited her again, and had told her the day and hour of her death.

She had many conversations in the hospital with Mother Godinho, who came every day. Once the *madrinha* mentioned a certain priest who had delivered a wonderful sermon, and was much praised by fashionable ladies for his theatrical voice and manner. "When you least expect it," said Jacinta, "you will see that that padre is wicked." Within a few months the great preacher left the priesthood under scandalous circumstances. This was only one of Jacinta's prophecies that came true. A doctor who asked her to pray for him when she went to heaven was surprised to hear her say that he and his daughter were going to die shortly after she did; and they did. To Mother Godinho, who wanted to visit Cova da Iria, she said, "You will go—but after my death; and so will I."

When Jacinta was taken to the operating room on February 10 she was so weak that local anaesthesia had to be given instead of chloroform or ether. She wept when she saw her body unclothed and in the hands of men. Dr. Castro Freire then proceeded to remove two of her ribs on the left side, leaving an opening large enough to contain his fist. The pain was terrible. "*Ai, Nossa Senhora!*" moaned the child. "*Ai, Nossa Senhora!*" Then she would murmur, "Patience! We ought to suffer everything to go to heaven. . . . It is for your love, my Jesus! . . . Now you can convert many sinners, for I suffer much." At last it was over, and they took her back to the ward, this time to Bed 60. Doctor Freire and his assistant felt that the operation had been successful.

Jacinta knew better. For six days she continued to have excruciating pains. Then on the night of February 16 she told Mother Godinho that she had seen Our Lady. "She told me she was coming for me *very* soon, and would take away my pains."

From then on she had no more pain. But she felt certain that the hour of her going was almost at hand. She sent urgently for Doctor Lisboa to tell him some secret, probably about himself. He was busy, and supposed there would be time to see her later. But at six o'clock on the evening of Friday, February 20, she called her nurse, Aurora Gomez ("my little Aurora") and told her she was about to die and wanted the last sacraments. Two hours later she made her confession to Father Pereira dos Reis of the Church of the Holy Angels, who promised to bring her Communion next morning.

Jacinta was not there the next morning. At ten-thirty that evening the nurse left her for a few moments, and returned just in time to see her breathe her last sigh, a rosy flush on her cheeks, a half smile on her lips. Perhaps the nurse's name was symbolic. It was night in the dingy hospital, but it was forever dawn in the soul of Jacinta as the Mother of God bent over Bed 60 and gathered her into the arms that had enfolded the Christ in infancy and in death.

The news quickly got about, and some Catholics who believed in the Fátima apparitions raised money to pay the funeral expenses, the burial to be on Sunday, February 22, in one of the cemeteries of Lisboa. The Marquesa of Rio Maior had the body arrayed in a white Communion dress, while the Marquesa of Lavradio added a blue cape; and thus, wearing the colors of Our Lady, it was laid in a white coffin and taken to the Church of the Holy Angels, where it was placed across two small benches in the sacristy.

In giving permission for this, Father Pereira dos Reis, the pastor of the church, had had no idea how many people in Lisboa had heard of Jacinta, and believed in the Fátima revelations. Nevertheless he received the first visitors with patience and kindness. It was only when more and more kept coming that he became uneasy. He asked them not to touch rosaries, crucifixes or images near to the body. When some of them refused to obey, he drove them out of the sacristy. They had not expected this, for he had the reputation of being a charitable and courteous priest; and there was a great deal of talk and resentment. Yet the Fátima devotion had not been approved or authorized, and the Church does not permit public honors to the dead until their sanctity has been recognized in some official way after careful investigation. Naturally, too, the Pároco did not wish to offend the Cardinal Patriarch. And the sanitation authorities might perhaps raise some objection, as in fact they did. To free himself from further responsibility, Father Pereira had the body removed to the Casa do Despacho of the brotherhood of the Most Blessed Sacrament, outside the sacristy, locked the door, and turned the key over to Senhor Antonio Rebelo de Almeida, an undertaker of the Rua da Escola Politecnica, in one of the old and tawdry quarters of the city.

Meanwhile plans for the burial in Lisboa had been given up when word came from the Baron de Alvaiázere, offering a grave in his plot in the cemetery of Ourem. On February 23 the undertaker allowed a few persons to see the remains before he inclosed them in a lead casket. All remarked an agreeable odor like that of flowers, and some insisted that the cheeks still had a faint roseate flush, giving an impression of life and health. Next morning the casket was sealed, taken to the Rossio and placed on a train for Chão de Maçás, thence to be driven to Ourem.

On that day there was a large annual assembly of the Saint Vincent de Paul Society in Lisboa. Many charitable rich men attended, for one must do something for the poor; and the Cardinal Patriarch, Dom Antonio Mendes Belo—a man with a strong purposeful face, that bore a striking resemblance to that of the actor George Arliss, though perhaps there was a little more rigor in it—presided. The chairman read a message from Dr. Lisboa, regretting his inability to be present, for he was busy with another work of charity concerning one ·of the children of the Fátima apparitions. The whole assembly, including His Eminence, burst into a loud and raucous laugh. This quickly got about the city, and gave no slight offense to devotees of Our Lady of Fátima. In anticlerical circles, on the other hand, it was whispered that both the Marto children had been murdered by Catholics to avoid unpleasant contradictions in their stories, and to leave only the affirmations of Lucia as the official version.

Jacinta was far beyond the reach of cold hearts and lying tongues in the cemetery at Ourem. A few persons went from Aljustrel to attend the simple funeral. Ti Marto was one of them, saying over and over:

"And you died there alone! You died there alone!"

CHAPTER XVII

Wherever Lucia walked, a dark silhouette between the moors and the sky, something reminded her of Jacinta or of Francisco. Every sheep, every star that twinkled into the night, every sunrise and sunset told her again that they would never return. The wind at Cabeço brought a dear imaginary voice saying, "I will never see you again, Lucia. . . . I am going to heaven, but you stay here—alone." The vagrant scent of rosemary or of wild mint had power to conjure up an invisible little girl who bent over her saying, "I do as the angels do, I give you flowers." On top of every wall there sat a pensive boy playing softly on his *pifaro* as he watched the red glare of the dying day on the water of the Lagoa.

Her mother and sisters tried in many ways to make amends for their former lack of understanding and sympathy. Maria Rosa could always be counted upon to do her duty when she saw it. Her eldest daughter, Maria dos Anjos, had a warm and affectionate nature; her fine, spiritual and motherly face is evidence that she could never have done wilful injury to anyone. Yet the very fact that the apparitions and miracles had now been verified was a new barrier between Lucia and the other members of her family. If a prophet is without honor in his own country, neither is a mystic ever completely at home in his own household. There was bound to be an unbridgeable gulf between a girl who had spoken with the Mother of God and had been charged by her with a mission on which the future of mankind depended, and older sisters, however lovable and admirable, who were devoted to dancing, gaiety, husbands and children. A girl with Lucia's past was doomed to loneliness in a human sense, no matter where she might wander in a world whose criteria were no longer hers. Thus even on that memorable day when her Aunt Olimpia took her to Ourem to visit the grave of Jacinta, her grief was her own and incommunicable, having overtones of hope and joy which the older woman could never have understood. Older? There is something eternally childlike in Olimpia even in her seventies. Her privileged niece, at thirteen, had the grave patience of one who knows what lies behind earthly appearances.

It made her lot no easier to realize that she was now the center of all the interest, favorable or unfavorable, that the extraordinary events at Fátima had evoked. She alone could answer the continual bombardment of questions and objections; and the only persons in whom she could fully confide were beyond her reach. Hers was no small responsibility before God and men. She had been given a part in something more than an ephemeral rustic drama. This was obvious from the revelations themselves. Little Jacinta had seen it, Francisco had known it.

It was implicit in some of the scenes that took place on the Serra. Men like her brother Antonio and Ti Marto needed no college degrees to be able to predict that if the tension between the pilgrims and the skeptical continued, a civil war might well be the outcome. The more the Government at Lisboa tried to suppress the devotion, the more fervently the followers of Our Lady of Fátima resolved to vindicate her honor.

There was a rather remarkable demonstration on the May 13 following the death of Jacinta. That was the day when the famous statue was set up in the shrine. A certain man had gone to Cova da Iria a year or two before with scorn instead of love in his heart. One story has it that he had a bomb in his pocket, with which he intended to destroy the chapel in the presence of all the crowd, but on putting in his hand he found a rosary instead. A more probable version is that his sister had left the rosary there for his unbelieving hand to encounter at the right moment. At all events, he was touched by grace and returned to the practice of his Faith; and out of gratitude he promised to have a statue made for the chapel. He went to great pains to ascertain from Lucia just how Our Lady had looked, and spared no expense to make the work accurate and beautiful. Whatever might be said of it as art, it had the power, especially in profile, to suggest something infinitely pure, simple and spiritual; it could awaken an almost fanatical devotion in the breasts of many who knelt before it or followed it in procession; and there were scenes of delirious joy when it was first set in its place of honor on May 13, 1920.

That was precisely the day when the Government, resolving to temporize no longer with an invasion of mysticism, had sent a couple of regiments of the regular army to Cova da Iria. When the pilgrims began to arrive they found rifles and bayonets hedging the scene of the apparitions. Undaunted by this, they formed a still larger cordon of the barefoot and the humble all about the men in uniform, and proceeded to recite the Rosary and sing Our Lady's songs with such passion that before long the guards themselves commenced to take part, as Roman legionaries used to join the unarmed Christians in the arenas. Soon their ranks were broken and they were on their knees with the others about the azinheira and the chapel when the new statue was borne tenderly and triumphantly to the place prepared for it, the place where it has been honored, with some interruptions, to this day. At one period of the persecution Maria Carreira used to keep it in her house, for fear of desecration, except on the days of pilgrimage. Once it was taken to Lisboa, where it was welcomed by the people with an enthusiasm to which some attribute the escape of the city thus far from the doom that Jacinta had foreseen.

Certainly all Portugal was in a sad plight morally, politically and economically in 1920. In the sixteen years following the Revolution of 1910 there were sixteen bloody revolutions and forty-three changes of ministry at Lisboa. The men who fomented and perpetuated that chaos were part of a revolt against Christianity which modern Popes have traced to the upheaval of the sixteenth century and even farther back, and which continues every year to pursue its goal of world domination. Pope Benedict XV saw plainly from the watchtower of Saint Peter by the Tiber a great deal of what has since occurred. "Morals are much more depraved and corrupt than formerly," he lamented in 1920. "The fond hope and wish of every renegade is the speedy rise of some universal state which is based on the complete equality of men and women and common ownership of property as a fundamental principle, in which neither any distinctions of nationality nor authority of parents over children, nor of public authority over citizens, nor of God over man living in society, is acknowledged. If these principles are put into practice, dreadful horrors must necessarily follow." [1] A few days later, appealing for help for the new Polish state against the mysterious Soviet power that had seized control of Russia only a few weeks after the last apparition at Cova da Iria, he made another prophetic observation: "Not only is the national existence of Poland in danger, but all Europe is threatened by the horrors of fresh wars." [2]

Revolutions are noisy, but God works quietly and patiently. On August 5, 1920, the very day when Benedict spoke these words, something occurred which was to have profound effects upon Portugal, the Fátima devotion, and especially the life of Lucia Abóbora. A bishop was consecrated as head of a new diocese of Leiria (including Cova da Iria, Aljustrel and all the rest of the Serra) which the Holy Father had made independent of the Patriarchate of Lisboa.

Dom José Alves Correira da Silva was a professor at the Seminary of Porto when Pope Benedict selected him for this important post. Born near Braga in 1877, he was of medium height, dark and rather corpulent. His face, like so many in northern Portugal, was more Celtic than Latin, and concealed, under an habitual expression of benignity, certain traces of suffering that were evident only to those who knew his history. Dom José had endured more than ordinary persecution under the Republic of 1910. Dragged from his rectory and thrown into prison, he had been tortured by being made to stand in icy water day and night, with the result

[1] Motu Propio, *Bonum Sane*, July 25, 1920.

[2] Letter, *Con Vivo Compiacimento*, August 5, 1920.

that he became permanently lame, and walks with great difficulty. This cross he cheerfully accepted. He had an especial devotion to the Mother of Sorrows, and had made six pilgrimages to her shrine at Lourdes, where, after his release, he had begged her, with other Portuguese refugees, to have mercy on his country. Later he had returned to give lectures at Porto, where his intelligence, his gracious and charming manners and his gift for friendship endeared him to students and fellow teachers, while his sound and scholarly articles in the Catholic press made him favorably known as far away as Rome.

One of the first acts of the new bishop when he arrived in the ancient city of Saint Isabel was the formal consecration of his diocese, on the feast of the Assumption, 1920, to the Mother of God. And if ever there was a man who needed her help, it was he. Ten years of persecution, following other years of complacency and indifference, had left the Church in a bad way, especially in the cities. Many clergy were still dispossessed, scattered, exiled, without incomes. The new diocese had no funds for building and other expenses. Through ignorance and neglect large numbers of people had given up Mass and the sacraments. Even the old episcopal residence, next to the Cathedral of Leiria, was being used for barracks and government offices, and the new bishop had to find quarters in a house at an inconvenient distance.

As if there were not enough problems already, there was this vexing affair of Fátima. Not long after his consecration, Dom José was presented with the 357,000 *reis* collected by Maria Carreira, with the request that he dispose of it as he might see fit. About the same time there came a delegate from the Patriarchate at Lisboa, who delivered to him the whole dossier of the case. It was now his problem. The Cardinal Patriarch was no doubt very glad to be rid of it.

Dom José saw that it was necessary to proceed cautiously. He had letters from enthusiasts demanding that he recognize the devotion at once and proceed to build a sumptuous shrine. Yet there were others from persons worthy of respect, including priests, denouncing the whole affair as a delusion or a deceit, and arguing that it gave the enemies of the Church one more weapon to use against her when she sorely needed a period of quiet in which to repair the ravages of the persecution. It was not easy for a newcomer to decide. Whatever course he took he was bound to give offense. It is likely, however, that such a man as Dom José would have acted promptly if he had been able to make up his own mind. But what was he to think? Two of the chief witnesses were dead. Lucia always made a bad first impression on anyone who met her, nor did she ever try to be ingratiating. When all was said, the story was strange and appeared to be improbable.

One thing seemed evident: something had to be done about Lucia Abóbora, the sole center of the controversy and the sole witness since the death of Jacinta. There was no doubt that such a girl, almost untaught, stood in danger from the possible violence of sectaries who decried the apparitions and from the certain flattery of devotees inclined to canonize her. It seemed best to have her leave the Serra for a considerable period. If the affair of Fátima had been due to any delusion or deceit on her part, her absence ought gradually to put an end to it. If, on the other hand, the story was true, devotion would doubtless continue, and a just decision could be made. After further inquiries and much reflection, and more than one conversation with Lucia and other memebers of her family, the Bishop asked Maria Rosa to visit him and to bring her daughter on the feast of Saint Anthony, June 13, 1921.

When they had chatted for a while, Dom José asked the child how she would like to leave Aljustrel and attend a good school. Lucia looked pleased. To be rid of all the questions and controversies, to be able to forget her grief and loneliness in new surroundings, to learn to read and write well, to travel—why not? Maria Rosa was even more favorably impressed. The continual strain of having such a daughter, even after the proof of the apparitions, had been almost more than she could bear. She was always wondering what was going to happen next. Her hearty acquiescence, so unflattering to her daughter, may have startled His Lordship a little, but it also pleased him. He said that Lucia could enter a school of the Sisters of Saint Dorothy near Porto, and that she had better leave in a few days.

"Yes, *Senhor Bispo.*"

"And you will tell no one where you are going," he added in his quiet voice.

"Yes, *Senhor Bispo.*"

"In the school where you are going you will tell no one who you are."

"Yes, *Senhor Bispo.*"

"You will say nothing more to anyone about the apparitions of Fátima."

"Yes, *Senhor Bispo.*"

On the way back to Aljustrel, Lucia and her mother passed groups of people returning from the pilgrimage at Cova da Iria singing, *"Ave, Ave, Ave Maria!"*

Her few preparations were soon made, and she spent her last day, June 18, in a series of farewell visits. She climbed the slope of Cabeço for a last look at the valley where she had first seen the Angel; and going to the cave, she prostrated herself on the ground beside the rock where he had knelt, and said the prayers he had taught her:

"O my God, I believe, I adore, I hope and I love You. . . .

"Most Holy Trinity, Father, Son, Holy Spirit, I adore You profoundly. . . ."

Lucia climbed over the rocks and went down the other slope to Valinhos. There at the break of the wall under the olive trees was what was left of the azinheira where she had seen Our Lady on August 19, 1917. Pious hands had raised a circle of field stones around it, to the height of about two feet. Usually there are some daisies there, left by children, and sometimes a *vinten* or two. Lucia knelt and poured out her grief and her love. It was not easy to leave these places! It would not have been easy even if she had had no memories but those of her games and conversations with Francisco and Jacinta.

"You will have much to suffer. But the grace of God will be your comfort. . . ."

She went down the road between the high walls to the Lagoa. Perhaps there were women washing there, men watering cattle on the other side; but Lucia saw Francisco and Jacinta, bending over to drink the brackish water of the *barreiro*. How many times they met there on their way to the Serra!

There was no one else at Cova da Iria, and she knelt alone by the plucked tree. Here five times she had seen the Mother of God; here too she had seen Christ and Saint Joseph. Yet except for the meagre chapel it was still almost a wilderness of undulating moors, too far and inaccessible ever to be of much interest to civilized communities. The heat was withering, the sky a vast glare of blue. How huge and uninhabited the world could be!

"I am the Lady of the Rosary. . . . Do you suffer a great deal? Don't be discouraged. I will never forsake you."

On the way home Lucia stopped at Fátima to say a last prayer in Saint Anthony's Church, where she had been baptized, where she had received her first Communion, were she had spent so many hours alone with the hidden Christ. She said goodby to Saint Quiteria, to Saint Anthony. As she left, the bell in the tower was beginning to ring the Angelus. "Behold the handmaid of the Lord: let it be done according to Thy word."

She crossed the road to the cemetery and knelt by the mount that showed where Francisco lay. The sun was already low in the west, and the old wall cast a cool shadow on the grave and on the kneeling girl.

"Goodby, Francisco; take care of me in heaven."

On the way down the street of Aljustrel she stopped to say goodby to her uncle and aunt. It was a sad moment, for these had been two terrible years for Ti Marto and Ti Olimpia. Not only had Francisco and Jacinta left them, but Florinda had died in 1920 and Teresa in 1921. Yes, Jacinta had been right again. Four children dead in something like twenty-three months! It was a high price that Olimpia paid to become a strong woman.

After a brief prayer in the room where Francisco had died, Lucia went home, wiping the tears from her eyes, and found her mother preparing the supper. They were to start before dawn for Leiria, said Maria Rosa, for no one must know they were going; besides, it would be a long journey to Porto. Manuel Carreira was coming to drive them there with his team.

Lucia slipped out to the well for a last look at the sky through the leaves of the fig trees. It was a serene and beautiful night, jeweled with stars. The lamps of the angels, she could hear Jacinta saying.

Maria Rosa was calling her to supper.

Afterwards she went to the corral, where two or three sheep remained after the flock had been sold. "Goodby, my little friends," she said, patting their woolly heads, and went back to the house. She remembered the rope girdle that Jacinta had given her before going to the hospital, and burned it. Now it was time for bed.

Her mother called her at two o'clock in the morning. Ti Carreira was already waiting outside with the cart. The moon had risen, paling the stars and making the Serra wonderfully alive and mysterious. The lamp of Our Lady, Jacinta had called it. Goodby, goodby! They were soon on the road leading westward through Chainca and Santocico to Leiria.

When they came to Cova da Iria Lucia said, "Let us stop here and say the Rosary."

The three got out of the cart, and went down to the chapel. There was an oil lamp burning in it at the feet of the statue. There they knelt and said the five decades. "Don't be discouraged. I will never forsake you." But Lucia wept again as she looked for the last time at the azinheira, plainly gleaming in the eerie light of the moon.

It was time to go, for they had a ride of nine hours ahead. By dawn they were far beyond Batalha, between the pines and the olive groves. At eleven o'clock they were at Leiria, where they were met by a lady sent by the Bishop.

Three hours later Lucia boarded a train for Alfarelos, thence to Porto. Maria Rosa watched her depart, the tears coursing down her heavy cheeks. "Goodby, goodby." The train started noisily.

Lucia Abóbora had disappeared from Fátima and from all the world she had known. To all appearances the Fátima episode was ended.

CHAPTER XVIII

Mass was being said when Lucia and her guide arrived early next morning at the Asilo of the Sisters of Saint Dorothy at Vilar, a suburb of Porto, and she was taken at once to the chapel. She was glad to be able to receive Holy Communion and to compose herself a little after a night of travel. The vaulted gothic roof with its ceiling of blue, spangled with gold stars, somehow made her feel more at home; it was like the one over the altar at Fátima. The Mass over, she followed the portress to the sacristy, where she was presented to the Mother Superior and to the Chaplain.

Reverend Mother was not favorably impressed by the tired girl of fourteen who stared at her rather sullenly from under dark brows, and seemed to have a fixed pout on her heavy, half-parted lips. She had refused to take her at first, telling the Bishop frankly that she wanted no simpletons in her house, because she did not want to make simpletons of the other pupils. "Yes, she is simple," Dom José had said, "but I don't think you will find her a simpleton, and I wish you would take her for a while." As she looked at the girl herself, Reverend Mother began to wonder if she should not have been firmer with her old friend, the former professor at the Seminary of Porto. But having given her word, she proceeded to carry out all his wishes.

"When they ask you your name," she said, "you will reply, 'Call me Maria of the Sorrows.'"

"Yes, Reverend Mother."

"When they ask you where you are from, you will say, 'I am from near Lisboa.'"

"Yes, Reverend Mother."

"As for what happened at Fátima, never again mention it to anyone, either by question or by answer."

"Yes, Reverend Mother."

"Not to anyone. Do you understand?"

"Yes, Reverend Mother."

"You will not go to walk with the other girls, but you will not say why you do not go. Do you understand, my dear?"

"Yes, Reverend Mother."

"That is all."

The new student was shown her room and given a uniform of black and white checked gingham such as the others wore. So she was to be called Maria of the Sorrows. She would have preferred Maria of Jesus, since she had been christened Lucia of Jesus. But patience! "You shall have much to suffer." This was only the beginning.

For the next four years Maria of the Sorrows led the quiet and ordered life of an average convent boarding-school student. Every day after early Mass there would be a succession of classes, recreation, manual work, prayers; manners to learn, themes to write, head-splitting declensions and conjugations to memorize, little speeches to be made. As the months passed she learned sewing, embroidering, typewriting, cooking, waiting on table, scrubbing floors, polishing brass and silver. Doubtless there were many blunders and heartaches at first before she was able to adapt herself to a routine so different from that of Aljustrel. But after a while the sense of haste and strain left her, and she became a faithful and obedient, if not a brilliant, pupil.

During the four years she never revealed her identity. She never mentioned Fátima; not even to her mother, who visited her twice, once at Porto and once at the convent of the order in Braga. Not once in all that time did any of the nuns or students suspect who or what she was. The wise Mother Superior had taken good care to carry out the Bishop's instructions. She understood perfectly why it had to be so. If the apparitions turned out to be illusory (so she explained later) Lucia would gradually forget them, and it was better so. If they were real, she would never forget and no harm would be done; but she would escape the danger of learning false pride through flattery until she had attained a certain degree of maturity. The young girl herself came to understand the necessity of this. She began to think of herself naturally as Maria das Dores. At moments it seemed as if Lucia Abóbora had been only a girl she had dreamed about. If now and then some journalist, investigating the phenomena of Fátima, traced a clue to the convent door, the portress would answer calmly, "No, there is no one here called Lucia." The Abóbora girl, for all practical purposes, was dead.

Yet there were compensations in this lonely existence. To the casual eye the Asilo de Vilar was a plain building on a hilly street in a rather dingy part of the town, with a drab seminary on one side, a factory on the other, and a cemetery near by. It was very different when one had passed through the quiet building and ascended the hill on the other side to the gardens that lay hidden, like all the secrets of the great King, from vulgar prying eyes. Surely Saint Dorothy, patron of horticulture, must be well pleased with those six gardens, flamboyant and fragrant with rare and gorgeous flowers of every color and description.

There was a wonderful view also from the upper windows of the house or from a nearby hill. One could see the River Douro coiling like a great flat silver snake as it finished its long course from the mountains of Spain to the harbor of Porto, where ships of all nations came and went. It was thrilling to glimpse the pine forest of Cavaco far away, and beyond the long yellow tongue of beach that defined the harbor, the sunlight on the vast and blue Atlantic. The ocean always reminded her of "the grandeur and the power of God."

Convent routine, which seems so oppressive to people of the world, becomes delightful and satisfying to those who accept it freely. Lucia learned to love the order and regularity of it, the freedom from the petty frictions and worries of family life, the sense of living only in the present, and leaving the past and the future in the hands of God. She came to love the good women who toiled so cheerfully and unselfishly so that she might have an education, far from the prying questions of pilgrims and the small daily vexations of Maria Rosa. Yes, they had faults, there, too; but their effect was lessened by prayer, and by the firm tact of a good superior.

Here in these cloisters there was peace. Lucia began to be glad that the Bishop had sent her there.

The sisters on their part soon discovered, what many others remarked, that first impressions of Lucia were deceptive, perhaps because her humility kept her from trying to make a favorable impression. As the Bishop had said, her simplicity was by no means that of a simpleton. They came to respect and love her ready obedience, her unselfish willingness to sacrifice her own convenience for others at all times, her extraordinary devotion to God. More than most girls of her age, she seemed constantly aware of His presence no matter what she was doing, and when she had leisure moments she liked to spend them in the chapel rather than playing or talking. She read and reread the Portuguese translation of "L'Histoire d'une âme," the autobiography of little Saint Thérèse of Lisieux, who was beatified in 1923. Lucia's own experiences helped her to understand the desire for suffering reflected in many such passages as this: "My heart thrills at the thought of the frightful tortures Christians are to suffer at the time of the Antichrist, and I long to undergo them all. Open, O Jesus, the Book of Life, in which are written the deeds of Thy Saints: all the deeds told in that book I long to have accomplished for Thee." [1] Yet Lucia, like the Little Flower, realized that her vocation was not martyrdom, but love. Her other favorite saint was the young Jesuit John Berchmans, who had given so perfect an example of the virtue of obedience, of small daily duties heroically performed. "I like these two saints," she said, "because I can imitate them."

After four years of this life of study, work and prayer at Porto and other convent schools of the order, Lucia was a well-bred self-contained young woman of eighteen. The time was coming when she must make up her mind what to do with the rest of her life. She had no desire to go back to the world. Perhaps it was her love for Little Saint Thérèse that made her think of becoming a discalced Carmelite. But the

[1] Chapter XI.

Mother Superior discouraged this. She had had every opportunity to study Lucia during those four years. "You are not strong enough for such austerities, child," she said. "If you really have a vocation, it would be better to choose some order with a simpler rule." Lucia accepted this with her usual humility as the decision of God, and after some further thought asked to be admitted to the Institute of the Sisters of Saint Dorothy.

"Why do you wish to be a sister of Saint Dorothy?" the Mother Provincial asked.

"So that I shall be more free to go to the chapel and pray."

The Mother Provincial made her wait another year. At the end of that time, finding her of the same mind, she accepted her as a postulant. This was in 1925, at the convent in Tuy, just across the Spanish border. It was the year of the canonization of Little Saint Thérèse of Lisieux.

A year later, on November 2, 1926, Lucia became a novice. During the following year, 1927, she had two visions in which Christ Himself appeared to her, confirming the requests of His Mother concerning the devotion to her Immaculate Heart, and giving her permission to reveal certain things, but not of course the Last Secret of the July apparition. On November 3, 1928, she took her first vows as a lay sister. It was not until six years later, on October 3, 1934, that she made these perpetual.

Lucia's mother, two of her sisters, some cousins and a woman friend traveled all the way from Aljustrel to be present on that occasion. It was the first time she had seen Maria Rosa in thirteen years. Three times the good woman had written to ask what she wanted as a present on her profession day. The third time Lucia had answered, "Some flowers and some bees." So Maria Rosa brought a large bunch of flowers, smelling of the Serra, and a honeycomb full of bees, no doubt carefully inclosed. Was there some symbolism in this, or was Sister Maria of the Sorrows human enough to tease her mother a little for those scoldings and spankings of other days? Perhaps she merely wanted to spare her an expense she knew she could not afford.

Since 1934 Sister Dores (as she is commonly addressed in the cloister) has performed her humble duties in various convents of the order. She is often heard singing softly to herself as she scrubs floors, waits on table, or peels potatoes. But she is most happy in the hours she spends before the Blessed Sacrament. She does not need images to arouse her devotion. She usually kneels with her head bowed, her hands open and crossed upon her breast. Thus she remains sometimes for hours, sometimes all night if permitted.

One day she and another lay sister were walking from the convent at Tuy in Spain across the international bridge to do some shopping at Valença, which is in Portugal. At the Portuguese end of the bridge they met three ladies who stopped them and said, "Aren't you Sisters of Saint Dorothy? From the convent of Tuy? Oh, how nice! We are going there. We hear that Lucia is there—the one who saw Our Lady at Fátima!"

The two Dorotheans looked at each other.

"It's true that she is in Spain, isn't it?"

"Oh, no, Senhora, I don't think so," said Sister Maria. "In fact I'm quite sure she is in Portugal now."

"Oh!"

When the ladies had gone on, Sister Maria das Dores chuckled very much as the three children had when they tumbled over a wall in 1917 to escape from questioners.

Just when her silence about her past and Fátima was broken has not been revealed. Certain it is that on the night of January 25, 1938 (the feast of St. Paul's conversion, on being blinded by light from heaven) the young lay sister looked out of the window of her cell and saw the sky aflame, the whole vault of heaven fearfully aglow with crimson fire which continued balefully from nine o'clock in the evening until two o'clock in the morning. Next day the newspapers all over Europe recorded it. People had seen it from the North Sea to the Adriatic. In south Germany especially it struck fear to many Catholic hearts. In Fribourg, Switzerland, the sky was said to be "like a furnace." The same sinister glare was seen on the Belgian coast, in Spain, Hungary, Norway, Italy, Poland, and Greece.

Sister Maria of the Sorrows was convinced at once that this was the strange light Our Lady had predicted at Cova da Iria on July 13, 1917. "When you shall see a night illuminated by an unknown light, know that it is a great sign that God gives you that He is going to punish the world for its crimes by means of war, hunger, and of persecution of the Church and of the Holy Father. To prevent this I come to ask the consecration of Russia to my Immaculate Heart and the communion of reparation on the first Saturdays. . . ."

So it had come at last! It was "nigh, even at the gates." Sister Maria was undoubtedly allowed to communicate her fears to the Bishop of Leiria at once. That she did so in good time is plain from what she wrote him at Tuy on August 8, 1941:

"Your Excellency is not unaware that some years ago God manifested that sign which the astronomers choose to designate by the name *Aurora Borealis*. If they look well into it, they will see that it was not and could not be, in the form in which it appeared, such an aurora. But be that as it may, God was pleased in this way to make me understand that His justice was ready to let fall the blow on the guilty nations, and in this way to begin to ask with insistence for the reparatory Communion of the first Saturdays and the consecration of Russia. His end was not only to obtain mercy and pardon for all the world, but especially for Europe. God in His infinite mercy made me feel that this terrible moment was approaching, and Your Excellency is not unaware how on opportune occasions I used to point it out. And I still say that the prayer and penance that are done in Portugal have not yet placated the divine justice, for they have not been accompanied by contrition or amendment. I hope Jacinta is interceding for us in heaven." [2]

Pope Pius XI was undoubtedly informed about this. Sister Maria Lucia was allowed to write him a letter which has not

[2] Memoir III, p. 7.

been made public, but a person worthy of all credit assures me he saw a copy of it at the beginning of 1939. Whether the Holy Father believed or doubted the Fátima story, or whether his last illness and many anxieties made him postpone consideration of it during those months of his great strain, I do not know. As everyone does know, he died early in 1939, and the impact of World War II fell upon Poland in September of that year. Stalin, having instigated the Spanish War as a prologue, had now given Hitler the green light for the destruction of a pivotal Catholic country in the east.

"I come to ask the consecration of Russia to my Immaculate Heart and the Communion of reparation on the first Saturdays. If they listen to my requests, Russia will be converted and there will be peace. If not, she will scatter her errors through the world, provoking wars and persecutions of the Church. The good will be martyrized, the Holy Father will have much to suffer, various nations will be annihilated."

CHAPTER XIX

Sister Maria das Dores was not long frightened by the strange illumination. She could see beyond the hellish thing that was descending upon Europe, and she knew that the Lady who had promised never to forsake her would conquer in the end. While statesmen toiled and lied, while the flower of youth was blasted, while old cities perished in flame and agony, the lay sister of Saint Dorothy went about her humble tasks and prayers as usual. Sometimes sorrow visited her, as when she learned that her mother had died on the feast of Our Lady of Mount Carmel in 1942; and the rule of all strict orders, prohibiting members from leaving to attend the funerals of relatives, must have augmented the grief of a daughter who had long since forgiven the severities of poor Maria Rosa. Yet there are many joys also in convent life. Not the least was the good news that came from time to time from Cova da Iria.

The cult had grown astonishingly since her departure in 1921. The Bishop's attitude had been one of encouragement from the beginning. Some say he received a secret message from Our Lady through Lucia. Others insist that he was won over by a miraculous rain of flowers that he saw at Cova da Iria. His unwillingness to publicize himself or to exploit Sister Maria das Dores during her lifetime makes it difficult to get at the exact truth. Certain it is, however, that only four months after her leavetaking he permitted the first Low Mass in the chapel of the apparitions, and purchased the surrounding land from the Abóboras and others. In November of the same year (1921) he set some men to work making a cistern near the shrine to collect rain for pilgrims, and was deeply impressed when a spring of pure clear water bubbled up from the dry rocky soil, increasing in volume until it filled thirty-six taps and became the main supply of the peasants roundabout, and a source of health to many sick persons who drank of it.

Opening the formal canonical investigation the following year, the Bishop wrote: "Of the three children who said they were favored by the apparition, two were dead before our arrival in this diocese. We have questioned the only survivor several times. Her account and her responses are simple and sincere and we have discovered in them nothing against faith or morals." Expressing doubt that any qualities or powers of an almost untaught girl of fourteen could have drawn such crowds to the scene (especially after her departure), or that any natural charms of that remote and barren place could have attracted them, he appointed a committee of investigation, and called upon his people to furnish any information they might have, whether favorable or unfavorable.

The number of pilgrims steadily increased. Cardinal Mendes Belo, who had laughed at the affair in 1918, changed his opinion before his death in 1922, and regretted that he could not go to Fátima. The unrelenting opposition of the Government and of the Liberals of Santarem and Ourem served only to whip the fervor of the devout to a steadier flame. On March 6, 1922, for example, the little chapel was destroyed by four bombs, though the altar and shrine were saved when a fifth failed to explode; but on the following May 13 some 60,000 believers assembled, despite the mobilization of the Republican Guard by the Governor of Santarem, and made humble reparation to Our Lady for the outrage. In 1927 the Bishop presided over a pilgrimage for the first time. The following year he welcomed 300,000 persons in one day. In 1930 he officially recognized and accepted the devotion, declaring the visions of the three children worthy of faith, and asking the people to show their gratitude to the Mother of God by the purity and sincerity of their lives. In 1931 he was joined by all the other Portuguese bishops, including the new Patriarch, Dom Manuel Gonçalves Cardinal Cerejeira, in honoring her.

Several hundreds of miraculous cures meanwhile had been registered: cures of tuberculosis, Pott's disease, blindness, deafness, spinal meningitis, cancer, paralysis and many other afflictions of which Father Fonseca, for example, gives ample accounts, with names, dates, and details, in his well-documented book. Only last June (1946) there was a great sensation over the instant healing of Miss Maria José da Silva of Tomar, of tuberculosis. The following September 13, when a lame youth threw away his crutches during a procession, and walked upright for the first time in many years, he was congratulated by a great throng of men and women, many of whom were weeping with joy, among them the ex-Queen of Italy and her daughter. Of the moral cures—the conversions, the broken homes restored, the return of hardened sinners to the practice of the Faith—there have been thousands.

To Our Lady of Fátima the Portuguese attribute many of the blessings, both spiritual and material, that have come to their country in recent years. The Republic which so long persecuted the Church and the Fátima pilgrims vanished in the anarchy of 1926. Three generals, amid popular acclaim, took over the government, and by various steps set up the dictatorship of Salazar which has since ruled the nation. It is not within the scope of this work to appraise any existing political regime. Whatever else may be said for or against the present government at Lisboa, it has at least maintained peace and order; hence the Church, purified by persecution, has found time for recuperation and restoration, for training new priests, building seminaries, bringing lapsed Catholics back to the fold. Tremendous progress has been made in many ways under a new and vigorous hierarchy.

Yet there is much evidence to support the fears of Sister Maria das Dores that her people have not done nearly enough by way of reparation for the blasphemies and indifference of former times. After all the marvels of Fátima, only 4,000,-000 out of almost 8,000,000 Portuguese pretend to be Catholics in any sense of the word. There are hardly more than 3,000 priests—about one for each 1,300 professing Christians. The *pároco* of Vimiero, birthplace of Mr. Salazar, told me that he usually had but 150 out of a population of 1200 at his

Sunday Mass. In the large cities there is bitter anti-clericalism, and much Communistic activity. Churches are still closed at sundown for fear of desecration; nuns do not dare appear on the streets in their habits; and the Salazar government still retains some of the church property confiscated by the Republic. Mr. Salazar limits his practice of the Catholic faith to a barely discernible minimum; and as one of his officials said to me, "It is a mistake to call our regime Catholic. So far as the Church is concerned we are neutral." This neutrality has helped in one way. However, when the clergy tried to extend Catholic Action to aid the underpaid and underfed workers, they were told in no uncertain terms to confine their labors to "spiritual" affairs. They are not allowed to apply the social principles of the great encyclicals of Popes Leo XIII and Pius XI. They are not permitted to make any effective appeal to the anti-clerical masses in the cities. The *Voz da Fátima* stands almost alone against a financial empire ruled from London when it warns the rich that in paying starvation wages they court the very red ruin they fear.

Nevertheless the priests and people are grateful for such freedom as they have received, and hope that the rest will follow in time. They are especially thankful that their country escaped the harrowing experiences of Spain in 1936. Anticipating the reign of terror that began there in July, 1936, and fearing its spread throughout the peninsula, all the Portuguese bishops made a solemn vow at Cova da Iria as early as May of that year, that if Our Lady protected their land from war and red revolution they would return to make a public thanksgiving. This promise they kept at the great national pilgrimage of May 13, 1938, amid scenes of incredible rejoicing.

There were similar manifestations in the subsequent years, when many had become convinced that Our Lady of Fátima had saved Portugal from World War II, as she had told the children she would. When the twenty-fifth anniversary of the apparitions was celebrated on May 13, 1942, a telegram came from Pope Pius XII with his blessing to all the pilgrims, and to Portugal. Before the end of that year he consecrated the entire world to the Immaculate Heart of Mary in the presence of 40,000 persons at Saint Peter's in Rome. Thus the Fátima devotion overflowed the boundaries of the *terra de Santa Maria* and became worldwide.

To Sister Dores it seemed the fulfilment of the prophecy of Jacinta a quarter of a century before: "The Holy Father in a church before the Immaculate Heart of Mary, praying, and so many people praying with him." It was a step also toward the final accomplishment of the wishes of Our Lady, even if the Holy Father did not mention Russia specifically. In his prayer he referred to "the peoples separated from us by error and by schism, especially the one which professes a singular devotion for you, the one in which there is not a single house which did not display your venerated ikon, to-day perhaps hidden and put away for better days." The public consecration of Russia was yet to be made.

Sister Dores meanwhile remains not only the sole surviving witness of the apparitions, but the only person in the world who knows the Last Secret, of which nothing has been divulged except that it means woe to some and joy to others. I heard in Portugal from a man of the highest credibility that when she was ill and in danger of death in 1939, she obtained permission from Our Lady, at the Bishop's instance, to write it out and seal it up in an envelope marked, "Not to be opened until 1960."

If this cannot be verified at present, there is no such mystery about the four memoirs she composed at the command of Dom José to make sure that her version of the events of 1917 would not be lost. These accounts, written on ordinary lined notebook paper in a precise, clear, regular, rather commonplace handwriting, suggest a sane and well-balanced personality. It is interesting to compare them with the manuscripts of Saint Teresa of Jesus in the Escorial. Both were written rapidly, with the intention of imparting truth rather than achieving literary effect. Neither has the smudges and other irregularities that betray neurotic or psychotic tendencies. And if Sister Dores lacks the individuality, the grand manner, the veritable genius of the Spanish mystic, at least she is not so disdainful of grammar and punctuation!

The first account, written in 1936, contains many of the incidents I have related, besides a touching little poem in memory of "dear Jacinta," somewhat after the pattern of Santa Teresa's lyrics:

O tu que a terra
Passaste voando
Jacinta querida
Numa dôr intensa
Jesús amando
Não esqueças a prece
Que eu te pedia
Se minha amiga
Junto do trono
Da Virgem Maria.

Lirio de candura
Pérola brilhante
Oh! lá no Céu
Ondes vives triunfante
Serafim d'amor,
Com teu irmaosinho
Roga por mim
Aos pés do Senhor.

This memoir concludes with a request that if the Bishop publishes what she has written, he will say nothing of her "poor miserable self," and assures him that if he burns it without reading it she will be happy, having composed it only out of obedience.

It was in the second memoir, of 1937, that Sister Dores first let fall a casual reference to the Angel of Peace. This was something like a bombshell after twenty-one years of silence, and in some quarters it provoked consternation and even indignation. How could this be explained? What would people think? One learned visitor went so far as to say:

"You will have to do many turns in Purgatory, Sister, for concealing such a thing all this time!"

"I haven't the least fear of Purgatory on *that* account," she replied calmly. "I have always acted under obedience, and there is no penalty or punishment for obedience." [1]

As a matter of fact the Angel story, confusing as it has been to some persons, supports her credibility. A pseudo-mystic or impostor clever enough to invent so remarkable a tale would never have drawn suspicion upon herself by a startling and uncalled-for addition many years later. And a psychopath suffering from delusions would have had other hallucinations, surely, in all that time. Yet her superiors and associates agree that she is a perfectly normal religious, who has never shown any inclination to parade her spiritual experiences.

The third memoir, written August 8, 1941, contains further details about Jacinta, and an account of the weird light of January 25, 1938.

When the Bishop demanded a fourth and definitive account, Sister Dores retired to the garret of the convent at Tuy on the morning of December 8, 1941, and after praying a long while for the grace to set everything down correctly and in order, sat on a trunk near a small window, and holding a pad of notepaper on her lap, began her fourth and longest manuscript, in which she recorded, for posterity, the exact words of the Angel and of the Lady of the Rosary, with all the circumstances she could remember of each apparition in succession. The beginning, in which she tells of opening the New Testament more than once in search of light, is somewhat long and self-conscious; here perhaps she dramatizes herself a little. Once under way, the narrative proceeds swiftly and objectively. At the end, she makes some trenchant criticisms of errors she has found in the best-known books about the Fátima apparitions.

It was only last year, after a quarter of a century, that she was permitted to return to the scenes she had described in

---

[1] Memoir IV, p. 30.

that historic document. Perhaps it was fitting that her triumph and vindication should be reserved for the memorable pilgrimage of May 13, 1946. The Second World War was over, and the Portuguese well understood from what futile horrors they had been saved. Although rain fell all night and in the morning, a crowd of more than 700,000 pilgrims gathered in the Cova da Iria to give thanks to Our Lady of Fátima. Almost a tenth of the population of the country was there.

A second-hand but unforgettable impression of that demonstration came to me in some motion pictures I saw two months later at the Bishop's house in Leiria. The expanse of black bobbing umbrellas, the Portuguese prelates and the Papal Nuncio humbly standing in the rain, the thousands upon thousands of handkerchiefs that fluttered like the waves of a white sea or the wings of innumerable angels beating the wind—there was something unheard-of, almost apocalyptic in the magnitude, the fervor and the patience of that prodigious host. For parallels one must go back to the children of Israel singing with Moses in the wilderness, or the medieval crusaders shouting back at a Pope Urban II or a Saint Louis, "It is the will of God!"

Of the crusading enthusiasm of that pilgrimage, too, I obtained some qualitative idea, at least, from the one I attended the following July; for the pattern is much the same month after month. On the twelfth, the roads are full of picturesque groups, men predominating and most of them poor. By nightfall they are scattered over the great bowl of the Cova da Iria, finding places to hitch their burros or lay down their packs, to eat, to rest. Loaves of tough brown bread and bottles of wine are drawn from wicker baskets, earthen water-bottles are passed around or replenished at the holy well, blankets are spread on the dry ground under the olive or carrasqueira trees. Here an old woman slowly advances toward the chapel on bare and bleeding knees. There a stunted peasant is warming some soup for his wife and children over four candles, which he shields from the breeze with his body and his sombrero.

All the crowd are well supplied with such tapers, each encircled with a paper guard. By ten o'clock thousands of these tiny orange-tinted lamps are burning as the procession begins to form; they look strangely dim and ethereal as the full moon mounts higher in the east, flooding the Serra with an unearthly radiance and lending a peculiar steely-blue cast to the infinite dome above. As the wind comes stronger from the far ocean and the western mountains, the torches flicker madly, yet few are extinguished.

Now they have assumed the order and form of a long straggling procession that slowly moves up the hill toward the main highway. The resonant voice of a priest is heard on a loud speaker, leading in the Rosary. Thousands of voices high and deep, male and female, respond with a thunderous and passionate rhythm; *Santa Maria, māi de Deus, rogai por nos pecadores agora e na hora da nossa morte!*"

The head of the procession has reached the top of the hill, has turned, and is coming down another road toward the basilica. The slow majestic pace, the dancing of innumerable lights, the hoarse and throaty voices convey an overpowering impression of an army not of blood but of prayer, a host of crusaders bearing the light of truth through the darkness of a hostile world, fearless of time and death, certain of triumph. What can resist these voices and footsteps of yesterday and of tomorrow?

Between the mysteries of the Rosary the marchers fling the Aves of their favorite hymn to the metallic sky:

A treze de Maio
Na Cova da Iria
Apar'ceu brilhanda
A Virgem Maria.

Ave, Ave, Ave Maria!
Ave, Ave, Ave Maria!

Individuals cry out between the strophes their own hopes and supplications, sometimes with heartbreaking sobs: "Lord, we adore you!" "Lord, we love you!" "Jesus, have mercy on us! Lord, you can cure me if you will!" Yes, these voices seem to belong to lustier and heartier times than ours. They come from the plain of Esdraelon, from the walls of Jericho and Constantinople and the fields of Tunis, like the pulses of faith and of human personality breaking through the mediocrity and regimentation of a machine age.

The column of lights finally dissolves at the basilica. The thousands slowly push their way inside to attend Benediction, and then to form in long cues by the confessional boxes, patiently waiting to tell their sins so that they can receive Holy Communion at dawn. The prayers, the songs, the exclamations continue through the night. But at two in the morning many thousands have already disposed themselves for sleep. Around every tree, around the well, around the concrete platform of the chapel of the apparitions, one sees them lying prone in circles, the heads toward the center, the bare feet of women and the hobnailed boots of men grotesquely forming the perimeters. Here under one blanket lie a young peasant and his wife. Under two or three others are huddled a man and a woman and their four children. A baby is inert on the breast of her sleeping mother. All are strangely silent and motionless in the deathlike slumber of those who labor in the fields and think nothing of walking fifty miles to honor the Mother of God.

On the morning of the thirteenth, after a humble breakfast of dry bread wherever they have slept, the people form another procession, which follows the same route to the highway and thence back to the basilica. This time the white statue of Our Lady of Fátima has been taken reverently from the chapel, and is born at the head of the column on the shoulders of six sturdy men; while in front, leading this second crusading army in the full glare of the summer heat, walk the Archbishop of Evora and the Bishop of Leiria. Dom José goes slowly and painfully, with stiff and swollen knees, an ungainly but heroic figure in crimson and gold. As he finally climbs the steps of the basilica he is smiling graciously, and few can guess what it has cost a gallant gentleman to pay his devoir to his Lady.

Perhaps the most moving of all the scenes is the one just between the High Mass and the noonday Benediction. In a special place roped off for them the sick are waiting patiently for this moment, some on stretchers, some in wheel-chairs with nurses, some hobbling on crutches; paralyzed children in the arms of mothers; the blind, the emaciated. A priest descends from the basilica carrying the Sacred Host in a monstrance. All who are able fall on their knees as he passes between the rows of the *doentes* and holds It up before the face of each, imploring the Lord to heal and to restore. I will not attempt to describe those faces, those eyes; there are no words for such love, hope, desperation, adoration. One can only think of the atmosphere of the Gospels, as Lucia has reminded us. "And Jesus went about all the cities and towns, teaching in their synagogues and preaching the gospel of the Kingdom, and healing every disease and infirmity. And seeing the multitudes, he had compassion on them, because they were distressed, and lying like sheep that have no shepherd." [2] There are no sensational episodes on this occasion; later, however, we hear that a man from the north has been cured of cancer.[3]

At last it is finished, and the statue is being borne back to its place in the small chapel. All the people wave their handkerchiefs up and down in farewell. The effect is tremendous; it is more eloquent than all the shouts and the final Aves. But when the figure of Our Lady has passed, the multitude quickly melts away. Only a few small groups are still gathered here and there. Still fewer have taken the trouble to follow the statue to its home. There they are, kneeling about the humble building, still muttering their love and their petitions —most of them women, and very poor ones too in dusty garb, with black kerchiefs over their heads, and bare feet. Among them on July 13 I saw Ti Olimpia, the mother of Francisco and Jacinta, earnestly saying her Rosary.

[2] St. Matthew, IX, 35–36.

[3] *Voz da Fátima*, August 13, 1946.

Such, on a much grander scale and despite the rain, must have been the atmosphere at the greatest of all the pilgrimages, the one on May 13, 1946. On that day, too, as a climax, the three-quarter-of-a-million pilgrims heard the voice of the Vicar of Christ speaking from Rome; and the force of all his words tended to heighten the impression of a modern Crusade.

"Your great concourse, the fervor of your prayers, the thunder of your acclamations, all the holy enthusiasm which vibrates without cease in your hearts, and finally the sacred rite which in this moment of incomparable triumph has just been performed," said the Pope, "call to Our mind another multitude innumerably greater, other cries of worship far more ardent, other triumphs yet more divine, another hour solemnly eternal, the endless day of eternity when the glorious Virgin, triumphantly entering the Heavenly Homeland through the nine blessed choirs of Angels, was raised even to the Throne of the Most Holy Trinity, Who placed upon her brow the triple diadem of glory, and presenting her to the celestial court seated at the right hand of the immortal King of Ages, crowned her Queen of the Universe. And the King saw that she was truly worthy of such honor, glory and empire, because more filled with grace, more holy, more beautiful, more divine—incomparably more so than the greatest saints and the sublimest angels; because she is . . . the first-born daughter of the Father, pure Mother of the Word and beloved bride of the Holy Ghost, because Mother of the divine King, of Him to Whom from her maternal womb the Lord God gave the throne of David and everlasting Kingship in the House of Jacob: He Who Himself proclaimed to have received all power in heaven and earth—He the Son of God decrees for His heavenly Mother all glory, power, and majesty of His Kingdom. . . .

"So the Church salutes her Lady and Queen of the Angels and Saints, of Patriarchs and Prophets, of Apostles and Martyrs, of Confessors and Virgins; she acclaims her Queen of Heaven and earth, most glorious, most worthy Queen of the

Universe . . . the light shining in the sky amid the tears of this exile. . . .

"You, by crowning the image of Our Lady of Fátima, signed as it were a document of faith in her supremacy, a loyal submission to her authority, a filial and constant correspondence to her love. You did yet more: you enlisted as crusaders in the conquest and reconquest of her Kingdom, which is the Kingdom of God, that is to say you bound yourselves before heaven and earth to love her, to venerate her, to serve her, to imitate her, so that with her blessing you may better serve the Divine King; and at the same time you bound yourselves to labor that she may be loved, venerated, and served all around you, in the family, in society, in the world." [4]

Sister Dores may have heard the Holy Father's words, but she did not see the demonstration. It was a week later, on May 20, that she arrived, with the Mother Provincial of her order, at Cova da Iria. She had left as an untutored girl of fourteen. She returned a calm and poised woman of thirty-nine. Most of the countryside was unchanged. But her brown eyes opened wide with amazement when she looked down on what had been the wilderness of Cova da Iria. It was partly inclosed by a wall. From two majestic gates descended roads that joined at the miraculous fountain, and then ascended to the lofty white basilica on the northern hill. The chapel of the apparitions had been completely rebuilt. To the left was an imposing hospice containing two or three chapels, the Bishop's quarters, and a seminary. On the opposite hill workmen were laying the massive foundations of another such building. Ground was being broken for an Italian seminary to the northeast. On another hill stood the new convent of the Discalced Carmelite nuns from Belgium.

Hardly anything was the same there except the carrasqueira tree to which the children had fled from the first flash of light on May 13, 1917. From one of its limbs hung

[4] *Voz da Fátima*, June 13, 1946.

an angelus bell, which João, the lame son of Maria Carreira, would ring at suitable hours; he also sold rosaries, and attended to the fountain. And hovering birdlike about the chapel of the apparitions at almost any hour one could see his mother—Maria da Capelhina, they now call her—removing withered flowers from the place where the azinheira had been, or going about on her hands and knees, dusting the concrete floor with a whisk-broom.

Ti Marto was very much in evidence those days, wearing a blue shirt, with a black tie on Sundays; and in the lapel of his well-brushed coat the button of the Catholic Action League of Farmers.

"Yes, I believed in it from the first," he would say. "Once a Spaniard came here and told me he could look at the sun any time. I dared him to prove it. He got under a fig tree and looked up through the leaves. 'Oho!' said I, 'come out here and look at it.' Of course he couldn't. Then there was a Communist here who said that it was all nothing but one great big stupidity. I said to him, 'Let me see you go back to your own town and make a stupidity as big as this one.'"

When I asked him if he still hoed his maize and dug his potatoes, he said apologetically:

"No, I don't do much work now. I'm only seventy-three, but my legs are no good any more—they're almost as bad as Dom José's."

Dom José, as the people affectionately call their Bishop, gives the impression of never allowing his affliction to stand in the way of anything he resolves to do; and the morning after the arrival of Sister Dores he came from Leiria to say Mass at the little chapel especially for her.

Meanwhile the news of her coming had created quite a sensation all over the Serra. Soon people were flocking from all sides to catch a glimpse of her, and a crowd followed wherever she went. Naturally she visited Aljustrel to speak with her sister Maria, her aunt Olimpia, and other old friends and neighbors. She went with Father Galamba, representing the Bishop, to verify all the scenes of the events of 1917. She pointed out exactly where the Angel had appeared at Cabeço and at the well. She watched the women washing their clothes at the Lagoa. A priest who saw her standing at Valinhos, gazing at the pile of stones where Our Lady had appeared in August, 1917, told me he was much impressed by her detachment and lack of vanity. She seemed wholly unaware that anyone was looking at her.

After a visit to the Church of Saint Anthony at Fátima, where she noted all the changes and improvements, she crossed the road and entered the creaking gate of the old cemetery. Where she had left the little cross on the grave of Francisco, she found an impressive monument inscribed:

HERE LIE THE MORTAL REMAINS
OF JACINTA AND FRANCISCO MARTO
TO WHOM OUR LADY APPEARED.

For Jacinta, too, had returned to Fátima, as she had promised, long after her death. It was in 1935 that her body was taken from the cemetery at Ourem, and laid in a common grave with her brother's. When both coffins were opened, nothing was found of Francisco but his bones, but Jacinta's face was intact and incorrupt; she seemed to be only asleep, waiting for the Resurrection, and the good odor of Paradise hung about her. Her mother was one of those who saw her. Ti Marto told me he was there, but could not get a very good look. "*Ai Jesús,* there was such a crowd! I couldn't get near enough."

Sister Maria das Dores went back to her convent. A few days later the Bishop ordered evidence taken in the cause for the beatification of those who, if these efforts succeed, will one day be known as Saint Jacinta and Saint Francisco of Fátima.

EPILOGUE

It was in the convent of the Dorothean Sisters at Vilar, near Porto, that I had the privilege of conversing with Sister Maria das Dores on the afternoon of Monday, July 15, 1946. She seemed uncomfortable at first, and probably was, for she dislikes such interviews intensely, and submits to them only when ordered to do so. She wrung her hands nervously. Her pale brown eyes looked rather guarded and unfriendly. There was not much conviction in the high and timorous voice.

A few moments later I had almost forgotten this first impression. She had begun to feel more at ease. She laughed readily; and when she smiled, a little dimple would appear on each cheek. The voice now sounded natural and sincere. There was intelligence in this face, too, and charm. It was impossible not to like her and to trust her.

First I presented a few questions from America, some perhaps a little obvious and unnecessary. One, from a sculptor, was whether the rosary in the hand of Our Lady had had five or fifteen decades.

"I didn't count them," she said quickly, with a mischievous smile.

"When the Angel of Peace gave you Holy Communion at Cabeço, did it seem to you like a dream or a vision, or was it like the reality of receiving Holy Communion in a church?"

She hesitated for the right word. "I cannot be absolutely sure of that, because I was not in any ordinary state of mind during such an experience, and there was something so intimate, so interior, so intense about the apparition of the Angel and what he said and did. But I believe it was like the real experience of receiving in a church, for I felt the contact of the Host."

"Did you see Our Lord in the year 1927?"

"Twice." The answer was prompt and matter-of-fact. I was

not permitted to question her as to what He said. Nor was I allowed to ask about the conversations she has had with Our Lady since 1917. It is well known that there have been several such apparitions. According to the *Voz de Fátima*, published at the shrine, the Blessed Mother said to her in her cell, on December 10, 1925: "Look, my daughter, at my Heart surrounded with the thorns with which ungrateful men wound it by their blasphemies and iniquities. You, at least, try to console me, and announce that I promise to assist at the hour of death, with the graces necessary for salvation, all those who, on the first Saturdays of five consecutive months, confess, receive Holy Communion, recite part of my Rosary, and keep me company for a quarter of an hour meditating on its mysteries with the intention of offering me reparation." Sister Dores made this known, and it has given great impetus to the Immaculate Heart devotion.

The interview continued:

"When you reported the words of the Angel and of Our Lady, did you give the exact words as they were spoken, or only the general sense?"

"The Angel's words had an intense and overpowering quality, a supernatural reality, that could not be forgotten. They seemed to engrave themselves exactly and indelibly upon the memory. It was different with the words of Our Lady. I could not be sure that every word was exact. It was rather the sense that came to me, and I put what I understood into words. It is not easy to explain this."

"Our Lady showed you many souls going to hell. Did you get the impression from her that more souls are damned than saved?"

This amused her a little. "I saw those that were going down. I didn't see those that were going up."

"Does the statue in the shrine at Cova da Iria look like the Lady you saw there?"

"No, not much. I was disappointed when I saw it. For one thing, it was too gay, too *alegre*. When I saw Our Lady she was more *triste*, or rather more compassionate. But it would be impossible to describe Our Lady, and it would be impossible to make a statue as beautiful as she is." She left the room a moment and returned with a small print of Our Lady on some sort of transparent plastic material, the most simple and unadorned I had seen, and handed it to me. "This is the picture that comes nearest to what I saw," she said. "Our Lady seemed to be made all of light, and her garments were also. There was no border of gold, no ornamentation."

"In many books about Fátima, the prayer Our Lady asked you to say after the decades of the Rosary is given in some such form as this: 'O my Jesus, pardon our sins, save us from the fire of hell, have mercy on the souls in Purgatory, especially the most abandoned.' Is that correct?"

"No, it is not," she replied positively. "The correct form is the one I have written in my account of the apparition on July 13: 'O my Jesus, pardon us, and save us from the fire of hell; draw all souls to heaven, especially those in most need." [1]

"Have you ever read the works of Saint Teresa of Ávila?" I was thinking especially of the descriptions of uncreated light in the *Libro de su vida*.

"No. Parts of them were read to us in the refectory."

"Have you had any revelation from Our Lady about the end of the world?"

"I cannot answer that question."

"Some persons believe that Jacinta's vision of a persecuted Pope referred to some particular Pontiff. Some believe the present Holy Father was the one she saw."

"Jacinta said it was a Pope. There was nothing to indicate any particular Pope."

"Why did you say nothing about the Angel of Peace for so many years?"

"Nobody told me to. I am under obedience. The priest to whom I mentioned it at the time told me not to speak of it again. I never did until the Bishop told me to write everything down."

---

[1] "*O meu Jesus, perdoai-nos e livrai nos do fogo do inferno; levai as alminhas todas para o Céu, principalmente aquelas que mais precisarem.*"

She explained the different effects of the apparitions of the Angel and of Our Lady in terms very similar to those she had used in her memoirs. She seemed very fond of such words as *"intimo"* and *"intenso."* Her recollections were clear and precise. "The Angel left us feeling exhausted, helpless, overpowered, and we remained lost to everything for hours. Our Lady always made us feel light and joyous."

Finally we came to the important subject of the second July secret, of which so many different and conflicting versions have been published. Lucia made it plain that Our Lady did not ask for the consecration of *the world* to her Immaculate Heart. What she demanded specifically was the consecration of *Russia.* She did not comment, of course, on the fact that Pope Pius XII had consecrated the world, not Russia, to the Immaculate Heart in 1942. But she said more than once, and with deliberate emphasis:

"What Our Lady wants is that the Pope and all the bishops in the world shall consecrate Russia to her Immaculate Heart on one special day. If this is done, she will convert Russia and there will be peace. If it is not done, the errors of Russia will spread through every country in the world."

"Does this mean, in your opinion, that every country, without exception, will be overcome by Communism?"

"Yes."

It was plain that she felt that Our Lady's wishes had not yet been carried out. People must say the Rosary, perform sacrifices, make the five first Saturday Communions, pray for the Holy Father.

"Did Our Lady ever say anything to you about the United States of America?"

She gave me a rather startled glance, and then smiled in faint amusement, as if to suggest that perhaps the United States was not so important in the general scheme of things as I imagined.

"No," she said gently. "She never did. But I wish you would have Masses said for me in the United States!" I promised, and she said she would pray for me.

It was almost eight o'clock, and we had been talking for

about three hours. Mother Pignatelli, who had been present at the interview, with Father Galamba, Father Rocha, Father Furtado and Mr. Daniel Sullivan, gave us all some lemonade and cakes. She and Sister Maria das Dores followed us to the porch. A black cat was sleeping there in the last warmth of the departing sun. The fragrance of roses and gardenias came down from one of the six beautiful gardens of the convent. As we took our leave, Sister Maria das Dores, who had entered that house as Lucia Abóbora, leaned over the railing and gave us a charming smile of farewell.[2]

[2] After my return from Portugal I wrote several questions which His Excellency the Bishop of Leiria was good enough to send to Sister Dores. Her answers, written February 17, 1947, reached me just too late for the first edition of this book. I summarize or quote the most important:

The more specific request of Our Lady, that *Russia* be consecrated to her Immaculate Heart "by the Pope and all the Bishops in the world on one special day" was made in 1927, ten years after the original revelations.

Q. "Is it your opinion that the Pope and the Bishops will consecrate Russia to the Immaculate Heart only after the laity have done their duty, in Rosaries, sacrifices, first Saturday Communions, etc.?"

A. "The Holy Father has already consecrated Russia, including it in the consecration of the world, but it has not been done in the form indicated by Our Lady: I do not know whether Our Lady accepts it, done in this way, as complying with her promises. Prayer and sacrifice are always the means necessary to draw down the graces and blessings of God."

Q. "Did you write the wishes of Our Lady to Pope Pius XI?"

A. "In 1929 I wrote the desires and requests of Our Lord and of Our Lady, which were the same, and delivered the writing to my confessor; he was then the Reverend Father Bernardo Gonçalves, a Jesuit, now Superior of the Mission of Zambesia Leifidizi: His Reverence transmitted it to His Excellency the Most Reverend Senhor Bishop of Leiria, and some time later it was transmitted to His Holiness Pius XI. I do not know the exact date when it was communicated to His Holiness or the name of the person of whom my confessor availed himself. But I remember well that my confessor told me that the Holy Father had heard the message graciously and had promised to consider it."

Q. "Can you give me a brief account of any other revelations you have received from Our Lady since 1917?"

A. "What has been published of the revelations later than 1917 appears to me sufficient to make possible the realization of the wishes of Our Lord, and I do not think the moment opportune to state anything further."